THE COMPLETE BOLIVIAN DIARIES OF

Ché Guevara

AND OTHER CAPTURED DOCUMENTS

EDITED AND WITH AN INTRODUCTION BY DANIEL JAMES

A SCARBOROUGH BOOK

STEIN AND DAY/*Publishers*/*New York*

R E V I S E D   E D I T I O N

THE COMPLETE BOLIVIAN DIARIES OF

Ché

Guevara

1968

(1980)

AND OTHER CAPTURED DOCUMENTS

THIRD SCARBOROUGH BOOKS EDITION 1980

First published in the United States of America by
Stein and Day/*Publishers* 1968

Copyright © 1968 Stein and Day Incorporated

Library of Congress Catalog Card Number 68-55642

Published simultaneously in Canada

Designed by David Miller

Printed in the United States of America

Stein and Day/*Publishers*/7 East 48 Street, New York, N.Y. 10017

Revised edition 1970

ISBN 0-8128-1229-8

For Jessica

CONTENTS

ILLUSTRATIONS

Following page 96

PREFACE

The purpose of Ché Guevara's insurrectionary expedition to Bolivia, beginning in the Fall of 1966 and lasting for eleven months, was to create a sufficient amount of trouble for the Bolivian Government so that it would be forced to ask for substantial American intervention. It was intended to force an American government honoring its treaty obligations to defend the Western Hemisphere into becoming bogged down in what Ché hoped would become "another Vietnam."

A substantial American military presence in Bolivia would have inflamed not only the pro-Communist left in many Latin American countries but many moderate groups as well, causing a continent-wide reaction against "Yankee Imperialism." Thus, Ché Guevara's minute guerrilla force would have served as the catalyst for a revolution of an entire continent.

The consequences for the West would have become massive. There is no denying the importance of Ché Guevara's attempt in Bolivia and the importance of his resolution.

This book begins with a section in which I have intended briefly to outline the background and course of the Bolivian campaign so that the reader will be able to grasp the import of the diaries and documents which make up the rest of the book. All of these documents were captured by the Bolivian Army. As a whole, they are a strange mixture of personal pique (stronger, curiously, than political fervor), the difficulties of guerrilla life, especially in the relations of Ché Guevara's band with other Communist groups, as well as descriptions of the battles they fought, comrades lost, and most intensively, the despair of one of the great revolutionaries of the twentieth century, who had won Cuba and then tried to win the rest.

There are two Ché Guevara diaries: the first from November 7, 1966 to December 31, 1966, the second from January 1, 1967 to the day before his final defeat on October 8, 1967. The first is of historical value though generally not highly readable. The second is moving and far more important. This is followed by the diary of Rolando who was killed half a year before Ché. In

Ché's diary we get what Ché thought and felt; in Rolando's, we learn from one of his most trusted lieutenants what he actually said and did; the counterpoint is fascinating. Pombo's diary reflects his great interest in the personalities and in the conflicts within the Communist movement. Braulio's diary, the first to be captured, is more personal.

There is also an illustrative section of human and political interest consisting largely of photographs taken by the guerrillas themselves, many of which have never been published.

All of this material was made available at a cost of Bolivian and Cuban blood. The diaries contain the day-by-day as well as the longer-range concerns of men taking lives and, with the exception of Pombo, going to their own deaths.

DANIEL JAMES
La Paz, Mexico City, and New York
1968

PREFACE TO THE REVISED EDITION

Every effort has been made to track down and correct, in this edition, errors of fact and translation that crept into the first. Most of the errors were, perhaps, unavoidable, in view of the lack of sufficient time before publication and the extraordinary difficulty presented by Ché Guevara's cramped handwriting and by the many "Bolivianisms" to be deciphered. Hopefully, not only have major errors been corrected but passages in the diaries rendered more idiomatically and, therefore, easier to understand.

It should also be noted that two of principal actors in the ill-fated guerrilla campaign, President René Barrientos of Bolivia and Ché's Bolivian lieutenant, Inti Peredo, have perished, the former in a helicopter crash and the latter in renewed guerrilla combat. A third, General Ovando, has since staged a coup and, in imitation of the Peruvian generals, has nationalized the Bolivian Gulf Oil Company and generally oriented Bolivia leftward.

Finally, after nearly two years of silence, Fidel Castro has gradually made public the identities of ten of the Cuban guerrillas who fought with Ché in Bolivia; they tally exactly with the information published in the first edition. Remaining yet to be identified are six more: Antonio, Arturo, Benigno, Moro, Pacho, and Urbano.

Daniel James
Mexico, D.F.
November, 1969

Ché's guerrillas operated in the Red Zone between Camiri and Santa Cruz. The dark line indicates the path of the campaign. The dotted line was followed by Pombo and his group after Ché's capture at Quebrada del Yuro, in their escape to Chile. (Also see map on page 70.)

INTRODUCTION   BY DANIEL JAMES

"A new stage begins today." In those simple words Ernesto Ché Guevara recorded his arrival in the wild and remote southeastern corner of Bolivia where he went to establish the *"foco insurrec-ional*—"insurrectional focus"—of the continental revolution he intended to launch in South America. The date: November 7, 1966.

Ché had traveled halfway around the world to reach Nancahuazú (nyan-kah-wah-zoo) where his advance party set up his guerrilla base. He had gone from Havana to Prague, then to Frankfurt, and from there back to Latin America, reaching São Paulo, Brazil, on November 3, 1966. From São Paulo, he flew directly to La Paz, the capital of Bolivia.

It was an audacious move, going to the capital of the country where he planned to make a revolution, but Ché was well disguised. He traveled with a false Uruguayan passport made out in the name of "Adolfo Mena González," and he was disguised to look like anyone but the famous guerrilla leader Ché Guevara; he appeared to be a stout, balding, bespectacled, middle-aged and rather ordinary man. His passport stated he was a *"comerciante"*—"merchant." At El Alto Airport, he was met by agents who escorted him past Immigration, past police and military officers, and into a waiting automobile.

Stopping in La Paz only long enough to confer with local and Cuban agents who had been working many months on his guerrilla project, Ché and four others got into two Toyota jeeps and began the tiring 400-mile journey that would take him to Nancahuazú. On the way, they avoided such heavily populated areas as Santa Cruz de la Sierra, a booming oil center of 100,000, not quite 140 miles northeast of the guerrilla base, and crossed the Río Grande, Bolivia's largest river, on a raft. It took him three days to reach his destination.

Ché's presence in southeastern Bolivia was such a well-kept secret that some of his own guerrilla followers did not know who he was. When one of them, a young Bolivian nicknamed "Bigotes"—"Whiskers"—suddenly recognized the bourgeois-looking

11

stranger who went under the name of "Ramón," he was so startled that he nearly drove his jeep over a cliff, much to Ché's amusement.

Ché had been out of public sight since March 14, 1965, when he returned to Cuba from a three-months' trip abroad spent mostly in Africa. His disappearance immediately became an object of world-wide speculation. He had been an international figure since 1959, the year the Cuban Revolution triumphed, and his absence from the news even for a few days was news in itself.

Ché had made headlines from the start of his trip, in early December 1964, when he made a fiery address before the United Nations General Assembly in New York. There, he had blasted Yankee Imperialism and other enemies of revolution, while a Cuban exile took a pot shot at the UN building. Then he had gone to Algeria, Mali, Republic of the Congo (Brazzaville), Guinea, Dahomey, Algeria again, Tanzania and Egypt, attacking not only America's imperialism but also the Soviet Union's, and making headlines everywhere. Suddenly, he dropped out of sight.

The world press immediately proposed a number of theories. Ché had been executed, jailed, hospitalized, purged, gone into seclusion, all of which eventually turned out to be wrong. But it is important to establish what Ché had been doing during the nineteen months between his return home in March 1965 and his reappearance in Bolivia in November 1966. The documents captured in Bolivia during the guerrilla campaign provide, for the first time, a fairly accurate account of this period.

When Ché was met at Havana's José Martí Airport by Cuban Premier Fidel Castro after his barnstorming tour of Africa, it was not exactly with open arms. A photograph taken at the time— the last published photograph of Ché until snapshots captured at Nancahuazú were printed—shows him looking dejected, defeated and tired. He knew as well as the others his mission had been a failure. Worse still, he knew he had embarrassed the Cuban Government and its Premier.

Nearly everywhere on his trip, most notably at an Afro-Asian economic seminar in Algiers, Ché had blasted the Soviet Union for following trade policies toward the underdeveloped countries that were virtually identical with those of American "imperialism." He had called for a radical overhaul of Soviet foreign economic policy which would have required financing the economic development of the underdeveloped countries without expecting a return on the investment. Ché's program did not sit well with a Moscow government which for years had been subsidizing Cuba with approximately one million dollars a day, and its displeasure was conveyed to Castro.

The Cuban Premier himself had been disappointed by Ché's disastrous performance as Minister of Industries since 1961. Trying to replace a policy of material rewards for highly productive workers with one of "moral incentives," Ché had committed so many errors—errors he frankly acknowledged—that the Cuban economy had verged on bankruptcy. Meanwhile he had become engaged in acrimonious arguments with the orthodox Marxist economists of the Old Guard Communists in Cuba and their counterparts abroad. His opponents included such highly respected figures as Charles Bettleheim of France, whom Castro had brought in to advise on reconstructing the shattered Cuban economy. Ché's writings and speeches on guerrilla warfare urged the export of Cuba's revolution to all underdeveloped countries and particularly those of Latin America, further aggravating relations between the Castro regime and Moscow.

To add to his problems, Ché had, before and during his African trip, made some pointed public criticisms of Fidel personally. He went so far as to describe mistakes Fidel had made back in 1953, during the famous assault on Moncada Barracks which had led to the founding of the July 26th Revolutionary Movement. In a fourteen-page article he published in a Peking-subsidized Paris magazine, Ché even made the charge that, of all the battles that had taken place in the Sierra Maestra, "Fidel Castro participated in only one and it was a complete failure."

Ché disagreed, of course, with Fidel's Soviet-oriented economic policy and particularly with his rapprochement with the same Old Guard Cuban Communists against whom he had been polemicizing earlier.

All this brought into play the undercurrent of rivalry that had existed between Ché Guevara and Fidel Castro since the Sierra Maestra period which both had been careful to keep down over the years.

The two men had always had an ambivalent attitude toward each other. Ché adored Fidel almost to the point of idolatry, but at the same time held little regard for him as military leader and political thinker. Castro, in turn, felt a deep affection for his younger lieutenant. But although Fidel respected Ché for his keen brain, he felt that the younger man was dogmatic, arrogant

and impetuous. Though Fidel copied Ché's ideological program
—and still adheres to it—he and other Cuban leaders were often
annoyed by the Argentine-born guerrilla expert's apparent bid
for the ideological leadership of the Cuban Revolution and his
condescension toward his colleagues in the revolutionary establishment.

By March of 1955 all these factors—Ché's criticisms of Moscow, the Old Guard and Fidel, his failures as Industries Minister, his lofty intellectual manner, his inflexible idealism—combined to make Ché's continued presence in the Cuban leadership
increasingly difficult. The time had come, Fidel and Ché both
agreed, for the restless revolutionary "twentieth-century soldier
of fortune," as Ché called himself—to seek other employ.

Ché, a man of deep insight, had of course realized that his
attacks on the Soviets would jeopardize his position in the Cuban
Government. Accordingly, while abroad he had laid plans for his
future. He all but announced what these would be when, on
February 12, 1965, he made a speech in Dar es Salaam, the
capital of Tanzania, in which he stated:

"I am convinced that it is possible to create a common front of struggle
against colonialism, imperialism and neocolonialism."

He decided to return to Africa to begin building his common
front. Africa, as he told Josie Fanon, the widow of the Third
World theoretician, Franz Fanon, "was one of the most important fields of battle."

In January 1965, Ché conferred at length with President Al-
phonse Massemba-Debat of the Republic of the Congo (Brazzaville) on the left-wing rebellion that had broken out in the adjacent Democratic Republic of the Congo (Kinshasa), which
Brazzaville was supporting. Ché agreed to throw in his lot with
the Kinshasa rebels.

He then visited Tanzania where he met secretly with Kinshasa rebel leaders, and accompanied them on an inspection trip
of their bases in the eastern Congo bordering Tanzania. Ché
promised them Cuban aid, apparently with the knowledge and
approval of Castro. He then returned to Havana where he reported to Castro on that phase of his mission.

In April, Ché wrote a letter to Fidel (not made public until
the following October), relieving himself of all official govern-
mental and political responsibilities. In it, he said:

"I renounce formally my positions in the leadership of the party, my post as minister, my rank as *comandante,* my status as Cuban citizen. Nothing legal binds me to Cuba."

That freed Castro and the Cuban government, as well as Ché, of any official responsibility for any future actions of the guerrilla leader.

Meanwhile Fidel surreptitiously helped Ché gather together a force of more than 125 Cuban guerrillas who embarked for the Congo to join the Kinshasa rebels, with Ché personally in command.

They filtered into rebel territory by crossing Lake Tanganyika between Tanzania and the eastern Congo. The rebels were well equipped and well armed by the Soviets, and also were receiving some expert guerrilla direction from the Algerians. Even so, Ché's contribution was welcomed.

All his experience and expertise, however, plus the fighting prowess of his Cuban contingent, could neither make good guerrillas of the Kinshasa rebels nor decide the rebellion's outcome. The trouble, Ché soon found, was that the insurgents were simply "unwilling" to fight, as he later put it, and were "chaotic." In many cases they were downright corrupt. When, in the fall of 1965, they proved unable to defend their well-fortified base at Atshoma, Ché gave up in disgust, urged Fidel to withdraw all aid, and returned to Havana.

Ché and his Cubans made their share of mistakes in the Congo; some of these were a preview of the Bolivian disaster to come. Ché and Pombo, in their Bolivian diaries, compare their unhappy experiences in both countries.

There was more than a superficial connection between Ché's Congo and Bolivian adventures. Eight Cubans accompanied him on both expeditions: Arturo, Braulio, Moro, Pacho, Segundo, Tuma and Urbano. This was half of the total of sixteen Cubans he took to Bolivia.

But if Ché's expedition to the Congo was a natural outgrowth of his statement in Algiers, his reasons for intervening in Bolivia are less obvious. The ultimate criterion for the guerrilla high command in Havana was: Which country offered the best possibilities for advancing the continental revolution? Bolivia, itself, was of secondary importance, as the leader of the Bolivian Communist Party (PCB), Mario Monje, recognized. Ché was quite blunt in telling his Cuban followers that, as far as he was concerned, Bolivia was purely and simply a sacrificial lamb to be offered on the altar of continental revolution. In the presence of Pombo, Pacho and Tuma, he stated, according to Pombo's diary:

"Bolivia will sacrifice itself so that conditions [for revolution] can be created in neighboring countries. We have to make [Latin] America another Viet Nam, with its center in Bolivia."

A more callous statement can hardly be imagined. One can only wonder how the Bolivian guerrillas in Ché's command would have reacted had they heard it.

Ché, Fidel, and the other guerrilla war planners in Havana saw Bolivia solely in terms of its importance to the continental revolution. From that point of view, Bolivia's over-riding advantage over other candidates for the role of "center" of "another Viet Nam" was, precisely, that it lies in the center of South America, at the heart of the continent. It offered by far the best strategic location.

Bolivia is bordered by five countries, more than any other South American republic except Peru. Argentina lies to the south and Brazil to the east and north. Two other countries of considerable importance are Chile, to the west and south, and Peru, to the west and north. To the southeast lies Paraguay, Bolivia's fifth contiguous neighbor. Though the least important economically, the overthrow of its perpetual ruler, General Alfredo Stroessner, would have had far-reaching political repercussions.

All five of these countries were the targets of Ché's continental strategy. One can easily see that establishment of a strong guerrilla *foco* in Bolivia could have produced a chain-reaction among her immediate neighbors.

Describing the then recently established guerrilla front in Bolivia, the official magazine *Tricontinental* in Havana stated:

"Its appearance is not just chance, for this focal point of guerrilla action—on analyzing the elements that surround it and that led to it—appears to stem from a coordinated tactical-strategic line, related to an all-round view of armed struggle: specifically for the Latin American continent." [1]

Tricontinental added that Ché felt, like Debray, that "military foci are more decisive for the future of Latin America than 'political foci,'" and his "Many Viet Nams" article in April 1967

1. "Bolivia, Time of the Furnaces," *Tricontinental*, No. 1, July-August 1967, Havana. The title is from a favorite quotation of Ché's, from José Martí: "Now is the time of the furnaces, and only light should be seen."

"could be considered an extension, on an international scale, of that proposal."

Political considerations then, which would require an accurate evaluation of the internal situation in Bolivia, were secondary to the military. Just as he rejected Monje's proposal to make the political chief of the revolution supreme, Ché Guevara insisted on the paramountcy of military over political considerations in the choice of Bolivia as the revolutionary center. As he declared in his *Guerrilla Warfare:*

"It is not always necessary to wait until all the conditions for revolution exist; the insurrectional focus can create them." [2]

That theory, which governed Ché's whole approach to Bolivia, proved to be the fatal flaw in his adventure there.

To be sure, neither Ché nor Fidel entirely ignored the political conditions in Bolivia at the time. All those involved in preparing the guerrilla war agreed, with Pombo, that "for the moment, conditions were better in Bolivia" than elsewhere. Monje thought "Bolivia was the ideal place" to start a revolt. And the young Bolivian volunteer, Loro, told Ché on his arrival in Nancahuazú that he had decided to join the guerrillas because he thought Bolivia had "the best conditions on the continent for guerrilla warfare."

But the dazzling goal of continental revolution blinded Ché and Fidel to the realities that had to be faced before they could come remotely within striking distance of it. For them, it was but a single leap from a tiny guerrilla *foco* secreted in the mountains to the conquest of the whole immense continent. In a sense, it did not matter too much to them whether Bolivia itself was ripe for revolution or not, since the country was to serve essentially as the staging area of continental revolution. It was not absolutely decisive that a strictly Bolivian revolution be made or that it succeed, though that was naturally to be hoped for.

In any case, as reasonably well-informed Latin American leaders, both Ché and Fidel had a fair working knowledge of recent Bolivian history.

The Barrientos Government was the outgrowth of a military coup which, on November 4, 1964, overthrew President Víctor Paz Estenssoro and ended twelve years of rule by his Movimento Nacionalista Revolucionario. The coup produced a military

2. Ernesto Ché Guevara, *Guerrilla de guerrillas,* in *Obra revolucionaria,* Ediciones Era, Mexico, D.F., 1967; p. 27.

junta with Barrientos and General Alfredo Ovando Candia, Commander-in-Chief of the Bolivian Army, as "Co-Presidents." In July 1966, Barrientos won 62 percent of the vote in a Presidential election the Organization of American States characterized as fair and honest.

These developments were seen by Ché and the Cuban leaders as a "farce" intended to deceive the Bolivian public. Even Barrientos' inaugural speech in August was considered "a fabric of lies," as Pombo termed it, deriding him for "calling for unity on the basis of love of country in order to achieve a new, industrialized Bolivia." The guerrilla high command were convinced that:

"The 1964 counter-revolutionary coup halted a process begun in 1952 which, in 1963–64, began to yield positive results. Víctor Paz Estenssoro left the country, and Bolivia entered on the political era of Barrientos and a military clique which leaned to the right." [3]

Bolivia in 1966 appeared to be so fragmented in all respects that it could not possibly be put together again. Until 1952, it had been little more than a collection of warring rival regions, classes, races and leaders. The MNR had initiated a process of "nationalizing" the country, of establishing a Bolivian nationality, which by 1966 had begun to affect many Bolivians, but was still far from completed.

Against this background, it was not surprising that discontent all too often took the form of violent demonstrations and strikes, which kept the country on the edge of chaos. The tin mines were particularly unstable following the 1964 military takeover, and seemed close to open rebellion.

The tin industry, which had traditionally provided Bolivia with her greatest source of income, was also the sickest part of the economy. Because it had long been a drain on the nation's finances, Barrientos totally reorganized it in early 1965, firing superfluous workers and adjusting wage schedules to reflect profits, eliminating featherbedding and padded payrolls. Strikes broke out in May and brought on the military occupation of the mines. Though Barrientos' action enabled them to show a profit for the first time since the Revolution, his toughness with the mine union—and particularly his exiling of such extremist leaders as Juan Lechín Oquendo—made him appear repressive and reactionary to the extreme left.

3. *Tricontinental,* No. 1.

Of all the miscalculations Ché and Fidel Castro made about Bolivia, their lack of understanding of the state of the nation, the state of its government, and the character of its two top leaders, Barrientos and Ovando, were among the most costly. Viewing Bolivia in terms of pre-revolutionary Cuba as they nearly always did, Guevara and Castro saw the ruling generals as a two-headed Batista. This was a dangerous illusion. Neither general had fought the revolutionary trend in their country, as Batista had. On the contrary, both had been part of it. The governments they led jointly and alternately from 1964 to 1966, and the one elected in the latter year, were based entirely on the popular policies of the National Revolution of 1952.

Had Ché and Fidel studied the background of President Barrientos, they would readily have seen he was in every respect a product of the long revolutionary process that had been going on in Bolivia since her shattering defeat in the Chaco War (1932–35). He aligned himself with the first of the revolutionary nationalist governments which followed the war, headed by Colonel Germán Busch, which foreshadowed many of the radical reforms to come.

When Barrientos was graduated from the Colegio Militar in 1943, he joined the successful revolution led by Colonel Gualberto Villarroel, a revolutionary social nationalist. Villarroel established the basis for the future agrarian reform, enlarged the Labor Code, and made education universal. Martyred in 1946 when an angry mob, egged on by the privileged classes he had dared challenge, hung him from a lamp-post just outside his office in the Palace of Government, he became a national hero.

When the Movimento Nacionalista Revolucionario (MNR) was formed in 1949 to further the programs of Villarroel and create a profound social revolution, Barrientos joined it. That year, he participated in the first revolt led by the MNR. Forming a revolutionary command in Cochabamba and seizing the airbase and military school there, he flew one of its planes over La Paz and dropped leaflets announcing the revolution's triumph. He was premature. The revolt was put down in blood and Barrientos had to flee for his life. He was also dismissed from the Army, and became one of four high-ranking officers belonging to the MNR who fought reactionary Army leaders during the six years his party was in the opposition.

From 1946 to 1952, Barrientos lived the life of a typical Latin American revolutionary. He was shunted from one jail to an-

other, sent to two concentration camps, and periodically starved.
Upon his release, he continued his revolutionary activities underground.

In 1952, after four consecutive post-Villarroel regimes had
exhausted every brutal means of suppressing a growing clamor
for change, the Bolivian people rose in revolt. This was one
of the very few truly popular upheavals of our time, with virtually the entire nation—workers, peasants, students, merchants,
soldiers, officers—rising up as one against the reactionary junta
in power. Barrientos, now a captain at El Alto Air Base in La Paz,
immobilized it the day the National Revolution began, April 9th,
in defiance of his superiors' orders. Three days later, he was
selected by the provisional revolutionary government to bring
home the leader of the National Revolution, Víctor Paz Estenssoro, from his exile in Argentina.

Barrientos remained a loyal supporter of Paz Estenssoro, but
when, in 1964, the MNR President showed himself to be increasingly corrupt and tyrannical and sought to perpetuate himself in
power by amending the Constitution, the students led a revolt
against him. The military, also opposed to his rule by now, moved
to take power on November 4th even though it was internally divided over that decision. Thus began what Barrientos and others
have called "the revolution within the revolution." As Barrientos
once explained his position: "I believe in the National Revolution but not in the MNR."

This is no place to assess Barrientos' record as President of
Bolivia. Obviously, he made his share of mistakes. The fact remains that he offered a revolutionary program that was popular
with the people, and thus undercut any appeal Ché Guevara
might otherwise have expected. In particular, Barrientos enjoyed
immense popularity among precisely the segment Ché deemed
most essential to his own success, the peasantry.

Barrientos, orphaned at 16, was fluent in the country's dominant Indian tongue, Quechua, and as a young revolutionary,
fought for such radical measures as agrarian reform. Though he
was already a man of 48 when Ché Guevara launched his guerrilla war, the Bolivian President did not hesitate to risk his own
life flying his plane into guerrilla territory to urge his troops on.
A jaunty man of medium height and stocky build, with a crew-
cut, Barrientos would land wherever the action might be and
step out of his cockpit with a submachine-gun slung over his
shoulders. Ché records that Barrientos once landed about 250

yards from where he himself lay hidden. This was more the act of an Errol Flynn than of a Batista.

Ché and Fidel Castro quite naturally carried their faulty assessment of the Bolivian government over to the Bolivian armed forces. This, however, was more understandable, because after the Bolivians' smashing defeat at the hands of the supposedly inferior Paraguayan army in the Gran Chaco War, they were never taken seriously at home or abroad. They were riddled with political factionalism during the period of postwar ferment, and thoroughly purged after Paz Estenssoro came to power. Paz Estenssoro also closed the Colegio Militar, which had trained the reactionary officer caste.

The Revolution meanwhile brought into being a workers' militia, largely made up of the militant mineworkers, and a new police force, both of which were encouraged and maintained by the revolutionary government as a counterweight to the truncated Army. They were intended to ensure that the military would never again dominate Bolivian politics.

An emasculated Army, however, represented a grave weakness to the republic in the eyes of some of the younger officers, as long as there was a separate militia responsive only to its own narrow interests rather than those of the nation. One of these officers was Captain Alfredo Ovando Candia, who took upon himself the task of quietly reconstructing the Army—but along different lines than before. The new Army would accept and defend the Revolution and would stay out of politics.

When Ovando became Commander-in-Chief, he continued to believe that the military should remain nonpolitical. It suited his personality, in any case, for in contrast to the loquacious, flamboyant Barrientos, he is fundamentally a reserved and somewhat introverted man. Unlike Barrientos, Ovando is more the professional military officer, having remained in military ranks continuously since his graduation from the Colegio Militar in 1931.

Despite the rebuilding of the armed forces under Ovando, they were in extremely poor fighting condition when the guerrillas appeared on the scene. Ché was filled with scorn for them. After the initial clash on March 23, 1967, he wrote of their "total ineffectiveness." It was an accurate appraisal at the time.

It was also, as events proved, a superficial one.

The armed forces of Bolivia were then back at their prerevolutionary strength of about 20,000 men, organized in the fol-

lowing services: Army, 16,000; Air Force, 2,500; Navy, 1,500. But
the figures were misleading. An antiquated conscript system usually kept the actual number of effective men in any given year
down to about half. They were expected to defend a country
twice as large as France, extending for some 425,000 square
miles, with borders touching five other nations.

After years of neglect by the Bolivian government, Bolivian
troops went into combat against Ché's guerrillas carrying Mauser
rifles of World War I vintage and other outdated arms. Some
modern armament had been obtained when Bolivia signed a
bilateral agreement with the United States in 1958, under the
latter's Military Assistance Program (MAP), but not enough
to outfit the entire Army. At the same time, to make both the
new Army and the bilateral agreement palatable to the people
and to its own adherents, the MNR laid heavy stress upon MAP's
Civic Action Program. By late 1963 one-fifth of the Bolivian
Army's man-hours were being allocated to civil works, building
irrigation projects, roads or other needed improvements. Thus
Rolando noted in his diary for February 11, 1967:

"Among the features of this area we find that a road is being built
by 300 soldiers assigned by the government . . ."

Civic Action was thus highly beneficial for the country, and
for the Army's image. But it did not produce trained troops.

Beset by both short- and long-range problems that impeded
its development into a modern, efficient fighting force, it was
no wonder that at first the Army was no match for the guerrillas it overwhelmingly outnumbered. The Bolivian leaders
and official American circles were concerned that the Army
might collapse under the blows of Ché's guerrillas and that they
might well over-run Bolivia. Although American military aid was
increased in May 1967, at the Bolivian Government's request,
there was no certainty that this could make a real difference in
the Army's performance.

Complicating the Army's job of dealing with the guerrillas
was the outbreak of a major crisis in the mines, in June 1967.
This was accompanied by student and teacher demonstrations
in La Paz and elsewhere. The Army's best soldiers, called "MAP
elements" because they had been trained under the American
Military Assistance Program, were sent to occupy the mines
and could not be thrown into action against the guerrillas.

The Bolivian generals, facing the possibility of losing the

country or at least its southeast region to the guerrillas while remaining in control of the mines, decided to mix some MAP with non-MAP elements and send them against Ché. But that didn't work, either. When the mining situation came under control, complete MAP units could be thrown into battle. Still, they could not do the job required, and as late as August we find Ché commenting: "The Army does not improve in effectiveness nor combativeness."

But in the middle of August, the Bolivian high command was able to send into action the first elements of the 650-man 2nd Ranger Battalion just completing a tough, four-month training course given by a 16-man Mobile Training Team from the United States 8th Special Forces Group. Armed with modern weapons, they began to turn the tide. On August 31st, they succeeded in cutting down Joaquín's guerrilla group. By September 16th, the last members of the battalion had completed their training and were in combat. Ché quickly felt the difference. At the end of September, he was compelled to acknowledge that "now the Army appears to be more effective in its actions." Three weeks after the 2nd Rangers went into combat at full strength, Ché was brought to heel.

The Army went in heavily, as we have noted, for civic action, performing tangible works that benefited numerous rural villages. In many cases conscripts came from the same villages or areas that had been helped by civic action units. This gave the Army a "progressive" image which belied Communist propaganda calling it "reactionary" and "a tool of the oligarchy."

The Bolivian Army was, in short, a people's army, and that is what Ché was up against. The fact that it was poorly equipped and poorly trained, at the outset, had blinded him and Fidel Castro from seeing how deeply rooted it was in the National Revolution and the Bolivian people.

Ché returned to Cuba from the Congo toward the end of 1965, after some six or seven months of disheartening combat in support of the Kinshasa rebels, and almost immediately plunged into the work of organizing his final guerrilla adventure: Bolivia.

Ché was working for the goal that he and Fidel had kept uppermost in mind since their 1959 triumph in Cuba: extend the revolution to the "Cono Sur"—the "Southern Cone"—of South America, which consists of   Argentina, Brazil, Chile, Paraguay and Uruguay. Over the years, they had made a number of attempts to start guerrilla warfare in Argentina, Ché's birthplace, with no success, and also in Bolivia. President Barrientos claimed, in a talk he gave in June 1967 at the height of Ché's guerrilla campaign, that its organization had been under way since 1963. There is evidence to substantiate his statement.

The guerrilla known as Camba, who served Ché till near the very end when he saw the cause as hopeless and deserted it, told the Military Court trying Régis Debray at Camiri, on October 5, 1967, that he had received guerrilla training in Cuba for about eight months, beginning as early as August 1962. Sent to Cuba by the PCB, Camba upon returning home was ordered by the Party to join in organizing "a military apparatus designed to overthrow the government." Camba did, in fact, turn up among the earliest cadres Havana formed in La Paz to prepare Ché's expedition.

In the same year Camba was graduated from a Cuban guerrilla school, 1963, another future member of Ché's Bolivian team, Antonio, showed up in Bolivia. He was with the Peruvian guerrilla leader, Hugo Blanco, who had fled across the border after his own revolutionary movement had failed in Peru. Antonio, whose real name was Captain Orlando Pantoja Tamayo, was then a high official in Cuba's G-2 Intelligence Service and worked directly under its chief and Minister of Interior, Comandante Ramiro Valdes. A former member of Ché's famous "Ciro Redondo" Column in the Sierra Maestra, Antonio was interested in the possibilities of continuing or spreading Blanco's guerrilla war to Bolivia.

The Cuban Embassy in La Paz was in those days up to its ears in subversive activities in Bolivia. The Chargé d'Affaires, Ramón Aja Castro, had been working with two PCB leaders, Jorge Kolle Cueto (who in 1966 discussed with Fidel Castro in Havana the possibility of the PCB aiding Ché) and Luis Leytón, on plans for establishing a "Bolivian Socialist Republic." Significantly, this was to be used as the base for "a socialist revolution in Latin America"—as one PCB document found by the Bolivian police phrased it—and this was precisely the goal Ché set for himself in the same country some two or three years later.

Aja Castro's failure deterred neither Ché nor Fidel. Deeply hidden in Bolivia, under perfect cover as a student, was one of the most fascinating and capable Communist agents ever involved in a clandestine operation. Posthumously famous in Havana propaganda as "Tania la Guerrilla," she was an attractive, blonde, blue-eyed, oval-faced girl of about twenty-seven who lived in Bolivia under the name of Laura Gutierrez Bauer. She had been operating there for years. Her importance to Ché's undertaking is shown by his reaction upon her exposure:

"Everything indicates that Tania is identified, which means that years of good and patient work are lost."

Tania's cover story in La Paz as Laura Gutierrez Bauer was that she had been born in Argentina on November 19, 1937 of an Argentine father and German mother. Her father was actually an East German Communist professor named Erich Bunke; her mother a Pole, Nadja Bider. Her real name in full was Haydee Tamara Bunke Bider.

In La Paz she registered in the School of Pharmacy at the Universidad Mayor de San Andrés, Bolivia's leading institution of higher learning. Nobody seemed to think it odd that an attractive Argentine girl would leave sophisticated Buenos Aires for provincial La Paz to study pharmacy, when her own city offered much better educational facilities. She was immediately accepted into the Bolivian capital's society and became popular with the younger set.

Posing as a poor girl who had to earn a living, Laura, as she was then called, taught German and Russian. One of her pupils was Gonzálo López Muñoz, a journalist by profession, who met her through an associate on a new magazine he had started. Taking pity on the charming Argentine girl, López Muñoz gave her a job as a bill collector for his magazine; but others say that she was also his secretary.

As López Muñoz described Laura:

"Laura was a nice girl, alert and intelligent, rather quiet. She was a bit Bohemian—she lived in a rundown flat and slept on the floor—but went to few parties and drank little. She loved folk music. She never discussed politics, as far as I recall."

That struck me as strange (by the time of our interview, "Laura" was known to the world as "Tania the Guerrilla"), and I pressed López Muñoz to dig into his memory to try to recall some political remark she may have made. But no, he insisted, he had never heard her utter a single word about politics—a truly peculiar thing, he now realized, in a country where politics is the favorite sport of young and old alike. "Not even in our house," he added, "where she came many times."

The only variation in her otherwise quiet surface life seems to have occurred when she fell in, briefly, with a somewhat fast crowd run by the attractive secretary of a Cabinet Minister. The crowd liked nudist parties, and the Minister's girl made Laura come and bring a bottle to one of them; this led to attendance at a few more. Whether Laura feared that refusal might endanger her cover (perhaps the ministerial employee would get her sacked from school or her job, out of spite) or not, she found it expedient to tag along for a while. Laura was able to build up a list of more than 200 guerrilla contacts in La Paz alone, who at the proper signal were to start an insurrection there to be coordinated with the guerrilla campaign in the southeast. An examination of her list, discovered among Ché's belongings, revealed that her contacts reached right into the office of the Bolivian Presidency.

Laura's importance in the guerrilla movement became known only piecemeal. Thus it wasn't until after the August 31st clash in which she was killed that those who had known her as Laura found out she was "Tania the Guerrilla," who had conducted an advice-to-the-lovelorn radio program in Santa Cruz which was a means of communicating information to the guerrillas in Nancahuazú. Sometimes she would read "lovelorn letters" so unintelligible that nobody in her audience could understand them, and for a good reason: these were coded messages aimed at Ché. Laura's information was useful and often vital, since Santa Cruz was a major station on the guerrilla underground railroad and a place where arms were cached.

Laura-Tania was more than a key Guevara agent in La Paz; she was also Ché's liaison with an Argentine group he was forming for the purpose of attempting another guerrilla war in his own country concurrently with the one in Bolivia. Tania's real identity became known only when the Cubans, who had decided to let her share the posthumous heroic aura they were building around Ché, released some pertinent details. Her job, however, was not that of a simple revolutionary. When she turned 21, Tamara, as she was known in Germany, was recruited by the East German Ministry of State Security as an agent. According to a former Ministry official who held the rank of first lieutenant at the time, Guenther Maennel, her task was to lure foreigners into enticing situations and the Ministry would then attempt to talk them into doing intelligence work.

In December 1959, Tamara met the dashing Latin American guerrilla leader who, as President of the National Bank of Cuba, arrived in her country at the head of a trade mission. She fell in love with him. The gallant Ché obtained an official Cuban Government invitation for her to visit Cuba and she arrived there on May 12, 1961. Ché promptly put her to work for various youth and women's organizations, got her into the militia, and gave her her first guerrilla assignment. She was to work with the Frente Unitario Nicaraguense, a Nicaraguan guerrilla group then being trained in Cuba for operations in its own country. Then came the Bolivian adventure.

Unknown to Ché, however, from the time she set foot in Cuba to her death in Bolivia, Tania continued to work for the East German Ministry for State Security. Only for this operation, she was attached to the Soviet KGB. Her job: to keep an eye on the unpredictable Castro people. Maennel should know. He recruited her for the job.

When Ché, who had been involved with Tania, selected her to go to Bolivia as his advance man, the Russians gave her orders through their East German counterparts to spy on Ché. Again, it was Maennel who originally assigned her. As he tells it:

"I myself assigned Tamara Bunke as an agent against Guevara. Through her, East Berlin and Moscow were kept informed of Guevara's thoughts and decisions."

So Tamara—or Laura, or Tania, or María, or Mary—was not only a clandestine agent of Ché Guevara's in Bolivia, but worked simultaneously for the East German and Soviet Intelligence Services, spying on Ché.

She was killed crossing the Lower Masicurí River, along with the rest of Joaquín's cut-off group, and her body, which floated downriver, was found five days later in a decomposed state. In her *mochila*—knapsack—there was a tape of some Oriental music she had recently made.

Ché's preparations for the Bolivian adventure got under way early in 1966. The basic decisions were made in January of that year, when three Bolivian Communist leaders attended the First

Afro-Asian-Latin American Peoples' Solidarity Conference—of which Ché was perhaps the main instigator, in Havana, January 3rd to 15th.

The three were Mario Monje Molina, First Secretary of the Bolivian Communist Party, Mario Miranda Pachéco, Executive Secretary of the PCB-inspired National Left Liberation Front (FLIN), and Gabriel Porcél Salazar, who represented both the miners' union and the Revolutionary Party of the Nationalist Left (PRIN) led by Juan Lechín Oquendo, Bolivia's left-wing former Vice-President and its most powerful labor leader. Of the trio, Mario Monje was to be the most prominent in the discussions and plans for forming the guerrilla movement.

Mario Monje did not see Ché Guevara in Havana. Nor did he have any idea for some months that Ché was going to lead the Bolivian guerrilla movement. He did not even know, until much later, that the guerrillas were going to fight in Bolivia. His impression (shared by his fellow PCB leaders) was that the guerrilla war was to be launched in one of the neighboring countries. (Fidel and Ché had, as a matter of fact, discussed the possibility of starting their "continental revolution" in a country other than Bolivia.)

Ché Guevara was still very much under wraps in 1966, and operated entirely behind the scenes. That is why Monje never saw him, never knew of his involvement in the guerrilla undertaking, did not even know if he still lived. The man he dealt with was the Cuban *jefe máximo* himself, Fidel Castro. That was good enough: Fidel controlled the purse strings, and he would, of course, relay to Ché whatever he and Monje talked about. We learn of this direct contact between the Cuban Premier and the Bolivian Communist First Secretary from the diary of Pombo, which discloses further that the contact continued well into the guerrilla operation in Bolivia. Fidel also maintained direct contact with Monje's sidekick, Jorge Kolle Cueto, and other PCB leaders.

Relations between the Bolivian Communist Party and the Cubans were, however, stormy and largely unproductive. Though individual members of the PCB, such as Luis Tellería Murillo and Loyola Guzmán Lara, cooperated with Ché and the guerrillas, and a handful of others, such as Bigotes, joined them at Nancahuazú, the Party as such never gave Ché its support—a fact that contributed, perhaps decisively, to his defeat. On the one hand, Ché refused to surrender his military command of the guerrillas to Monje, while on the other the PCB resented the Cubans' intrusion in their country's affairs. Not least, they resented the Castro-Guevara decision to make Bolivia the scene of the revolutionary war without consulting them.

The directing role Fidel Castro assumed from the start in his relations with Monje, Kolle Cueto and other PCB leaders amounted to *prima facie* evidence that the Cuban Government was the sponsor and sole directing force behind the guerrilla movement Ché led. Cuba, in other words, was planning an armed intervention, surreptitiously, in a neighboring Latin American republic. But that is far from being the only evidence.

Ché sent two trusted emissaries, Pombo and Tuma, to oversee preparations on the ground in his behalf. Pombo, like the other Cubans, was a veteran of the Sierra Maestra. Born in Yara, Cuba, on May 10, 1940, now married, with young children, he worshiped Ché and joined the Bolivian expedition more out of his profound feeling for the man than for any other reason. Ché, in turn, had great confidence in him, which he showed in such ways as appointing him Chief of Supply, Services and Transport for the guerrilla band, a general-staff post. Pombo abundantly demonstrated his own sterling qualities as a guerrilla during the trying campaign, but most dramatically after it ended, when he led the only other Cuban survivors, Urbano and Benigno, on a perilous 500-mile trek across Bolivia to Chile and safety. In March of 1968, the last of the eighteen Cubans who went to fight in Bolivia managed to reach Havana, thanks to Pombo. This was the man whom Ché dispatched to Bolivia in July 1966.

Pombo arrived with a false Ecuadorian passport, No. 45908, issued in the name of Carlos Suárez González. Like many of the others, he went from Havana to Prague, then to Frankfurt, where he took a Lufthansa flight that stopped at Zurich, Dakar, Rio de Janeiro, and finally São Paulo. His companion was another trusted Guevara aide, Tuma—sometimes called Tumaini—whose relationship with the chief was in some respects closer than Pombo's. This we learn from Ché himself who, when Tuma is killed on June 26, 1967, pours out his grief in one of the truly tender passages of his diary.

Toward the end of the preparatory phase, Ché sent still another trusted lieutenant to La Paz to inspect the operation there. This person was Pacho, who arrived in the Bolivian capital by still another route—train from Chile—on September 3, 1966. Like all the other Cuban guerrillas, he traveled with a false passport, made out in the name of Antonio Garrido Garcia. All told, they had a total of 21 false passports, some of them, like Ché, carrying two at the same time, issued in different names. Besides, they all carried such additional false documentation as vaccination certificates and tourist cards. Havana, which maintains a veritable false-passport mill on a permanent basis, performed meticulously.

One of Pacho's principal missions was to settle the confusing issue of a suitable site for the location of the guerrilla base. Involved was a prolonged search of several months that took Ché's advance men over a considerable slice of Bolivia. They inspected four regions from south to north: the fertile Alto (Upper) Beni region in the northeastern Department (state) of Beni; Los Yungas, a lush subtropical province in the eastern part of La Paz Department bordering the Beni; Cochabamba, the central Department, also subtropical; and the Department of Santa Cruz in the southeast. One can only venture a wild guess at the number of guerrilla representatives, including the Frenchman Régis Debray, who explored those sites.

The master plan called for terminating the preparations and beginning the "first phase" of the guerrilla movement before the end of 1966. Yet until October, the month preceding Ché Guevara's own entry onto the scene, nobody, not even Ché himself, knew where the guerrillas were going to base themselves. At that, a decision was finally all but forced on Ché.

The situation became confused when Pombo arrived in July with instructions from Ramón to Mbili "to acquire a farm farther north." Mbili, or Ricardo, was stunned. He had, just that month, purchased a farm in the south at Nancahuazú. Why would Ché now want to buy another "farther north"?

Ricardo's new property at Nancahuazú comprised 1,227 hectares (some 3,000 acres), and had cost 30,000 Bolivian pesos (about $2,500). The actual purchase had been concluded by Coco Peredo who, as a Bolivian, would arouse no suspicion. Coco had been prowling about the southeast since June in a Toyota jeep, sometimes in company with a girl the neighbors described as his sweetheart, who may well have been Tania. Coco had finally found what appeared to be exactly the right piece of territory in the possession of a local landowner, Remberto Villa. Posing as a farmer interested in raising pigs and growing corn, he made the deal with Villa. The guerrillas had decided that a farm actually being worked would provide them with perfect cover.

As a location, Nancahuazú was in many respects ideal. As Pombo describes it in a report to Ché on September 11, 1966:

"The Nancahuazú property is located in the southwest region of Santa Cruz Province [he meant Department] in a mountainous area of exuberant vegetation but scant water in the general area. The property itself has plenty of water. Nancahuazú is in a canyon between the Serranías de las Pirirendas to the east and the Serranías Incahuasi to the west; their highest peaks are its eastern and western borders."

The property was about as isolated as it should have been, according to guerrilla specifications, yet not totally removed from all civilization. It was approximately 225 kilometers (137.5 miles) southwest of Santa Cruz de la Sierras, the chief city of the region, and 80 kilometers (some 50 miles) northwest of the oil center of Camiri. The only habitations nearby were the Terrazas *finca* where Remberto Villa lived, the little village of Lagunillas, and the farm of their nearest neighbor, Ciro Algarañaz.

Ché's instructions "to acquire a farm farther north" galvanized Ricardo into action. On July 30th, he sent three men to roam the vast Beni in search of land, then promised Ché to have a farm "within twenty days."

None of them could very well disobey Ché's order. Not directly. In typical circumlocutionary Latin fashion, they praised the Beni as a "very good" place for the farm, though to buy it would have involved endless red tape and there was no escape route. It bordered one of the most forbidding regions in the world, the rough Cordilheira dos Parecis in Brazil. At the same time, they also sang the praises of Nancahuazú and advised Ché that they had already bought a farm there, in a message on September 10th. They listed the reasons why they thought it much better than the Beni, among them because "it is a tropical zone" and "an economically important" one because of its location in oil and cattle country.

But after plugging so hard for Nancahuazú, Ché's men in La Paz then turned around and assured him:

"As for the arms, when we get the farm in Alto Beni, we will transfer them."

On October 2nd, they actually took steps to purchase the Beni site, sending there to complete the transaction the veteran

Bolivian Communist, Rodolfo Saldaña, who served as one of Ché's principal liaison men in La Paz and at this writing is in hiding.

A day later, however, Ché stunned them all with this message:

"The present farm is good. Get another without transferring the arms to it until I notify you."

Ché had, in other words, done an about-face—almost a complete one, anyway, for he still wanted "another" farm. But the "present" one was good, and the arms were not to be moved from the southeast.

What had made Ché decide to look for a farm "farther north," in the first place, when Nancahuazú had already been purchased? From the available facts it seems that the French Castroite Régis Debray had perhaps had a decisive hand in the switch.

When Pacho reached La Paz he told Pombo and Ricardo "about the visit of Danton [Debray's alias], whose mission is to make a geo-political study of the selected 'zone' in the Beni." Ché meanwhile had requested "military maps of the country," which Debray acquired when he reached Bolivia in September: obviously they would be needed for any "geo-political study."

Debray carried out Ché's orders and went into the Beni to look for possible campsites. While there he stumbled on Ricardo and other comrades doing the same thing. Ricardo, however, as Pombo reported on September 16th, "did not stay all the time necessary because the Frenchman is in that area and it is inadvisable that he see them often."

Mario Monje charged that it was Debray who "ordered a change of location of the farm to the Alto Beni region, an area from which a guerrilla cannot move out to other countries." Monje, a Bolivian, knew very well that there was no way out of Bolivia from the Beni.

As events turned out, the guerrillas did not fare much better in Nancahuazú. That choice turned out to be as fateful as the Beni would have been. The guerrilla base at Nancahuazú was perched on the edge of a rocky canyon nearly twelve miles long and more than 309 feet deep. Below was a river 30 feet wide which hugged the canyon walls, leaving no path for man or animal to tread. The forest above was so thick that nothing was visible from the air but treetops. Game abounded: jaguar and deer and bear as well as smaller animals like monkeys and iguanas, and also parrots and wild turkeys and *visna*, the small blackbird common to this remote southeastern region of Bolivia.

Along the canyon's edge ran a road, little more than a path, at the end of which was a small house. Its only unusual feature was a tin roof, which led people to call it the *Casa de Calamina*—house of the tin roof—a name that would become popular, especially with the foreign press. Beyond it, on a small hill next to a ravine, was an encampment not visible from house or road, for its entrance was covered by thick branches and logs. This was the base of Ché and his guerrilla band, the projected *foco insurrecional* of continental revolution.

Only four men inaugurated the *foco*. Besides Ché, there were Pacho, Pombo and Tuma, all handpicked comrades of his from the Sierra Maestra days. Soon, others would be coming (in twos, to ensure security), the first three pairs in a fortnight or so. Within a short while, Ché was confident, his little band would swell into a peoples' army with the peasants flocking into it from all sides, eager to follow those who had selected themselves to lead a peoples' liberation movement.

But first the wild terrain had to be subdued and prepared for the role it would play. As Pombo observed when he saw it, "it has the specifications" for guerrilla work, "but not on a large scale as yet."

At the end of a week they were digging the first of a series of tunnels and caves in the ravine, in which they cached, Ché reports, all "items which could be compromising." These included the guerrillas' false passports and other false documents, coded messages and reports to and from Havana and La Paz, some diaries, and a large quantity of arms, equipment and canned food. In two days they finished Tunnel 1, as it was named, and Ché made a sketch of it to insert in Document I, the first of a series he had begun.

Soon, a crude but serviceable little community replaced the jungle. Ché and his men had built structures for nearly every human requirement, forming a basic complex similar to that which he had constructed in the Sierra Maestra and recommended in his *Guerrilla Warfare* manual as standard procedure. On a hill where the camp sat they put up an open *cabaña* and around it a number of rustic log tables and benches not unlike those found in picnic grounds. Nearby were a round mud oven for baking bread, a lean-to for hanging meat, another serving as a dispensary (and stocked with a wide variety of imported antibiotics, medicines and surgical supplies). A good fifty yards higher up they built a latrine. The big radio transmitter they had brought with them was kept in a cave.

The camp was not constructed overnight. Ché and his men took until the end of 1966 to finish it. Most of December, for example, was spent in digging more caves and building Camp No. 2, into which Ché moved eight guerrillas on December 15th. Meanwhile, the men tried to familiarize themselves with the surrounding terrain and there were daily scouting expeditions in which all participated at one point or another.

The original four guerrillas were slowly augmented, during this period, by new arrivals, usually in the prescribed team of two. The first pair, who were of prime importance, reached Nancahuazú on November 20th. One was Marcos, Ché's choice as second-in-command, who in real life was Antonio Sánchez Díaz. Like Ché, he held the highest rank in the Cuban Revolutionary Armed Forces, *comandante,* and was also a member of the Central Committee of the Cuban Communist Party. The other was Rolando, real name Eliseo Reyes Rodríguez, also a CC member and Cuban Army officer, who was one of Ché's most intimate comrades and author of one of the guerrilla diaries.

A week later, on November 27th, two pairs arrived in rapid succession. They included two Congo veterans: Braulio, who was really Comandante Israel Reyes Zayas of the Cuban Army and another diary author; and Urbano, who was Captain Leonardo Tamayo Nuñez and had been Secretary to the Cuban Delegation, headed by Ché, to the Alliance for Progress charter meeting at Punta del Este, Uruguay, in 1961. The other pair consisted of Joaquín, whom Ché appointed second-in-command over Marcos and who had commanded a guerrilla school in Matanzas as Comandante Juan Vitalio Acuna Nuñez and was a CC member; and Miguel, Captain Manuel Hernández of the Cuban Army, whom Ché made chief of his vanguard.

On the same day, two Bolivian guerrilla recruits arrived: Inti (real name Guido Peredo Leigue), Coco's older brother and one of the only two Bolivians to survive the guerrilla defeat; and Ernesto, or Freddy Ernesto Maimura Hurtado, a medical student, both fresh from training courses in Cuba. Noted Ché happily that same day: "We are now 12 insurrectionists." Of the twelve, only two were Bolivians; the rest, including Ché, were Cubans.

Ricardo now brought the "unpleasant news" (as Ché characterized it) that other foreigners wanted to join the band. The

Peruvian revolutionary leader, Juan Pablo Chang Navarro, known as El Chino, was offering him twenty Peruvian recruits, at which Ché noted with concern: "This causes us some difficulty because we internationalized the struggle before we involved Estanislao." He was referring to the First Secretary of the Bolivian Communist Party, Mario Monje, and was understandably worried that too many foreigners were joining him before the PCB could come in and provide the guerrillas with an authentic Bolivian base.

With each new arrival, Ché's concern about prematurely "internationalizing" the struggle increases. In his November monthly analysis, Ché notes that already "half the personnel are here," but the Bolivians constitute only a handful. He continues, hopefully:

"The plan is to wait for the rest of the group, increase the number of Bolivians to at least 20, and then begin to operate."

The situation improved little in December. By the end of that month, a total of 24 guerrillas were in Nancahuazú but only nine were Bolivians; the rest were all Cubans. The total number of natives never rose higher than 29, out of a maximum total of 50 guerrillas before the first clash with the Army on March 23rd. Of the 29 Bolivians, two drowned and three deserted before that battle, leaving Ché with 24 Bolivians when he went into combat, as against 21 foreigners: barely half his force. If one reckons, as Ché did, that four of the Bolivian group were "dregs," as Ché calls them—his exact word is "*resacas*"—we must calculate, as Ché did, that during the combat phase he never had more than 20 Bolivian effectives to depend on; the real proportion thus drops to less than half of the total of 41 guerrillas (including himself) in his band at that time.

All the Cubans were not only veteran guerrillas but officers in the Cuban Revolutionary Armed Forces and men who had served with Ché in military and/or civilian capacities, or were close friends. Five, including Ché, held the top rank of *comandante* in the Cuban Army; four (not all *comandantes*) were members of the Cuban Communist Central Committee. (Ché, though on the six-man Secretariat of the PCC's predecessor, the United Party of the Socialist Revolution, had not been named to the CC, for by the time it was formed, in October 1965, he was in the Congo and no longer in Cuban politics.)

Though Ché prided himself, in the beginning, on having a

better bunch of Cuban guerrillas than any that had ever been put together (see Pombo), he was to change his mind before long. Most of his recruits did not measure up to expectations, and he not only regretted having praised them but criticized them as "the first to be a problem."

Pacho, who was so close to Ché that he alone was privileged to be his traveling companion from Havana to Nancahuazú, was the first to weaken. After only a week in camp, Ché began to note that "Pachungo seems somewhat unacclimated and sad, but he should recover." He never did. He made trouble repeatedly, usually in tandem with another prized Cuban guerrilla, Marcos, who was Ché's original choice for second-in-command. Both men, who may fairly be considered the cream of the Cubans Ché brought to Bolivia, came in for severe public criticism from their commander.

Violations of discipline began to occur during the first fortnight in Nancahuazú. Before a month was out, Ché felt it necessary to deliver a lecture on the subject. As Pombo records the occasion, on December 4th, Ché began by telling the Cubans that it is "our duty to be an example to the Bolivians." He also announced that henceforth the Cubans "will temporarily occupy positions of leadership to start developing the Bolivians."

By the end of January 1967, Ché was ready to take his little band out on a training march whose purposes were to become accustomed to all sorts of hardships, to familiarize themselves with the terrain of the region, and to win over peasants. When they started out, on February 1st, Rolando recorded with some excitement:

"The second phase of the first stage of L. [Liberation] begins now."

The phase did not begin auspiciously. Ché, Joaquin and Moro were ill from the outset. Trouble dogged them all through the 48 days the march lasted—nearly twice as long as planned, largely because they were unable to find their way back to Nancahuazú through the inhospitable region north of the Río Grande they had set out to explore.

The band returned to Nancahuazú on March 19th, footsore, half-starved, dejected, and minus two of their number who had drowned in a rain-swollen river. Worse than anything else, perhaps, was their failure to achieve the objective of winning peasant support. Not a single peasant they encountered showed any real sympathy for their cause, much less joined them. They tottered into the base, low in spirit, only to find that the Army had already discovered and reconnoitered the camp.

In the early morning of March 23rd, the guerrillas ambushed a 32-man Bolivian Army patrol in Nancahuazú, killing seven, wounding six and capturing eleven (the rest managed to flee). It was not much of a fight, but the March 23rd ambush represented a big victory for the guerrillas. Besides the casualties they inflicted on the Army, they captured, according to their own count, 16 Mausers with 2,000 rounds of ammunition, three 60-mm mortars with 64 shells, one 30 cal. machine-gun with 500 rounds, two BZ submachine-guns, two UZI machine pistols, two radio sets, and the Army's operations plan. "The beginning of the struggle phase," Ché proudly notes in his March monthly summary, "[was] characterized by a precise, and spectacular attack."

The guerrilla victory and accompanying worldwide publicity were naturally a source of pleasure and satisfaction to Ché and his men. Coming after the disheartening 48-day trek through the rugged southeast, these developments heightened morale and brightened the future. But Ché had second thoughts. He ends his March summary with the pessimistic statement, "The situation is not good . . ."

Why? The key to his thinking is this observation at the beginning of the last paragraph of the summary:

"Evidently we will have to get going before I had planned to."

The March 23rd encounter had been, in other words, premature. By the month's end, Ché came close to realizing that it had been a mistake. More than anything else, it had cost them the secrecy they had hitherto enjoyed—an irreplaceable weapon. Now everybody in the world knew that a guerrilla movement was operating in Bolivia and knew it before the guerrillas were prepared for the discovery.

Ché had laid down the dictum in his manual: in the first stage of guerrilla warfare the guerrilla's sole task is to keep himself alive. This implies avoiding contact with the always numerically superior foe of the regular army. The dictum was reinforced in the manual's sequel, *Guerrilla Warfare: a Method*, published three years later (in 1963), wherein he emphasized that guerrilla warfare is "a war of the people, a struggle of the masses." He then warned sharply:

"To try to carry out this kind of war without the support of the population is the prelude to inevitable disaster." [4]

Ché's men had only just returned from their extremely fatiguing march and were physically under par or sick. Moreover, they were quarrelsome, somewhat depressed, and the Bolivians were still unschooled in guerrilla warfare. Ché himself was sick, and generally not up to the rigors of guerrilla life (a fact which may have affected his assessment of the situation when he got back to Nancahuazú). And what was the situation? They had not won over a single peasant. Their urban organization, as we know from Ricardo's pitiful complaints to Pombo, was in disarray. The PCB and its pro-Peking offshoot, half-jokingly known as PCB-II, were hanging back. So were other leftwing groups. In all Bolivia at that point, Ché could honestly count upon perhaps only twelve to fifteen really first-rate guerrillas, and they were almost entirely foreigners. Were these the best conditions for Ché to take on the Bolivian Army?

Régis Debray maintains that Ché had no choice, since the Army already knew of his existence in the southeast anyway. He adds that it was three of Moisés Guevara's men, who had deserted and fallen into Army hands before the battle on March 23rd, who had betrayed Ché's presence in Nancahuazú. He had no alternative, so the reasoning continues, but to take the "strategic defensive"—attack first.

Actually, even then the Army had no proof that Ché was leading the guerrillas, though it had its suspicions. A lot of high-placed Bolivians, in fact, including President Barrientos himself, believed that Ché was dead.

The Army had obtained, however, some valuable information from the three deserters, which subsequently enabled it to locate some of the guerrilla caves and find a mass of documentation and photographs which unlocked many guerrilla secrets. Antonio, whom Ché had left in charge of the camp during the training march, was indiscreet enough to show the trio the large collection of photos Ché and his comrades had taken since the day they had set foot in Nancahuazú. The deserters also saw in camp a number of interesting visitors: Tania, Debray, Bustos, El Chino. But the incriminating evidence could only fall into Army hands *after*, and as a result of the March 23rd ambush.

It was Marcos, Ché's third-in-command, who unwittingly gave the guerrillas away. At a post-mortem session on March

4. *Guerra de guerrillas: un método*, in *Obra revolucionaria*, p. 551.

25th, two days after the ambush, Ché indicted Marcos publicly on that score. In punishment, he replaced Marcos with Miguel and gave the former the choice of returning to Cuba in disgrace or remaining in the guerrilla band as a private. Marcos chose the latter alternative.

The Army, even after the windfall of information it obtained from the deserters, moved cautiously. It finally decided to send a small unit to look in on Coco Peredo's Casa de Calamina on March 17th. The unit might well have departed after a cursory spot check, as a Lieutenant Carlos Fernández of the police had done months earlier. But, unluckily for the guerrillas, there occurred one of those incidents that always seemed to dog them in Bolivia.

Loro, whom we originally met as Bigotes and who was the student, Jorge Vásquez Machicado Viaña, got trigger happy and killed a soldier who was leaving the Casa de Calamina for his sentry post. Ché paid only scant attention to the incident when he returned to camp from the training march, but the soldier's death led directly to the dispatch of a bigger patrol to the guerrilla base on March 23rd. When that patrol was ambushed, the cat was out of the bag.

Ché was angry when he found that Marcos and Rolando had been arguing about where to lay the ambush, but he was particularly furious at Marcos who had wanted to withdraw. "It was unbelievable to retreat without a fight," is how Rolando paraphrases Ché's reaction. Ché thereupon personally took command and ordered that the ambush be organized.

Why? Did he not thereby expose the Nancahuazú base that had been established at such great cost? Why did he not, instead, first destroy all the incriminating matter it contained, and then, as his guerrilla manual urges, melt away into the woods? "The fundamental characteristic of the guerrilla is mobility," the manual states, "which permits him to be far from the specific theater of action in a few moments and far from the region itself."

The only possible answer to this puzzling question is given by the diaries of Ché and his comrades. They make this clear: The guerrillas came to Bolivia intending to go on the offensive as early as possible. They arrived convinced that the Bolivian Army would be a pushover, and, putting aside hard-earned guerrilla lessons, went looking for a fight from the very start. Pombo, for example, was anxious to attack an Army barracks only one week after he and Ché arrived at Nancahuazú. Ché refused, but only for tactical reasons: it was risky to attack anything but a "small" barracks. He was worried about "starting out with a defeat," but not about the consequences that could follow victory, such as exposure of his base.

Marcos, when called on the carpet for his own errors, openly challenged Ché's judgment, "alleging that Ramón's tactic was in error," according to Pombo.

The aftermath of the ambush found the guerrillas in disarray. Their main problem was internal tension—and dissension.

Ché was satisfied neither with the results of the training march nor the behavior of his men in their first battle. At a general assembly on March 25th, he singled out Inti, Miguel, Pombo and Rolando as among the few who had distinguished themselves on the trip and gave a critique of the action of March 23rd.

Throughout the spring and half the summer of 1967, Ché Guevara and his small guerrilla band had the Bolivian Armed Forces on the run. They struck pretty much at will up and down a 75-mile-wide corridor extending for a length of about 200 miles, from just north of Camiri to Samaipata, 60 miles southwest of Santa Cruz (see map on page 10).

The high point of the guerrilla drive came on July 6th, when the band audaciously entered and took Samaipata, on the key Cochabamba-Santa Cruz highway, and blockaded the road itself. That dramatic episode, coming on the heels of a string of unbroken victories for the guerrillas, had a profoundly demoralizing effect upon Bolivian soldier and civilian alike. Troops which could have been sent against the guerrillas were occupying the mines as the result of a violent strike. Student and teacher sympathy movements grew in a rising popular discontent. It seemed that the Barrientos government could survive only by the sheerest miracle.

But survive it did. It hung on till the tide turned in its favor on August 31st, when the Army finally scored a victory. This was of major proportions, resulting in the annihilation of about one-third of Ché's band, commanded by Joaquín, at Vado del Yeso on the northern bank of the Río Grande. As luck would have it, an almost straight line moving slightly northwest leads from Vado del Yeso to the scenes of the guerrillas' two final stands close by: La Higuera, at the end of the line, on September 26th, and Quebrada del Yuro, midway between the two, on October 8th. These three were the decisive engagements of the eleven-month guerrilla war in Bolivia.

They ended one of the most extraordinary political experiments of our time: an experiment in organizing a continental revolution from abroad in strict accordance with a thoroughly worked out, "scientific" guerrilla doctrine backed up by meticulously planned organization and strategy, and supported by great material resources, behind all of which lay the power of a foreign government. Its failure was produced by that inveterate foe of scientific conformity: the unpredictability of man and nature.

If the Barrientos government was lucky to weather the guerrilla onslaught from March through August, so paradoxically, were the guerrillas themselves. Victories did not bring them what they most needed to survive and grow: food, rest, health, hope, support. Lacking all of these, they suffered untold torment even as they were winning, and it was only the poor quality of the Bolivian Army that saved them from a quicker end.

Several skirmishes took place during the last days of March and the second week of April, but none was significant. The second clash of importance was on April 10, 1967, in the region called Iripití, a little north of the Cañadón of Nancahuazú. The Cañadón was the precise point where the March 23rd ambush occurred.

The battle commenced badly for the guerrillas. Rubio (Captain Jesús Suárez Gayol of the Cuban Army) had taken up "a very bad position since he was clearly visible from the river" where the soldiers were, reports Ché, and was shot. At a memorial service for Rubio on April 12th, Ché saw fit "to point out that the first blood drawn was Cuban." But apart from the death of Rubio, the Iripití ambush was another lightning victory for the guerrillas. As Rolando reports, they killed three soldiers, wounded one, and captured seven, together with a large quantity of weapons. At five in the afternoon a sequel took place, resulting in a total of 35 more losses for the Army: 8 dead, 3 wounded, 24 taken prisoner including the major commanding the unit of 120 men. The guerrillas this time captured a Browning, a mortar, 15 Garands, 5 Mausers, 4 M-3s and 2 M-1s.

The guerrillas learned from their prisoners that the Army had occupied the guerrilla camp at Nancahuazú, which Ché had had to evacuate on April 2nd. The prisoners said that the Army had taken a group of newspapermen into the camp with them, but that nothing of consequence had been discovered—a version Ché preferred to believe although "the radio spoke of photos and documents found there."

The radio was right, the prisoners wrong. The Army had found the first of the guerrilla diaries, Braulio's, which opened its eyes to many things: the Cuban government's sponsorship of the guerrillas, their surreptitious means of entering Bolivia, their organization, and so on. Also discovered were several field orders, one of them signed by Rolando, and a collection of photographs, some of which were of Ché. One, since become famous, was taken in the very early days at Nancahuazú, for it showed Ché still beardless, wearing a cap, sitting on a rustic bench smoking a pipe.

The guerrillas had evacuated Nancahuazú hurriedly, but not in disorder. There had been time to burn some papers, judging by the charcoal remains of them around. But in their haste they left behind an odd assortment of items: razors, flashlight batteries, Argentine and Dominican ammunition, elastic bandages, empty Coca Cola bottles, homemade bombs, women's deodorants and shoe heels (doubtless Tania's), Communist propaganda tracts, a book from the library at Catavi (a mining town), an article by General Vo Nguyen Giap, a love letter from a guerrilla to his sweetheart. . . .They also abandoned a large amount of medical supplies: plastic surgical gloves, hypodermic needles, quantities of American, British, Italian and West German instruments, bandages and antibiotics, the loss of which was to spell prolonged and unnecessary suffering for the guerrillas, particularly Ché.

An important consequence of the April 10th Army defeat was the proscription the next day of the Bolivian Communist Party, the Trotskyite POR, and other Red groups—a superfluous measure, as it developed, for their aid to the guerrillas was virtually nonexistent. The Government also expanded the emergency zone, unofficially called the "Zona Roja" ("Red Zone"), to take in five provinces ranging over the southeastern Departments (states) of Chuquisaca and Santa Cruz. These constituted the theater of war (see map on page 70).

After Iripití the guerrillas returned to their Nancahuazú base to see what they could salvage. The Army had not yet located all the caves and they were able to rescue some arms and canned milk.

What was to be the next move? Ché, we gather from his diary, had no specific plan. On April 14th, he writes vaguely:

"It is not clear how the operation is to be effected, but it would appear to be that it would be best for everybody to go out and operate for a while around this area of Muyupampa but later draw back to the woods."

If we can discern no clear tactical nor strategical objective in heading for Muyupampa, a town of 1,500 population 15 miles due south of Ché's location, there appears at least to be a personal one: to drop off, on the road to Camiri, the Frenchman Debray, the Argentine Bustos, and the British journalist, George Andrew Roth, who had just stumbled upon the guerrillas, all of whom were anxious to leave the guerrilla camp.

Even so, it was not finally decided to go on to Muyupampa for two or three more days, during which the guerrillas discussed alternate plans of maneuver. Ché, on the 17th, described his own state of mind frankly:

"The news kept varying and with it our decisions. Ticucha is a waste of time according to the peasants, and there is a road directly to Muyupampa (Vaca Guzmán) which is shorter and on the last portion of which vehicles can travel. So we decided to go on directly to Muyupampa, after much hesitation on my part."

Just before reaching Muyupampa, Ché committed one of the costliest blunders of his guerrilla career. On April 17th, he ordered Joaquín to "remain around the area" they were in, a hamlet called Bella Vista, for three days "and await our return." With Joaquín was most of the rearguard, plus Tania and Alejandro, who had been suffering from high fever and were consequently lagging behind.

We can only guess why Ché gave Joaquín such an order. He offers no explanation for it in his diary, and we are left to speculate on the purpose he could have had in dividing his small force.

The appointed three days' waiting passed, but Ché was unable to find Joaquín. The days stretched into weeks and the weeks into four months, during which both guerrilla groups scoured the entire region north and south of the Río Grande searching for each other, to no avail. They had lost each other for good. This of course suited the Army perfectly. It picked off Joaquín's tiny band first. Then it had to contend with only about two-thirds of the original force, small enough to begin with: the group left with Ché.

According to Rolando, the guerrillas reached Muyupampa on the night of April 19th and arrested a patrol of four residents, from whom they learned that three truckloads of guards had arrived in town. At 3:00 a.m., his notes continue, they withdrew, "leaving Carlos, Danton, and the British newsman hidden in the vicinity of the village." Then Rolando recorded what was to be the final entry in his diary: "At 0900 hours we arrive at Don Nemesio's house."

The townspeople were worried over the guerrillas' presence so close, fearing trouble, so at midday they sent some officials and a German priest in a station wagon flying the white flag to "negotiate" a "peace." The delegation came offering cigarettes and, Ché reports, "the news that the three outbound ones had been captured." So the main purpose for which the guerrillas had entered Muyupampa, to drop off their "visitors" safely, had been frustrated.

Now tragedy struck. It was April 25th, "a black day," as Ché records. While ambushing some soldiers in "tiny El Mesón," Rolando was mortally wounded and died when Ché began to administer plasma. The loss struck Ché hard. He considered Rolando, only twenty-seven, "the best man in the guerrilla band," and had planned to give him command "of the eventual second front."

Ché tacitly admits that he committed serious errors in laying the ambush.

During the summer Ché showed definite signs of physical deterioration and emotional strain. Clashes with the Army were few and unimportant. Nature replaced the human foe and caused the guerrillas far more trouble than the Army. Their trek across the mountains was inhumanly difficult, and as often as not they lost their way. Many times Ché or Pombo would write, as the former did on May 2nd, "A day of slow progress and much confusion about our geographic position." They were constantly asking themselves such questions as, "Where is the Iquiri?" (Ché on May 5th), or forced to admit, "Our calculations on reaching the Oro River turned out to be wrong" (Ché on May 6th).

Hunger dogged them. "We ate our penultimate poor meal," Ché records on the 6th. And the next day, "We ate the last of the soups and meats"—which they had found in one of their caves along the Oro River. Meanwhile they learned that soldiers had taken the supply of corn left at the little farm.

Ché's guerrilla campaign was six months old on May 7th, but he barely made passing mention of it. Perhaps he was aware that the half-year had not made a vast improvement in the quality of his little band. Mistakes continued to be the order of the day. Wandering about seemingly without plan, they crossed the Nancahuazú and, after hacking their way through the forest with machetes, reached Pirirenda on the other side, "with almost everybody sick."

Food, or rather lack of it, created a disciplinary problem: The men would steal whatever they could from the collective larder. The situation became so serious that Ché, before starting out for Lake Pirirenda on May 14th, called everyone together "and gave them a talk about the problems facing us; principally about the food situation."

By the end of June, Ché was so ill and weak that he could no longer keep up with his men on foot. The once doughty guerrilla commander was forced to conduct war from mule-back. He was to continue mounted on a mule or a horse for most of the war's duration.

Around this time, too, Ché's chronic and increasingly acute asthma became a serious problem.

Ché was very disturbed when the taking of Samaipata, on July 6th, failed to yield the medicines he needed for his asthma, one of the main reasons for the expedition. Finally, to get some relief, he had to resort to makeshift drug concoctions he put together himself.

At the end of his ninth month in Bolivia, on August 7th, Ché ruefully counts the toll that has been taken:

"Of the first six men, two are dead, one has disappeared, two are wounded, and I with a case of asthma which I am unable to control."

While they were heading to Samaipata farther to the northwest, Pombo had been hit in the leg and Tuma fatally in the stomach.

Ché felt Tuma's loss as keenly as he had Rolando's, if not more so. "With his death I lost an irreplaceable, truly loyal comrade of many years standing," he mourned, "and I miss him as I would a son."

A third death Ché might have included in the same context was that of Ricardo. Though he did not belong, strictly speaking, to the six who started out at Nancahuazú, he was most certainly a charter member of the guerrilla band and one who had been working for Ché in Bolivia longer than anyone but Tania. He was killed in the same clash in which Pacho was wounded on July 30th.

The taking of Samaipata was the high point of the guerrilla drive in Bolivia. But paradoxically, it accomplished nothing of lasting value for the guerrillas. It dramatized their presence in Bolivia and gave the world the impression that they were winning the war, and by the same token had a demoralizing effect upon the Bolivians. But these were ephemeral gains that did nothing to change the basic relationship of forces, much less frustrate the process already under way of strengthening the opposing Bolivian Army.

A further paradox is that the guerrillas seemed not to have had in mind even the temporary aim of seeking publicity when they took Samaipata. Nor did they seek a local objective such as the cutting of the Cochabamba–Santa Cruz highway, which ran through the town, in order to halt military traffic into the area. Since Samaipata had no intrinsic value, possessing no oil, no industry, no major utilities, nothing of economic or military worth, the question may fairly be asked: What, then, was Ché's intention in occupying it for a few moments?

The answer his diary gives is: None. None, that is, of any military or political importance. The only statement that can pass for an objective is the following, recorded on July 6th, the day Samaipata was entered:

"The plan was to steal a vehicle that might come from Samaipata, ask about existing conditions, go to Samaipata with the driver of the vehicle, take over the DIC [Departamento de Investigación Criminal, more or less equivalent to the FBI], buy some things at the pharmacy, continue to the hospital, buy some canned goods, gasoline and return."

Ché sums up the results of the victory:

"In terms of getting supplies, the action was a failure; Chino let himself be dominated by Pacho and Julio and bought nothing of any use and when buying medicines bought nothing of the items necessary for me, even though he *did* buy the most essential medicines for the guerrillas. The action took place before the whole village and many travelers in such a manner that the news spread like fire."

Whether Ché intended it or not, the impact of Samaipata

on Bolivia was also explosive. It made worldwide headlines. Many Bolivians got the impression that the guerrillas were about to over-run the entire southeast, while some elements of the international press inflated the event to the proportions of a near-Armageddon for the Bolivian government.

Samaipata seems to have shocked Government and Army into the realization that they could lose this war (though actually they came nowhere near doing that at any time during the guerrillas' activity), and that they had better go on the offensive if they intended to beat the guerrillas. Accordingly, a change of strategy and tactics was dictated.

For General Ovando, the Armed Forces Commander-in-Chief, the guerrilla war went through five crucial phases: the March 23rd ambush, the Muyupampa raid, the El Espino clash, the taking of Samaipata, and finally, the Army offensive against the guerrillas. For him, and for the armed forces of Bolivia, Samaipata was the watershed. As he describes that critical juncture:

"For the Armed Forces, the phase that lasted till the *coup de main* at Samaipata was critical. The enlistment of new conscripts and the discharge of the old ones undoubtedly had lessened the fighting capacity of the Armed Forces. Once this difficulty was corrected, and the soldier was acclimated to the terrain in which he had to operate, there commenced what could be called the offensive phase of the Armed Forces, which tries to reduce the area of guerrilla operations and liquidate the groups operating in them."

The immediate reaction of the Army to Samaipata was to launch, on July 9th, the first of two offensives. This was given the original name of "Operación Cynthia," after the daughter of the man who conceived and led it, Colonel Luis Reque Terán, who had replaced Colonel Rocha as Chief of the Fourth Division. It encompassed Nancahuazú and the whole region south of the Río Grande. In early August, a companion offensive was launched north of the river under the name of "Operación Parabanó," after a town in the area; it was commanded by Colonel Zenteno of the Eighth Division. The two *"operaciones"* disposed of Joaquín and Ché, in that order.

Ché, after committing the fatal error of splitting his forces in two and spending weeks vainly searching for Joaquín south of the Río Grande, then compounded the error by marching north in the hope of finding him. But Joaquín had stayed south of the river. Finally, in a climax of cross purposes, Ché went in search of

Joaquín south of the river at precisely the time when the latter, evidently figuring (correctly) that Ché had gone north, went looking for him there. And there he met his doom.

Since the day "Operación Cynthia" was announced, Joaquín had the Fourth Division constantly on his heels and there it clung tenaciously till the end. From time to time there were clashes, but nothing of major importance before the final encounter on August 31st.

Meanwhile, Joaquín was having trouble with his men, as Ché was with his. We learn from Braulio's diary that Marcos and Víctor disappeared on June 2nd. Early in July, the "visitor" Serapio was killed. Braulio adds:

"From this time we abandoned Nancahuazú and began to operate on our own."

In a surprise clash with the Army on the road to Taperillas, Braulio records, the "dregs" Chingolo and Eusebio desert, a truly major disaster, for thanks largely to their information the Fourth Division was able to find and locate another guerrilla cache in the Nancahuazú area: the third to fall into Army hands. This one contained a big haul: a Johnson Ranger 150-watt transmitter with complete antenna and coaxial cable; two radios, an AN-PRC-5 and a GRC-9, used by the Bolivian Army for divisional-company communication; a three-way walkie-talkie system; dark-room chemicals for developing film; a bag with surgical instruments; eight suitcases filled with books; six French-language course texts, and a tape recorder with reels of tape. One of the latter was a recording of a musical program broadcast on the Peruvian National Radio, probably made by Tania.

Joaquín and his tiny group were bested by troops of the Eighth Division, not the Fourth, since by then they had crossed over into "Operación Parabanó" territory on the other side of the Río Grande. The exact location was Vado del Yeso, just north of the river.

As Captain (later Major) Mario Vargas subsequently recalled, on August 30th he and a 31-man patrol were in La Laja, a tiny place on the Masicurí River, a tributary to the Río Grande, when he was informed that Joaquín's band had crossed the Río Grande. Two soldiers, disguised as peasants, had successfully tracked the rebels, been captured and held, but escaped when they went to catch fish for the guerrillas. Since the soldiers knew the terrain, they led Vargas, who was quite familiar with the area himself, to the place where Joaquín was encamped.

The soldiers arrived in the vicinity at dawn next morning after a forced march, and learned that the guerrillas had reached the house of one Honorato Rojas the night before. They were interested, informants told Vargas, in buying a calf. (Like Ché's group, Joaquín's had suffered almost constant hunger.) Knowing this part of the southeast well, Vargas proceeded to deploy his men on high ground "to permit us to dominate the terrain and prevent flight," as he explained. He selected Vado del Yeso, on the Lower Masicurí just above its juncture with the Río Grande, as the best site for an ambush. He placed his men in the "U" formation, the northern mouth of which was blocked by three soldiers. It was a perfect trap. Vargas related:

"We knew it would go badly for them. Rojas had told us of their hunger and lack of equipment, that they had been discussing their next moves. The group was disconnected from the central body and seeking to make more contact."

At 5:20 on the afternoon of the 31st, as the guerrillas were crossing the Masicurí, holding their weapons and clothing above their heads to prevent them from getting wet, Captain Vargas gave the order to fire. The guerrillas made such prominent targets one wonders why Joaquín, an old guerrilla instructor and a veteran of Vietnam, had not taken the elementary precaution of sending scouts on ahead or, at least, letting his people cross one at a time at intervals.

Tania was among the first three who fell at once, Vargas reports. She wore a green and white striped blouse that made her stand out prominently (but was otherwise dressed like the others in fatigue trousers and army boots.) She dropped into the water before she could raise her own weapon. Her body floated downriver and could not be recovered for a week. In her *mochila*, besides her identification card, there were a notebook with the names and addresses of guerrilla contacts, and the titles of several songs, mostly Argentine zambas.

Everyone in Joaquín's group but Paco and the Peruvian, Negro, was killed on the spot. The dead included: Joaquín, Ernesto (the Bolivian physician), Walter, Braulio, Moisés Guevara, Toro, Tania, and Alejandro. Al the bodies (except Tania's, carried off by the water) were taken to the Señor de Malta

Hospital in Vallegrande, where Ché's would soon be on display.

Paco and Negro escaped but very soon the former was captured and the latter killed. Paco, another of Moisés Guevara's "dregs," immediately turned informer, and among other things identified Ché and charged that Debray carried arms. "He should be made an example," a furious Ché wrote in his diary after listening to the radio report of Paco's betrayal.

Ché, when he first heard of the fate of Joaquín's group over the Voice of America 48 hours later, refused to believe it.

The next day, however, September 3rd, he begins to think differently:

"Again the Voice of America gave more reports about clashes with the Army and this time named José Carrillo as the only survivor of the group of ten men. Since this Carrillo is Paco, one of the 'dregs'; and the annihilation took place in Masicurí, everything seems to indicate that it is a mess."

But a day later, when he hears reports of a "new" clash at Vado del Yeso "near where the group of ten men were annihilated," that "makes the report about Joaquín appear like a fraud."

Even when Tania's corpse is fished out of the river and definitely identified, to him the report "does not have the ring of the one about Negro." It isn't until the month is over and he sits down to write his regular summary that he can find it in him to admit, "There may be truth in some of the news about deaths in the other group, which can be considered liquidated," but then he adds this reservation: "although it is possible that there is a little group of survivors wandering about. . . ."

Ché, though the facts were in, remained unconvinced till the day he died.

Ché's group had meanwhile wandered into the inhospitable Province of Vallegrande, a mountainous terrain with difficult *quebradas*—canyons—where living off the land was next to impossible because crops and cattle and game could not thrive there.

In this country even "the animals suffered a great deal," Ché reports, finding it very difficult to cross the broken ground they were traveling.

The Army maintained a stubborn pursuit of Ché. On July 30th, the formidable Trinidad Detachment of the Eighth Division, which was in charge of "Operación Parabanó" north of the Río Grande, caught up with him near Moroca (spelled "Moroco" by Ché). The encounter went disastrously for the guerrillas.

Negro (unidentified, but not to be mistaken for the Peruvian of the same nickname in Joaquín's band) got lost "with the hatchet and mortar that had been captured," then "some bundles fell" and caused the guerrillas to lose time, and finally, rushing to escape across the Moroca River, they came under heavy fire from the soldiers, "who had become very bold."

Blunders and disregard of orders typified the retreat. Miguel and Julio had crossed the river "without receiving my instructions and shortly thereafter Camba reported that the soldiers had overtaken his group together with Miguel and Julio." Ché continues:

"The developments were as follows: Ricardo and Aniceto had foolishly crossed an open space. The former got hit. Antonio organized a line of fire and between Arturo, Raúl and Pacho, rescued them, but Pacho was wounded and Raúl was killed by a bullet through his mouth. The withdrawal was difficult. The two wounded men had to be dragged and there was little collaboration from Willy and Chaparo, especially the latter. Later they were joined by Urbano and his group with the horses and Benigno with his men, leaving the other wing unprotected, for which reason Miguel was overtaken. After an arduous march through the woods they came out on the river and joined us."

Ricardo, the second wounded man, was carried to safety in a hammock, while Pacho was able to ride horseback. Ché proceeded to treat both of them. He reports:

"Pacho has a superficial wound through his buttocks and the skin of his testicles, but Ricardo was gravely ill and the last plasma had been lost in Willy's knapsack. At 2200 hours Ricardo died and we buried him near the river in a hidden spot, so that the police will not find him."

Nor were Ricardo, Raúl and Pacho the only casualties. The guerrillas also lost irreplaceable supplies, whose importance can best be appreciated by reproducing the list of them Ché made in his diary for July 31st:

"We lost 11 knapsacks containing medicines, binoculars and equipment such as the tape recorder used for copying the messages from Manila, Debray's book with my notations, a book by Trotsky, not to mention the political significance that the capture of these items has for the government and the confidence that it gives the soldiers."

Perhaps of all the items listed, the most important was the tape recorder. How would they be able to record coded communications from Havana, for accurate deciphering later, without it? Its loss obviously meant that they would be deprived of crucial information and instructions from command headquarters.

The second of the three decisive battles that destroyed Ché Guevara's guerrilla movement occurred on September 26th.

"Defeat" is the single, ominous word with which Ché opens his diary that day. A day which had begun, as others had of late, rather quietly. Even, one might say, on a happier note than most other days, for upon reaching the little *pueblo* of Picacho at dawn they found a *fiesta* going on.

Then . . . "everything changed."

They got to La Higuera to find it almost empty. Ché became suspicious:

"All the men had left and there were only a few women. Coco went to the telegraph operator's house, where there is a telephone, and brought back a message dated the 22nd in which the subprefect of Valle Grande tells the Mayor that there are reports of guerrillas in the area and any news should be communicated immediately to Valle Grande, which will pay expenses. The man had fled but his wife assured us that they had not sent a message today as there was a *fiesta* in the next town, Jagüey."

The guerrillas decide to head for Jagüey. Shortly thereafter, while Ché is talking with "the only man" in La Higuera, a coca dealer arrives and tells him that he "had not seen anything," that is, no soldiers in the area. He seemed to Ché to be "very nervous," but the guerrilla leader attributed that to his presence. "We let them both go in spite of the lies they were telling us."

Half an hour after the vanguard's departure, at 1:30 p.m., Ché was on his way toward the top of a hill with his center group when "the sound of firing all over the ridge told us that our men [in the vanguard] had fallen into an ambush. I organized the defense . . . and designated as the retreat route a road which would lead to the Río Grande." (La Higuera is situated on the Pirainambi River, a small tributary of the Río Grande, near its mouth.)

Ché's record continues:

"A few minutes later Benigno arrived, wounded, and soon after him Aniceto, and Pablito with his foot in very bad condition. Miguel, Coco and Julio had fallen, and Camba disappeared, leaving his knapsack behind."

León, he soon learned, had also deserted. Inti had seen him

discarding his fieldpack in a nearby canyon and "walking very hurriedly" through the canyon.

The defeat at La Higuera sent Ché into a depression. He seems to have sensed, for the first time, doom threatening himself and his movement and, also for the first time, thought seriously of escape. Added to his problems was a police roundup of his La Paz contacts in mid-September, as a direct result of the discovery of their names and addresses in a notebook of his seized by the Army.

Ché had arrived too late at his decision to escape. Had he reached it at the end of August, when Joaquín's group was finished off and he was left with only 22 men—far too few to hope for victory—he might have succeeded in leading his men to safety. Now he had even fewer: only 17.

Ché's health continued its steady deterioration throughout August and into September. He alludes to his failing health in seventeen different entries in his diary for August—the same number as in July—clear enough acknowledgment of how weak he was physically and how much it affected his mental and emotional state. The asthma became so insupportable that, early in the month, he was driven to the extreme of sending three men to Nancahuazú "to get my medicines." This was a serious risk to take on two counts: the lives of three guerrillas were jeopardized, and their departure weakened by more than 10 percent the already depleted guerrilla band.

Ché suffered not only from the asthma but from other ailments as well. Thus he complains on August 9th:

"I had a carbuncle in my heel lanced and now I can put down my foot, but it is very painful and I have a fever."

His men were in not much better physical condition. All of them suffered from malnutrition to one degree or another. And no wonder. Here is the kind of food they were reduced to eating, as Ché recounts on August 24th:

"At dusk the *macheteros* returned with the traps; they caught a condor and a rotten cat. Everything was eaten together with the last piece of the anteater meat."

Even the mare Ché had been riding for two months had finally been butchered to supply the near-starving guerrillas with food.

The men are "collapsing for lack of water," he reports on

August 29th. And on the next day, he observes that the shortage of both food and water is causing the *macheteros* (whose job was to hack open paths through the brush with machetes) to have "fainting spells," while other guerrillas suffer from dizziness, diarrhea and cramps much of the time.

The perennial shortages of food and water could not fail, of course, to have a profound adverse effect upon guerrilla morale. As Ché is forced to admit in his August summary, "Our subsequent march on a horsemeat diet demoralized the men."

It was no wonder that during September, the last full month of Ché's Bolivian adventure, quarrels and breaches of discipline became ever more frequent. From the 11th to the 19th, for example, he devotes almost every entry to incidents of that nature.

It was no wonder, too, that the guerrillas in their deteriorating physical and emotional condition were prone to all kinds of mishaps and blunders. Again, this is increasingly the case toward the last, extremely difficult days.

Then, finally, there were the peasants and the Army to contend with.

It was the peasants of the locality who gave away Ché's position at La Higuera on September 26th, and at Quebrada del Yuro on October 8th. In the former instance, it was when the guerrillas stopped at Alto Seco—"a little village of 50 houses at 1,900 meters altitude, which received us with a balanced mixture of fear and curiosity"—that the Eighth Division began to receive information tracing the rebels' progress toward La Higuera practically every inch of the way. Colonel Zenteno posted a company under Lieutenant Eduardo Galindo at Laja, on the Lower Masicurí. Captain Vargas had destroyed Joaquín in August, and when Galindo got word there from peasant informants that Ché had left Alto Seco, he was ordered by Zenteno to pursue him. Zenteno himself, to be as close as possible to the operation (which he and his superiors fondly hoped would finally trap Ché Guevara), moved his field headquarters to Vallegrande.

The stop at Alto Seco was almost gratuitous, for the hamlet had nothing to offer the guerrillas, not even the medicines Ché had hoped to find there. They tarried there through September 21st, the day they had arrived, then continued on to another tiny *pueblo*, Santa Elena, since it had "a beautiful ofange grove." The guerrillas spent all September 22nd there "resting and sleeping."

Ché had begun to recognize, as he admitted in his September summary, that "now the Army appears to be more effective in its actions, and the peasants do not give us any help and are turning into informers." But he had received no aid from the peasants from the very beginning of the Bolivian adventure, and the Army's increasing effectiveness dated from mid-August when it received the first of a batch of 650 native Rangers fresh from months of rigorous training in anti-guerrilla fighting. Yet Ché had made no effort to escape from the closing circle.

The Eighth Division's strategy for trapping Ché, as outlined by Colonel Zenteno, proceeded in three phases. The objective during the first phase was to isolate Ché in a well-defined area, for which reasons Zenteno deployed his men to the north of the Cochabamba-Santa Cruz highway, blocking his egress there, and along the Río Grande, blocking any effort he might make to escape southward. (In any event, had Ché managed to cross the river he would have fallen into the arms of Colonel Reque Terán's Fourth Division.) The goal in the second phase was the penetration of the narrowing "Red Zone" itself, for which Zenteno posted men to the east of Ché, along the Yacuiba-Santa Cruz railroad, from where they would work their way westward. Thus, Ché, from about September 26th on, found himself in an ever-tightening noose.

Phases One and Two of Zenteno's strategy were completed by the first week in October, and the eve of the final battle found him in the third and last phase. The objective here was starkly simple: to destroy the guerrillas. The units Zenteno employed to accomplish that were Companies "A" and "B" of the tough 2nd Ranger Battalion. These he deployed just west of Vallegrande, the capital of the province, and around such satellite villages as Higuera.

The strategy of the Eighth Division found the Army and the guerrillas in positions exactly the reverse of those assigned to them by Ché Guevara in his manual on *Guerrilla Warfare*. In the section where he stresses that mobility is the "fundamental characteristic of the guerrilla," he continues:

"Characteristic of this war of mobility is what is called the minuet, because of the analogy with the dance of that name: the guerrillas encircle an enemy position, for example a column that is advancing: they encircle it completely at the four cardinal points, with five or six men in each place and at a convenient distance so that they in turn are not encircled. The fight begins at any of the points and the

Army moves toward it; the guerrillas then retreat, always keeping the enemy within view, and attack at another point. The Army repeats its previous action and the guerrillas likewise. Thus, successively, it is possible to keep the enemy column immobilized, forcing it to expend great amounts of ammunition and weakening the morale of the troops without running any great danger." [5]

By substituting "guerrillas" for "Army," and vice versa, wherever those words appear in the above paragraph, we obtain from Ché an almost perfect description of the respective situations of his own and Zenteno's forces in the first week of October 1967. It was Ché, in other words, who was being encircled, and Zenteno who was doing the "minuet."

How did Ché permit himself to become trapped, against all the rules he had laid down in *Guerrilla Warfare?* The answer, obviously, is that he did not, or could not, obey his own rules, due to the numerous weaknesses that had come to afflict his band, not least among which was a nearly total ignorance of the geography of the region. Probably what finally trapped him was one factor, above all: a virtually complete lack of intelligence concerning the enemy's movements. In contrast, the enemy knew everything he was doing.

Ché Guevara had only a very slight idea of the Army's precise movements, acquired largely from radio reports which were heavily censored and never revealed much, and from minor skirmishes with military patrols. The rumors he picked up from peasants were rarely trustworthy. He knew, however, that the Army was well posted on his movements; in addition to regular peasant reports, it had also gotten an earful from the two latest deserters, Camba and León. As he ruefully observed in his diary for October 3rd:

"They have both given abundant information, about Fernando [Ché], his sickness, and all the rest, and who knows what they have revealed that has not been published."

He realized that his southern escape route was blocked when, next day, he heard the news that the Fourth Division had transferred its headquarters to Padilla, only fifty-odd miles due south of Higuera. That knowledge, plus ignorance of the Eighth Division's strategy, may have impelled him to keep pushing in a northwesterly direction—that is, toward Cochabamba and La Paz —in the belief that there lay the only possible route of escape.

5. *Guerra de guerrillas,* p. 34.

Unfortunately, that only threw him into the arms of Ranger Companies "A" and "B."

It is not unlikely that Ché, lacking certain knowledge, nevertheless sensed the closing of the enemy ring about him. That, at least, is what one suspects from reading these opening words of his September 28th entry:

"A day of anguish. At times it seemed as if it would be our last."

Food and water remained, of course, the central problem to the very last. And exhaustion and sickness slowed the guerrillas down, perhaps fatally. On the night before the final battle at Quebrada del Yuro, they had to stop marching at 2:00 a.m. This may well have cost them the game, for they awoke in the morning to find themselves trapped. They had had to make the halt because Chino, "a real burden when we have to hike at night," had bad eyes and was unable to see much in the darkness.

They had bedded down for the night in a canyon—this was the Quebrada del Yuro—where there were "patches of potato plants watered by ditches" so that they could quench their raging thirst and quiet the pangs of hunger. Next morning they looked up to find soldiers deployed on top of the ridges surrounding them. It was October 8, 1967.

The fighting began about 1:30 in the afternoon. It started with a brief clash, followed by a long one that saw a lot of firepower used by both sides. The whole battle lasted hardly longer than two hours, terminating around 3:30 p.m.

It was during the second encounter that Ché was wounded, in the leg. He was dragged up a hill from the bottom of the *quebrada,* or canyon, where they had been attacked, by a Bolivian guerrilla named Willy who meanwhile covered him with rifle fire. At the top he found a tree to cling to, and from there, though wounded, Ché continued to give his men orders. He was anxious to have them scramble out of the *quebrada* somehow and climb to a height where they could be more effective against the soldiers, who were shooting at them from ridges around the canyon.

When Ché's weapon, identified later as a carbine with the markings, "744,520 Land Division United States" and "D" (on the butt), was shot out of his hand, four Bolivian soldiers surrounded and captured him.

Typically, Ché, if one is to believe an eyewitness account, went into a violent asthma attack and could hardly breathe for some moments.

Captain Gary Prado Salmón, commanding Company "B" which had attacked the guerrillas, asked their leader to identify himself, and he answered simply:

"I am Ché Guevara."

Next morning, Monday, October 9th, Colonel Zenteno announced that the guerrilla leader had been killed in battle. But a formal communiqué issued the same day by the High Command in La Paz only said vaguely:

"The Reds suffered five casualties, among them presumably is Ernesto Ché Guevara."

The communiqué did not say that Ché had *died* in battle or was even dead at the time it was issued.

Actually, as the world later learned, Ché did not die until 1:30 p.m. on October 9th.

The official report on the manner of Ché's death, as stated first by Zenteno, was subsequently contradicted by many conflicting facts and became a serious point of dispute. The belief became widespread, and was substantiated by investigation by reputable journalists and others, that Ché had in fact been executed by the Bolivian Armed Forces. The Armed Forces' decision to execute Ché had been made well in advance of Ché's capture and was not the outcome of a last-minute discussion. It was a matter of policy, the military believing that, after the tremendous worldwide publicity campaign directed against Bolivia over the case of Régis Debray, the country could not afford the greater uproar if Ché Guevara were brought to trial. As the distinguished Bolivian journalist, Alberto Bailey Gutierrez, wrote in the liberal La Paz daily, *Presencia*, concerning the execution:

"What happened is natural, unfortunately, in a guerrilla war born of an armed rebellion coming from abroad and that obeys no kind of law. The Bolivian Army would have been very wrong, from its point of view, to have given Ché a world tribunal to enable him to stir up guerrilla passions."

Ché would have done the same to the Bolivian Army leaders, of course, had he won. He had methodically destroyed the pre-revolutionary Cuban Army in the blood bath he initiated after the Castro guerrillas had triumphed in 1959.

Why did Ché fail in Bolivia?

The simplest explanation is that he did not follow his own theory of guerrilla warfare, either on the military or the political levels.

The first and most fundamental mistake he made was the selection of Bolivia. On the surface it seemed to be most logical site for the *foco insurrecional;* in actuality, it was the least logical.

The National Revolution had radically transformed the life of the Bolivian Indian, who constitutes more than two-thirds of the country's 4,250,000 inhabitants, and that was probably its greatest single accomplishment. It had done so, first, through an agrarian reform law enacted in 1953, which made landholders of the hitherto virtually landless Indian peasantry and gave them pride of ownership, even if it was but a little plot they were given. Second, the whole body of revolutionary legislation had the effect of raising the Indian out of age-old serfdom and enabling him to exert his rights as a citizen. Before 1952, the Indian had always been considered and treated as a chattel. Now he did not have to stand aside to let the *patrón* pass first, or let the *patrón* sample his daughter before marriage, or let himself be subjected to countless other indignities and abuses.

Guerrilla war, according to Ché, is a war of the people, and the guerrilla is essentially an "agrarian revolutionary." The particular region Ché selected for his base of operations, the southeast, was precisely the one where "agrarian revolutionaries" were least needed. The peasants there had, as a rule, far more land than they could hope to work even with the help of their children. And any peasant, anywhere in Bolivia, who happened to have no land and wanted some, could have it for the asking in the southeast. What, then, could Ché offer the local peasantry? Still more land they could not use?

The revolution of 1952 is called the *National* Revolution. Fragmented during most of its history, Bolivia in modern times has been a nation largely in name; the Revolution sought to correct that weakness. By the time Ché started his *foco,* the "nationalizing" process was far from completed, but it was well enough along to have penetrated important groups in society and to have given them a stake in *la patria.*

It may seem curious to those with prefabricated theories of nations and classes to learn that, in Bolivia, the leading nationalistic force is the great peasant majority. When word got around that there were indeed foreign guerrillas operating in the southeast, and that they had torn this and that Army unit to shreds

—this was in the early days—peasant organizations throughout the country held meetings at which they not only denounced the invaders but proceeded to organize armed peasant detachments to send into battle against them.

In July 1967 the Fourth Peasant National Congress was held, representing the vast majority of Bolivian peasants. It called upon its followers to back the government against the guerrillas with arms if necessary. This was supplemented by a formal "Pacto Campesino-Militar," an alliance of the peasantry with the Armed Forces, which itself is made up almost entirely of peasant conscripts.

Ché was faced, then, not with a peasantry that was merely passive and apathetic to his appeals but one that actively opposed him, at least insofar as its organized expression was concerned.

Furthermore, Ché found that in the southeast he and his guerrillas, including even the Bolivians amongst them, were regarded as intruders. If the peasants there were not very conscious of a sense of nationality, they expressed the much narrower attitude of regional parochialism.

When Ché and his men would walk into some populated place (the majority of "towns" and "villages" in the southeast can scarcely be called more than "places"), or in the Spanish word, mere *poblados,* they would usually be greeted with a combination of surprise and fear because they looked like nothing anybody there had ever seen before.

Their physical appearance alone, even before they opened their mouths, aroused suspicion. Dressed in dirty jungle fatigues, carrying field packs and fearful-looking firearms, wearing beards and long hair, they might well have seemed like an invading force from another planet. It must be kept in mind that the Indians are not hirsute, that the faces of their men are practically hairless, and beards are something they seldom see. Nor did the Indians have ethnic features in common with most of the guerrillas, few of whom were of the "Andean Indian" type who generally has an epicanthic eyefold, high cheekbones, deep brown skin (in the south), and short stature.

When the guerrillas opened their mouths to speak, it was not often that the southeastern peasant understood a word they said. Ché had instituted classes in Quechua, Bolivia's dominant Indian language, when he arrived in Nancahuazú, hoping to become able to communicate with the largest single peasant grouping.

But—and this is typical of the guerrillas' generally inadequate preparation for their task—the spoken tongue of the region was Guaraní. Not one of the guerrillas, including the Bolivians could speak it. As Ché remarked upon entering the village of El Espino, they encountered a problem finding someone who could speak some Spanish.

Ché often complained that the peasants informed on him to the Army. Why the Army? There were several reasons for this. One was the ingrained fear and respect for established authority and power which has been beaten into the Indian since time immemorial. But also there was now a sense of identification between peasant and Army which had not existed before the Revolution of 1952. Literally an army of peasants, it was made up of youths, many of them born since 1952, who shared the country's generally revolutionary outlook. When a peasant told a soldier or officer where he had spotted the guerrillas, he was talking to his own kind, and in some cases, to a recruit from the same or a neighboring region.

On the purely political level, Ché violated another of his own guerrilla precepts in going into a country which had some form of popular government. As he writes at the very beginning of his manual on *Guerrilla Warfare:*

"Wherever a government has come to power through some form of popular consent, fraudulent or not, and maintains at least an appearance of constitutional legality, it is impossible to produce a guerrilla outbreak because all the possibilities of civic struggle have not been exhausted." [6]

The Barrientos government was a perfect example of what Ché was talking about. He felt Barrientos was "fraudulently" elected, but there could be no doubt that there had been an election on July 6, 1966 and that Barrientos had come to power "through some form of popular consent." Nor that he governed with "at least an appearance of constitutional legality."

With the peasants, the Armed Forces and a recently elected and fairly popular government all arrayed against him, Ché's only hope of getting his *foco* off the ground was to enlist some measure of serious support among the miners, students, and Communists. Had he been able to attract only a few hundred from all three elements combined, that would have given him several times larger a group of guerrillas than he had. He failed,

6. *Op. cit.* pp. 27-8.

however, to enlist their support, as much because he did not follow the right tactics as for more objective reasons.

June 1967 saw a major national crisis when the tin mines were struck. On June 24th, the Army was forced to occupy them, a bloody clash with the mineworkers ensued, and students, teachers and others in the cities organized big demonstrations in sympathy with them. Any spark might have touched off a national upheaval. Bolivian leaders and U.S. officials feared most of all that the miners, a militant crowd in possession of many arms, and the guerrillas would effect a juncture.

Sympathy for the guerrillas existed among both the miners and the students, who also have a militant tradition in Bolivia. They declared certain mines and schools *"territorios libres"*— "free territories"—in the Castro manner. Yet, and this was one of the strangest events of the guerrilla war, not a single miner or student sneaked off to Nancahuazú to join Ché.

Why they didn't is a long story, which I have discussed elsewhere.[7] Suffice it to say that Ché had never been able to establish a serious and effective contact with either the miners or the students. In dealing with the miners, he relied upon the rather ineffectual Moisés Guevara, who, as we shall see in the diaries, supplied Ché with a handful of guerrillas so poor on every level that he called them *"resacas"*—"dregs." All but two, M. Guevara and the one called Willy, deserted or performed badly.

As for the students, Ché did not have even a Moisés Guevara to do proselytizing work among them. Though they shouted loud "Viva Ché's!" after the guerrilla chieftain was dead, they gave him the cold shoulder when he was alive and could have used their help.

The baffling story of Ché's relations with the Bolivian Communists of all shades is also too long to relate here, and forms part of another book, but enough should be put on record now to make our present volume as complete and informative as possible.

Fidel Castro has bitterly indicted the Bolivian Communist Party for having failed Ché, and he is right. But the PCB is far from being the sole guilty party. Castro himself bears a large part of the blame for Ché's defeat.

Pombo indicates that the decision to establish the *foco* in Bolivia was a unilateral one taken by Fidel and Ché, perhaps to-

7. See Daniel James, *Ché Guevara, a Biography;* Stein and Day Publishers, 1969.

gether with other Cuban leaders, without consulting the Bolivian Communists whose aid they sought. This was one of Mario Monje's chief complaints, and was continually at the bottom of his refusal to yield supreme authority over the "liberation movement" to Ché. Ché was, after all, a foreigner. Though Monje was no great Bolivian patriot, he was enough of a nationalist— and egotist—to feel slighted at the fact that foreigners had decided to make his country a crucible of revolution without his knowledge or consent, and the further fact that they had preempted the leadership of it.

At a meeting Ché's agents in La Paz had with Monje, as reported by Pombo on September 28, 1966, the PCB chief made it clear "that this commitment to Leche [Castro] was to organize the matter of the south," meaning the Southern Cone countries, and "that the strategic plan gave secondary importance to the matter of Bolivia." Monje added "that the organization and direction of the [Bolivian plan] was his responsibility." Pombo further paraphrases Monje:

"He believed he was fulfilling his part of the agreement and that there had been meddling in the affair on our part."

The La Paz Cubans resented Monje's attitude and reminded him, in Pombo's words, that "two months back we informed Comrade Estanislao that the plans for the south today are secondary and that the headquarters was here because it was thought that this country, at the moment, was the one that had the best conditions (he agreed with this)."

It was probably true, as Pombo reports, that Monje had been told two months earlier—that is, in July— of Havana's decision to begin the continental revolution in Bolivia instead of elsewhere. But why wasn't he informed of the decision at the moment it was made, which was well before July? And why, more importantly, wasn't the Bolivian Communist Party included in the discussions concerning the fate of its own country?

By ignoring the Bolivian Communist Party during the decision-making phase, Fidel could blame no one but himself if the PCB refused to become involved in the guerrilla phase, when he and Ché intended to use it only to provide them with combatants and other means of material support.

That was not the only reason the PCB dragged its feet. Fundamentally, it did not subscribe to Ché's *foco* theory. It saw the revolution in more orthodox Leninist terms, as emerging from a

mass uprising in the cities. This it said it was ready to help
bring off. In a long document Monje issued semi-clandestinely
on December 9, 1967, explaining tortuously his and the Party's
role in the whole guerrilla affair, he reveals that he presented
a plan to Ché "which I regarded as more adapted to national
reality," consisting of the "preparation of the Communist Party
of Bolivia and other revolutionary forces for the armed struggle," and the "coordination of simultaneous actions in the cities,
mines, countryside, and mountains" as soon as a national crisis
occurred.

Monje and the PCB, in other words, saw the Bolivian Communist revolution almost exclusively in Bolivian terms. Fidel
Castro and Ché Guevara, who had had only slight contact with
Bolivia, thought of it essentially in Cuban terms, as they did the
guerrilla operation from beginning to end.

The famous dispute Ché had with Monje over which of them
was to lead the Bolivian Revolution ended in a deadlock which
saw the PCB pull away entirely, though not formally, from
supporting the guerrilla struggle. Though Ché could hardly be
blamed for not wanting to entrust the military command to
Monje or any other PCB leader (this was the fundamental
point at issue), Monje's insistence upon subordinating the military to the political leadership obeyed a classic Communist for-
mula dating back to Lenin.

In the preparatory phase, which lasted from early 1966
until November 7th, when the guerrillas settled in Nancahuazú,
Fidel supplied them with virtually everything they required
in the way of money, transportation, communications and rear
support in general. He allowed Ché to pick the Cuban veterans
he wished to take with him.

Fidel continued to help Ché into the first Nancahuazú phase,
but mostly in a political manner, exerting pressure upon the PCB
to join the guerrillas. However, judging from Ché's request to
Debray (which the latter was unable to execute because of his
arrest), on March 21, 1967, to obtain for him in Havana "every
means of assistance, especially money, medicine, and electronics
in the form of an engineer and equipment," Fidel appears to
have fallen short of giving his field commander full material
support during that phase.

Equally, or perhaps more importantly, Castro failed to maintain close communication with Ché during the combat phase
which began with the March 23rd battle, and in the last months

had no contact with him at all. Ché complains of his "isolation" for the first time in his April 1967 summary. In May, he speaks of the "total lack of contact with Manila" (the code name for Cuba). In July, Ché finally receives "a long message from Manila," but after that, virtually nothing.

Fidel wasn't entirely to blame for the communications breakdown. Ché's receiving equipment was run down and apparently his transmitter wasn't working at all. But his radio could hear Radio Havana, as we know from his mentions of its news broadcasts. Why, then, didn't Fidel use Radio Havana's powerful transmitter to get through to Ché? Surely he need not have worried about the enemy monitoring him, since that could no longer make a substantial difference one way or the other. (By this time, September, the Bolivian Army had captured most of the incriminating documents, knew where Ché was, and was already drawing its net around him.) Yet, with practically nothing to lose, it appears from the known record of the guerrilla war that Fidel did not make any attempt to restore the communications link so vital to Ché, while Ché obviously had no way to repair his equipment himself.

Fidel did nothing to aid Ché politically, either. In April, Havana published and widely disseminated Ché's last formal piece of writing, an article called "One, Two, Many Viet Nams— That is the Slogan," which explained why he was in Bolivia. Ché indicates, in his diary, that he expected his presence in Bolivia to be publicized as a result: "After the publication of my article in Havana there must not be any doubt about my presence here," he states in his April monthly summary. But there was no announcement. For reasons of his own, Castro did not give the world the slightest hint of Ché's whereabouts.   ✳

At the end of July and beginning of August, Fidel conducted the first Latin American Solidarity Conference, a Latin outgrowth of the Tricontinental Conference of January 1966, and Ché had been scheduled to attend it. It seemed to be a good occasion to broadcast to the world the news that Ché was in Bolivia heading up a guerrilla movement. At that time, though the guerrillas were suffering many misfortunes, they had a military record of unbroken victories over the Bolivian Army. But once again Fidel made no announcement of Ché's struggle.

Yet there is little doubt that had Fidel reported Ché's presence in Bolivia, as Ché evidently expected him to, the guerrillas would have received aid and support, and perhaps much-needed manpower as well, from all corners of the globe as well as from Bolivia. That alone could have enabled Ché and his guerrilla band to survive. Had they been able to, the story in Bolivia might be a different one today.

Fidel Castro certainly realized this. Why, then, did he leave Ché to fight and die alone in the wilds of the Bolivian southeast? It would be interesting if Castro dared to discuss these questions, instead of berating the rather dense Mario Monje for his obvious errors.

For what it's worth, the Bolivian officer who captured Ché Guevara at Quebrada del Yuro, Captain (now Major) Gary Prado Salmón, stated that Ché told him that Fidel had failed him at a crucial time.

Fidel was well aware of the stake he had in Bolivia. Why, then, did he not take some drastic action to protect it, to give Ché decisive aid, or at least to find some way of rescuing him? That Fidel did not can only mean that he did not wish to. He apparently left Ché to sink or swim on his own: a decision he might have made reluctantly, but perhaps necessarily, once he thought he had done his duty in seeing Ché through the preparatory and training phases. Once the battle was joined the Cuban leader preferred to continue the puzzling game of keeping Ché's whereabouts a mystery, allowing his life and his men's lives to be snuffed out in isolation.

Considering the long-standing rivalry between Ché and Fidel over leadership of the Latin American revolution, it is perhaps not surprising that Castro allowed Ché to fail in Bolivia. His success might well have jeopardized Castro's future position and the precarious relationship begun with Ché's removal from the Cuban government and his appointment as a roving revolutionary. There can be little doubt that with a victory in Bolivia, it would have been Ché, not Castro, who would have directed the projected continental revolution and emerged the greater leader.

The underlying fallacy behind the Castro-Guevara attempt to establish a *foco* in Bolivia is the theory of the *foco* itself, which stemmed from their Cuban experience and proved inapplicable in Bolivia. Though Ché inveighed against Cuban "exceptionalism," as he called it, the fact is that the "lessons" derived from the Cuban situation that he thought applicable elsewhere were unique to Cuba. The first of these lessons, for example, holding that "popular forces can win a war against the Army," [8] can find no support in the experience of any other country. (Even in China, Mao triumphed only after he had created a regular army of his own.)

The second lesson of the Cuban Revolution, writes Ché, is that "it is not always necessary to wait until all the conditions of revolution are present; the insurrectional focus can create them." Again, this has been true of no country other than Cuba, and the Bolivian experience shows that the *foco* can be eradicated, even by relatively weak and inefficient opposing forces, before it can be properly organized. That has been the experience, so far, of other Latin American countries as well, such as Colombia, Guatemala, Peru and Venezuela.

The third basic lesson Ché believes Cuba has taught the world is, "In underdeveloped Latin America, the scene of the armed struggle must be fundamentally the countryside." But Ché found that to be untrue, in practice. In Bolivia, it was precisely the lack of support from the city (as he often complains in his diary) that prevented him from transforming the countryside into a battleground. As for the peasants themselves, though Pombo noted after his escape that Ché expected them to be unfriendly in the first phase of guerrilla warfare, by the third he knew he would have won them over. The trouble was, Pombo added, that the guerrillas could never emerge from the first phase.

It was Ché's and Fidel's overemphasis of their Cuban experience, preventing them from seeing Bolivia in realistic terms, rather than as it appeared in theory, that in the last analysis explains why Ché's last attempt at guerrilla war was a failure. It is the essential reason why, to date, Cuba has been unable to "export" her revolution to a single other Latin American country. Perhaps the most disappointing aspect of the guerrilla defeat was the destruction of the myth of Ché Guevara as a great guerrilla technician. The author of the most widely used book on guerrilla warfare in Latin America proved singularly unimpressive as a commander. Ché allowed himself and his men to take a large number of photographs of one another, and let Bustos make a series of sketches, which as caricatures were far more revealing of identifying features. All of this was invaluable to the Army. He permitted the keeping of

8. *Op. cit.* p. 27.

detailed diaries by members of his command: another uncalled-
for assist to the Bolivian forces in their pursuit of the rebels.
The diaries provided an accurate index of the morale and equipment of the guerrillas at any given time, as well as an estimate
of their total strength. The guerrillas saw the risk they were
taking. Pombo objected to Debray's photographs, and Ché himself realized the value of these captured materials to Army
efforts to destroy him. But men who viewed themselves as
moving toward historic victory could not deny themselves the
pleasure of recording it, even though that record jeopardized
their final success.

As a guerrilla commander in Bolivia, Ché was remarkably
unaggressive. While located within easy striking distance of
relatively undefended oil fields, and major lines of transportation,
communication and electric power, Ché wandered about the
countryside with little overall concept of his objectives. He repeatedly ignored opportunities to destroy Bolivian troops, and
his continual habit of releasing entire units of captured Bolivian
soldiers unharmed, though humane, is unparalleled in the history
of guerrilla combat. Those battles which his guerrillas did fight
were often accidents which cost them more by revealing their
position than they gained by a few Army casualties. Events
seemed to be indicated more by Ché's circumstances than his
will. He was to achieve his greatest victory at Samaipata in pursuit of medicine for his asthma, but there is no record that Ché
ever caused the Bolivian government so much as the inconvenience of a cut telephone line.

It appears that Ché lacked the ability to plan a military campaign. He did very well as a field commander in Cuba, particularly in his brilliant victory at Santa Clara, but he was carrying out orders from Castro and seemed to be more successful
establishing a fixed guerrilla base than in planning his own strategy even then. In Bolivia under vastly more difficult circumstances, he was not able to enlist even a single peasant, and it is
significant that this seemed to preoccupy him far more than
the ineffectiveness of his forces, which he appears not to have
noticed.

But there is no denying Ché's fascination. Exiled in effect
by his adopted homeland and the apostle of the Communist revolution in Latin America, Ché had little choice but to attempt to
exploit whatever explosive situations appeared in Latin America.
He needed a revolution far more than the revolution needed him;

without one, he would fall by the wayside and become lost to history. But returning to guerrilla life at 39 after seven years of chauffeur-driven limousines and comparatively rich living cannot have been easy. Though Ché was at first to enjoy the physical rigors of Nancahuazú, it is evident that as the campaign wore on the constant pressures of primitive living destroyed his health and seriously impaired his judgment.

Nevertheless, Bolivia proved to be a fortunate thing for Ché. Without a power base of his own, and unable to put his abilities to work without direction, Ché might have wandered around for any number of years until he met some obscure end. His record in the Congo and Bolivia was poor and it is doubtful that Castro would have supported him for many more such crusades. If his military activities there seemed to be conducted at random and without any recognizable objective, one might suspect that by dying in the service of his beliefs, Ché was to achieve a more important objective of his own.

CHRONOLOGY

1966

January — Tricontinental Conference, Havana, January 3-15; Mario Monje Molina, First Secretary of the Russia-oriented Communist Party of Bolivia (PCB) and Cuban Premier Fidel Castro and other Cuban leaders discuss establishment of base in Southern Cone for continental revolution.

February — Cuban agents Ricardo and Tania, already in Bolivia, make arrangements with PCB and other Communist factions for support of forthcoming guerrilla operations.

March — Guerrilla training in Cuba of future Bolivian guerrillas such as Inti and Benjamín.

June — Coco purchases farm at Nancahuazú. Other campsites (in Beni and elsewhere) also being explored. Arms, food, and other supplies stockpiled in Santa Cruz and La Paz.

July — General René Barrientos elected President of Bolivia with 62% of vote, July 6. Later in month, Pombo and Tuma arrive in Bolivia, representing Ché carrying his instructions to Ricardo. Confusion over where guerrilla base is to be located. Pombo and Tuma inform PCB that Bolivia is to be the center of the guerrilla struggle not merely a staging area for continental revolution. Monje agrees to supply 20 guerrillas. Peruvians El Chino and Sánchez told of Havana's decision to concentrate on Bolivia instead of Peru as they had hoped. Discussions with Maoist labor leader Moisés Guevara requesting recruiting of miners.

Pombo diary begins July 14

August — El Chino opposes "giving priority" to Bolivia. President René Barrientos inaugurated. Training of Cuban members of Ché's band gets under way in Cuba. Pombo, Tuma, other Cubans in La Paz feel PCB will not support guerrilla struggle. Monje threatens

Rolando diary begins August 11

71

	to withdraw four guerrilla recruits he has enlisted. PCB youth recruited by Monje refuses to go into mountains, believing Bolivia unripe for revolution.
September	Pacho arrives by train from Chile to inspect operations and report back to Ché. He announces arrival of Régis Debray "to make a geopolitical study of the selected zone." The advance party awaits Havana's instructions on breaking off with PCB; Moisés Guevara supplies ten recruits. Equipment accumulated now includes uniforms, canteens, radios, tents, hammocks and machetes. Monje summons Ricardo to a meeting, "brought about by the activities of the Frenchman," since Debray has been negotiating with the PCB's archenemy M. Guevara.
October	Ché accepts his advance party's desire not to relocate in the Beni, despite Debray's advice, and settles the question of the guerrilla base. It will be the farm at Nancahuazú. Pombo and Ricardo direct supplying of Nancahuazú base and routes of infiltration for incoming guerrilla force. Strong conflicts develop between Monje and his PCB and the advance party of guerrillas over Monje's continual reneging on PCB commitments to Ché and Castro. This is compounded by the guerrillas' negotiations with Moisés Guevara.
Braulio diary begins October 25	
November	November 3, Ché arrives in La Paz with Pacho via Havana, Prague and São Paulo.
Ché diaries begin November 7	November 7 Ché arrives at Nancahuazú. Construction of defenses, storage, housing, and radio facilities at the base. Patrols sent to scout the neighboring areas. Curiosity of local landowner Algarañaz forces guerrillas to camp away from the main buildings of the base.
December	Guerrillas continually arriving, including Chino, Alejandro, Moro, and Benigno. Training classes held for the growing camp. Construction of defenses, facilities and reconnaissance patrolling continues. December 31 Monje meets with Ché and reaches a

deadlock in their alliance over the issue of leadership of the guerrilla movement. Ché insists upon his leadership of the military campaign, and the subordination of political considerations despite Monje's offer of PCB cadre support if Ché accepts his leadership.

1967

January Training and stockpiling of supplies continues. Many guerrillas sick. Minor disciplinary problems among the men and occasional friction between Cubans and Bolivians. On January 19, Algarañaz's suspicions of cocaine operations at guerrilla base result in a police detachment visiting it, but they find nothing. Slow recruitment of Bolivians disappoints Ché.

February Ché begins training march on February 1 planned for 25 days which is to last 48 days over terrain in which the guerrilla force is continually becoming lost. It rains constantly and Benjamín and Carlos (during the return in March) drown in crossing swollen rivers. Ché encounters major language problem as natives primarily speak Indian dialects unfamiliar even to most of his Bolivian guerrillas. Serious friction between various individuals under severe hardship. Ché often ill. The peasants show no interest in supporting or enlisting in the insurrection.

March Bolivian Government issues statement denying existence of guerrilla groups in the country. Border military force is ordered into state of alert. March 17, Bolivian Army searches camp at Nancahuazú, discovers Braulio's diary, Bustos' portraits of Ché and other guerrillas, and other photos and documents. March 19, the training march finally ends up at Nancahuazú. Two guerrilla deserters are captured by the Army; one of them confirms Ché's presence in Bolivia earlier. Barrientos recognizes the presence of guerrillas in the areas of Camiri and Monteagudo. March 23, Ché successfully ambushes Bolivian troops at Nancahuazú in the first battle of the Bolivian campaign. A second lieutenant, six soldiers and a civilian guide are killed by the guerrillas in the fight. President Barrientos issues a call to the nation "to join in the fight against local and foreign anarchists with arms and money from Castro-communists." Dr. Gilberto Flores, the head of the Red Cross group which recovered the remains of Lt. Rubén Amézaga and five soldiers killed by the guerrillas reveals that "the guerrillas are young foreign and Bolivian men . . . They carry automatic weapons . . ." March 27, Ché prepares the manifesto of his ELNB, the National Liberation Army of Bolivia.

April   Barrientos believes Ché Guevara has been dead for some time. Army planes bomb the guerrilla zone. Military missions from Argentina, Brazil, and Paraguay have arrived in Bolivia to study the movement of the guerrillas in the southeast. Almost nothing known of guerrillas; they seem to have no program, no manifesto and they have no visible connection with any of Bolivia's four Communist parties. The Army announces that on April 5, the 4th Division of the Army took control of Nancahuazú after a short combat. In Havana, on April 6, Hoang Bich Son, Chief of Mission of the Vietnamese National Liberation Front declares that the armed struggle in Bolivia constitutes "a stimulant for the South Vietnamese revolution." Gen. Ovando announces that the Castro-communist guerrillas have been extinguished. The second fight between Army and guerrillas takes place on April 10 in the zone of Iripití, 12 miles from the Nancahuazú Canyon. The Army has 19 casualties. Four provinces are declared zones of emergency by the government. The activities of the Communist Party are suspended by the Government. "El Diario" of La Paz publishes fragments of a diary written by the guerrilla Braulio which indicates that Cuba sent the guerrillas to Bolivia; it is confirmed in part by photographs of camp showing many foreigners. On April 19, a new guerrilla group appears between Muyupampa and Yacunday about 44 miles from Camiri. On April 17, the guerrillas accidentally split into two groups under Ché and Joaquín. New encounter of Army and guerrillas estimated at 50 men in the Yacunday zone. April 20, Régis Debray, George Andrew Roth and Ciro Roberto Bustos captured by the Bolivian Army. U.S. military advisors are insisting that the Bolivians introduce basic changes in the organization of their forces. Barrientos has personally flown reconnaissance missions over the rebel region in an AT-6 two-seat jet trainer. On April 21 the three foreign prisoners, Debray, Roth and Bustos are moved to Camiri. On April 22, a clash takes place in Caripote between Muyupampa and Monteagudo; the guerrillas suffer 4 dead and various wounded. April 25, other encounters in El Mesón and Itia, during which Rolando is killed. The Minister of Government says that "some political parties like the PRIN and the MNR" are preparing an "insurrectional climate to assist their political declarations." Ché has lost radio contact with Havana, evidently able to receive but not transmit for the duration of the campaign. He is unable to send communications except by courier.

Rolando diary concludes April 20

May Estimates of the guerrillas' strength put at 30 to 50 in early April have risen within the last month to 100 or 120. Sixteen U.S. Special Forces troops have arrived in Bolivia to train a battalion of more than 600 men. There are reports of trouble brewing among Bolivia's tin miners. Now the Government has both the miners and the guerrillas to cope with. May 8, another encounter between Army and guerrillas at Pincal, 44 miles north of Camiri. Army casualties to date total 23 dead. Bolivia is attacked by international intellectuals for imprisoning Régis Debray for his activities as a "journalist" in Bolivia. May 13, guerrillas attacked a ranch in Pirirenda. In Havana, Ecuadorian labor leader Raúl Guzmán Ortega calls for the complete support of the guerrillas of Bolivia, Colombia, Venezuela and Guatemala. May 16, two more battles in the regions of La Manga and El Platanal, one guerrilla shot and many wounded escape. Colonel Federico Arana, Chief of the Military Intelligence of Bolivia, tells officals of 16 American countries that there are important reasons to believe that Ramón, the Cuban leader of the guerrillas, could be Ché Guevara. In the battle that takes place on May 27 the Bolivian Julio Velasco Montano is killed. On May 29, Jorge Vásquez Viaña, the captured guerrilla Loro, is executed outside the hospital of Camiri. Battle on May 30 in Muchiri; result: one guerrilla and five soldiers dead. Another encounter takes place in El Espino where six soldiers are killed.

Pombo diary concludes May 29

June   Two small battles reported on June 3 and 4 in the oil region of Abapó near Santa Cruz. An encounter takes place in Ipitá causing three casualties. Guerrillas transmit a communique through Radio Havana announcing they will soon start popular revolutionary tribunals in Bolivia. The Army announces that to date 17 Cubans, 14 Brazilians, 4 Argentines and 3 Peruvians have been identified among the guerrillas. On June 7, Barrientos declares a state of siege and 60 radical politicians and labor leaders are arrested. Agitation in the mining area of Siglo XX and Oruro, Army troops are sent to keep order, but a clash between Army and miners causes 21 dead and 70 wounded. On June 24 the miners of Catavi and Siglo XX declare a 48-hour strike to protest the Army intervention. Another clash between Army and guerrillas takes place on June 26 causing three dead and two wounded near Florida, and another

encounter near the Gulf Oil property in
Santa Cruz. Ché begins to have increasingly
frequent asthma attacks, often incapacitat-
ing him, from June to his death in October.

July   In a press conference on July 1, Barrientos
states that Ché Guevara is in Bolivia. In a
newspaper interview Régis Debray reveals
the presence of Ché Guevara in Nancahuazú where he talked to him on three different occasions. Debray insists he came
to Bolivia to interview Ché. July 6, high-
water mark for the guerrilla campaign: Ché
takes over Army garrison at Samaipata.
Army announces beginning of "Operacíon
Cynthia" designating six Army units with
air cover to round up guerrillas. Army captures another guerrilla camp, El Dorado
near Río Grande. Another encounter with
guerrillas in Iquira causes the death of one
guerrilla. On July 29, Barrientos proposes a
joint intervention with the OAS against
Cuba. On July 30, guerrilla fighting at the
Río Moroca. Work back to normal in the
mining districts as the strike is called off
after signing an agreement favorable to the
state-owned company. July 31, Ché loses the
tape recorder that enabled him to decode
messages from Havana. His isolation becomes more complete.

August   August 8, led by two guerrilla deserters,
Chingolo and Eusebio, the Army captures
two guerrilla caches containing arms and
ammunition. On August 9, there is a
battle in Taperillas against the guerrillas resulting in a number of casualties, the guerrilla group commanded by Joaquín flees
toward the west. August 27, unsuccessful
guerrilla assault against a military unit in
Loma Mansa near Tatarenda. After tracking Joaquín's group since April when it had
been cut off from Ché, the Army finally
destroys the guerrilla group led by Joaquín
on August 31, in Masicurí Bajo (Vado del
Yeso); guerrillas killed: Joaquín, Ernesto,
Walter, Moisés, Tania, Negro, Alejandro,

*Braulio
diary
concludes
August 9*

Paco, Paulo and Braulio. This was the first of three fatal battles which destroyed Ché's Bolivian insurrection.

September Barrientos states on September 10 that Ché Guevara died a long time ago. However, on September 11, he states that there is proof Ché is in Bolivia and offers a reward of $4,200 dollars for his capture with leaflets air-dropped into the Red Zone. Second crucial battle in campaign at La Higuera on September 26; three guerrillas are killed: "Coco" Roberto Peredo, "Julio" Mario Gutierrez Ardaya, and "Miguel."

October Army clash with guerrillas on October 1 in Abra del Quinal in the southwest of Vallegrande province. In a final battle on October 8 at Quebrada del Yuro, two soldiers and four guerrillas are killed: El Chino, Pacho, Antonio and Arturo. Ché Guevara is executed on October 9 with Willy and Aniceto. The ten remaining members of the guerrilla band led by Inti and Pombo escape toward the border. On October 14, four more guerrillas, (Moro, Chapaco, Eustaquio, Pablo) are killed in a clash with Bolivian Rangers about 20 miles from La Higuera. The six surviving guerrillas are spotted south of Vallegrande in Los Gitanos. There are three Cubans: Pombo, Urbano and Benigno, and three Bolivians: Inti, Darío and Nato.

Ché diary concludes October 7

October 1967- January 1968 Many small engagements as the six guerrillas attempt to escape from Bolivia. Nato is killed on November 15 near Mataral.

February 1968 The Cubans, Pombo, Urbano and Benigno escape into Chile. Inti and Darío still remain in hiding in Bolivia.

March 1968 Pombo, Urbano and Benigno arrive in Havana via Prague.

CHE GUEVARA'S DIARY

Written in what Fidel Castro has described as "the small and almost illegible letters of a doctor," Ché Guevara's diary begins upon his arrival at Nancahuazú on November 7, 1966 and concludes October 7, 1967, two days before his death. Ché left two diaries. The first was kept in a spiral notebook and concluded December 31, 1966. The second diary was an appointment book given out by a German pharmaceutical company and used until Che's final entry. Examples of both diaries are included in the picture section.

Ché's style is crisp and restrained, highly literate, and evidences an excellent, dry sense of humor. It is interesting to contrast the monthly analyses entered by Ché with the cumulative effect of his diary for any given month. He often seems to ignore his daily impressions for a more hopeful summary of them. But Ché does not attempt to conceal either the course of his campaign or his growing desperation, and the daily reports become increasingly moody until towards the end he is considering means of escape. His courage, his mistakes in judgment, his illusions, and his ideals are honestly set down.

The following entries of those contained below were missing in the Cuban text released by Fidel Castro on July 2, 1968: January 4, 5, 8, and 9; February 8 and 9; March 1 and 4; April 4 and 5; June 9 and 10; July 4 and 5; all of 1967. There are numerous aliases and codewords used throughout Ché's diaries and the other diaries following them. Because of code changes during the course of the Bolivian insurrection, many of the guerrillas have more than one alias, and some of them as many as three. These are listed with a key in the Appendix.

There are a number of inconsistencies or errors in Ché's spelling of names and places which have been retained from his diary.

1966

November 7

A new stage begins today. We arrived at the farm at night. The trip was quite good. Upon reaching Cochabamba, appropriately disguised, Pachungo and I made the contacts and traveled by jeep for two days, in two vehicles. As we approached the farm we stopped the cars and only one of them went on to preclude arousing the suspicions of a neighboring landowner who was speculating on the possibility that our business there was the making of cocaine. As a curious sidelight the ineffable Tumaini is indicated as the group's chemist.

While heading toward the farm on his second trip Bigotes, who had just discovered my identity, almost drove off a cliff leaving the jeep stuck on the edge of the precipice. We walked about 20 kilometers to the farm where there are three Party workers. We arrived after midnight.

Bigotes showed himself willing to collaborate with us whatever the Party might do but he is also loyal to Monje whom he respects and seems to like. According to him Rodolfo feels the same way and so does Coco, but we must try to convince the Party to fight. I asked him not to inform the Party until Monje, who is traveling in Bulgaria, arrives and to help us. He agreed to both things.

November 8

We spent the day in the jungle beside the arroyo, some 100 meters from the house. We were attacked by some sort of insects which are annoying but do not bite. So far we have found the gnat, the *maragui,* the mosquito and the tick.

[The house referred to is one at the end of the road before the camp, called "Casa de Calamina"—"House of the Tin Roof." It was generally inhabited by Coco Peredo, who had purchased the Nancahuazú farm for the guerrillas and was its nominal owner.]

Bigote rescued his jeep with the help of Algarañaz, from whom he promised to buy a few things, such as pigs and chickens.

I intended to report on what has been going on, but I shall leave it until next week when the second group arrives.

[Ciro Algarañaz was the owner of the farm next to the guerrillas'. He was intensely curious about them, assuming that they were manufacturing cocaine and hoped to do business with them. He was formerly Mayor of Camiri, the oil town nearby, where he also owned a butchershop. He would eventually betray the guerrillas to the authorities.]

November 9
An uneventful day. Tumaini and I surveyed the area, following the course of the Nancahuazú River (actually a small stream), but we did not reach its source. It runs through narrow canyons, and the area fortunately is little frequented. With proper discipline, one could possibly stay there a long time.

In the afternoon a heavy rain drove us back into the house. I removed six ticks from my body.

[Ché used the spelling "Nancahuasu" or "Nacahuasu," for Nancahuazú, as it is generally spelled by the Bolivians.]

November 10
Pachungo and Pombo went exploring with Serafin, one of the Bolivian comrades. They went farther than we did, and found the fork where the stream branches out, into a little canyon which might be good. During the rest period they loafed around the house. Algarañaz' chauffeur [Ché spells this name several ways] who was bringing the men with the supplies they had purchased from him, saw them. I threw a tremendous fit and we decided to move into the jungle tomorrow where we shall set up a permanent camp. Tumaini may allow himself to be seen since he is already known as another employee of the farm. The situation is deteriorating rapidly. We must find out whether they will let us bring in at least our men. With them here I will be more at ease.

November 11
An uneventful day spent at a new camp on the other side of the house, where we slept. The insects are dreadful, and a hammock with the protection of mosquito netting is necessary (and only mine has it). Tumaini went to visit Algañaraz and bought some chickens and turkeys from him. There is no reason yet to suspect his movements.

November 12

A completely uneventful day. We did some good scouting to prepare the area to be used for a campsite when the six men of the second group arrive. The spot selected is about 100 meters from the head of the grade, on a small elevation; close by there is a ravine where we can build caves to store food and other things. By now, the first of the three two-man groups into which our party is divided should be arriving. By next weekend they should be at the farm.

My hair is growing, although very sparsely, and the grey hair is turning blond and beginning to disappear. My beard is growing and in a couple of months I shall start looking like myself again.

[Che's hair had been dyed grey as part of his disguise upon entering Bolivia. It was now "turning blond" because it had been bleached before dyeing. As time passed, the bleached hair was replaced by his natural, chestnut-colored hair.]

November 13

Sunday. Some hunters pass by our dwelling: Algañaraz' laborers. They are men of the mountains, young, unmarried, ideal for recruitment. They cordially hate their boss. They reported that there are houses 8 leagues away along the river and that there are some water-filled gorges. There is no other news.

November 14

A week in camp. Pachungo seems somewhat unacclimated and sad, but he should recover. Today we started excavating to make a tunnel for storing everything that could be compromising. We shall camouflage it with a grating of logs and protect it from humidity as much as possible. A pit measuring 1½ meters has been dug and the tunnel is under way.

November 15

We continue to work on the tunnel, Pombo and Pachungo in the morning, Tumaini and I in the afternoon. At 6, when we stopped working, the tunnel was two meters deep. Tomorrow we hope to finish it and put all the compromising objects in it. During the night the rain made me flee my hammock, which got wet because the nylon cover is too small. There was nothing else new.

November 16

The tunnel was completed and camouflaged; only the path remains to be disguised. We moved the things to our little house and tomorrow we will put them away, covering the entrance with a network of logs and clay. The layout of this tunnel, marked No. 1, is in document I. There is no other news; from tomorrow on we can reasonably expect news from La Paz.

November 17

The tunnel is filled with the articles which could be compromising to the people in the house, and some canned food, and is fairly well disguised. There was no news at all from La Paz. The fellows in the house spoke to Algañaraz, from whom they bought some things, and he again told them he wanted to participate in the cocaine-making enterprise.

November 18

No news from La Paz. Pachungo and Pombo again explore the arroyo but they are not very convinced that this is the proper camp site. Monday I shall look at it with Tumaini. Algañaraz came to repair the road and get rocks from the river. He spent a great deal of time at this task. He does not seem suspicious about our presence here. Things are very monotonous, the mosquitoes and ticks are beginning to cause annoying sores when the bites get infected. It is now getting cold in the early morning.

November 19

Nothing new from La Paz. Nothing new here. We stay indoors because it is Saturday, the day the hunters come out.

November 20

Marcos and Rolando arrived at noon. We are now six. They immediately gave an account of their trip. It took them so long because they got the word only a week ago. They were the ones who traveled most quickly, via São Paulo. We cannot expect the other four to arrive before next week. With them came Rodolfo, who made a very good impression on me. He seems to be more decided to break with everything than Bigote. Papi told him and Coco of my presence here, thus violating instructions; it seems to be a case of lust for authority. I wrote to Manila making some recommendations (documents I and II) and also to Papi, answering his questions. Rodolfo started back in the early morning.

November 21

First day with the larger group. It rained quite hard and the move to our new camp resulted in a good soaking. We are now installed. The tent turned out to be a canvas tarpaulin for a truck and is not rainproof, but it protects us somewhat. We have our hammock with its nylon netting. A few more arms arrived: Marcos has a Garand and Rolando will be given an M-1 from the stock. Jorge remained with us, but stays in the house. From there he will direct the work of improving the farm. I asked Rodolfo to look for an agronomist we could trust. We shall try to keep this going as long as possible.

November 22

Tuma, Jorge and I followed the river bank (the Nancahuazú) up to the newly-found arroyo. After yesterday's rain the river was entirely different and it took a lot of effort to reach the desired place. This is a little stream of water with a very narrow mouth; properly set up, it could be used as a permanent camp. We returned shortly after 9 in the evening. Nothing new here.

November 23

We set up an observation point overlooking the little farmhouse so that we can have some warning in case of any inspection or annoying visit. While two of us go scouting, each of the others gets three hours of guard duty. Pombo and Marcos surveyed the terrain of our camp site all the way to the arroyo, which is still flooded.

November 24

Pacho and Rolando went out scouting along the arroyo; they should be back tomorrow. In the evening, two of Algañaraz' laborers "strolled" over: a strange visit. It would have been nothing out of the ordinary, but Antonio was out with the scouts and Tuma who officially is part of the household was out also. Pretext: a hunting expedition. Today is

Aliucha's birthday.

November 25

From the observation point we got word that a jeep with two or three persons in it had arrived. They turned out to be a malaria-control team. They left as soon as they had taken blood samples. Pacho and Rolando came back very late at night. They found the arroyo indicated on the map and explored it; they also followed the main course of the river until they came across some abandoned fields.

November 26

Because it was Saturday, we all stayed in camp. I asked Jorge to go on horseback to explore the river to its very end. No horse was available so he went on foot to ask Don Remberto, who lives some 20 to 25 kilometers away, to lend him one. By nightfall, Jorge had not yet returned. No news from La Paz.

["Don Remberto" is Remberto Villa, from whom the guerrillas bought the Nancahuazú property. He remained their neighbor, living on the Terrazas farm to the south.]

November 27

Jorge still has not returned. I ordered an all-night sentry duty. At 9 the first jeep arrived from La Paz, bringing Coco, Joaquín and Urbano, together with a Bolivian who was to stay: Ernesto, a medical student. Coco drove back and brought Ricardo, with Braulio and Miguel, and another Bolivian, Inti, who is also to remain with us. We are now 12 insurrectionists, plus Jorge, who acts as the householder. Coco and Rodolfo will handle contacts. Ricardo reported some unpleasant news. Chino is in Bolivia. He wants to see me and to send me 20 men. This causes some problems because we will be internationalizing the struggle before taking Estanislao into account. It was agreed that he would be sent to Santa Cruz; Coco would pick him up and bring him here. Coco left at dawn with Ricardo who will take the other jeep and continue to La Paz. Coco will stop by Don Remberto's house to inquire about Jorge. In an initial conversation with Inti, he expressed the opinion that Estanislao will not take to the mountains but seems determined to break away.

November 28

By morning Jorge still had not returned, and neither had Coco. Then they both showed up. They had simply decided to stay at Don Remberto's for the night. Somewhat irresponsible. In the afternoon I called the Bolivian group together to tell them of the Peruvian offer to send 20 men. Everyone agreed to accept them, but only after the action had begun.

November 29

Tumaini, Urbano, Inti and I went out to measure the river and scout the arroyo where our next camp will be. The arroyo is very safe, but quite gloomy. We shall try to find another one that is an hour away. Tumaini fell and apparently fractured his ankle. We returned to the camp at night, after having measured the river. No news here. Coco left for Santa Cruz to wait for Chino.

November 30

Marcos, Pacho, Miguel and Pombo went out with orders to explore an arroyo which is farther away. They should be gone for two days. It is raining rather steadily. Nothing new at the house.

ANALYSIS OF THE MONTH

Everything went off rather well. I arrived without difficulty. Half of the personnel is here. They also arrived without trouble, although a few of them were somewhat delayed. Ricardo's main collaborators will take to the mountains against any odds. The prospect looks very good in this remote area, where everything indicates we can stay practically as long as we wish. The plans are to wait for the rest of the group, increase the number of Bolivians to at least 20, and then begin to operate. We still have to check Monje's reaction and learn how Guevara's people will conduct themselves.

[The Guevara referred to here is Moisés Guevara Rodríguez, a Bolivian, no relative of Ché's. See list of guerrillas in appendix.]

December 1

The day passed without news. At night Marcos and his companions returned from their exploration, having made a longer trip than ordered. They were wandering through the hills. At 2 in the morning I was informed that Coco has arrived with a companion; I leave that for tomorrow.

December 2

Chino arrives early, very effusive. We spend the day chatting. These are some important points: He will go to Cuba to give a personal account of the situation. Five Peruvians can join our group within two months; that is, when we begin to act. Right now they can send us two Peruvians: a physician and a radio operator who will stay some time with us. He asked for arms, and I agreed to give him a BZ-30, some Mausers, grenades, and to buy an M-1 for them. I also decided to help them send five men to establish contacts to pass the arms in a region near Puno, from the other side of Lake Titicaca. He told me about his troubles in Peru, including a bold plan to free Calixto which seemed rather fanciful to me. He believes that some survivors of the guerrilla units are still active in the area, but this is not a sure fact since no one has been able to get to the zone. The rest of the conversation was chit-chat. Chino left with the same enthusiasm, heading toward La Paz; he took some photos of us with him. Coco had instructions to prepare contacts with Sánchez (whom I shall see later), and to contact the Chief of Information of the Presidency, who has offered to provide them, since he is Inti's brother-in-law. The network is still in its infancy.

[The "troubles in Peru" refer to the destruction of the guerrilla movement there the previous year, in the course of which its most important leaders were either killed or arrested; Calixto was among the latter. El Chino, one of the handful to escape, wants Ché to help him resurrect the Peruvian movement. (Pombo's diary contains more discussion of this subject.)]

December 3

Nothing new. No scouting, today being Saturday. The three farm laborers leave for Lagunillas on some errands.

December 4

Nothing new. Everyone is quiet, since it is Sunday. I give a talk on our attitude toward the Bolivians who are to come, and on the war.

December 5

Nothing new. We intended to go out but it rained all day. There was a slight alarm caused by some shots Loro fired without any warning.

December 6

Apolinar, Inti, Miguel, Urbano and I went out to begin the

second cave in the first arroyo. Miguel is taking the place of Tuma, who has not yet recovered from his fall. Apolinar said he will join the guerrilla unit but wants to go to La Paz to settle some personal affairs. I told him he may go but to wait a little while. We reached the arroyo about 11; we made a hidden path and combed the area for an adequate spot for the cave, but the ground is all rock and when the arroyo dries to a trickle it passes between sheer rock banks. We left the rest of the exploration for tomorrow. Inti and Urbano went out to try to hunt deer since we have very little food and must make what we have last until Friday.

December 7

Miguel and Apolinar found an appropriate site and are dedicating themselves to the construction of the tunnel; their tools are inadequate. Inti and Urbano returned without a kill but at nightfall Urbano shot a turkey hen with the M-1. We had already eaten so we kept it for tomorrow's breakfast.

Today is actually the end of our first month here, but for convenience I shall write the complete analysis at the end of each calendar month.

December 8

Inti and I climbed up to a height above the arroyo. Miguel and Urbano were still digging the pit. In the afternoon Apolinar relieved Miguel. At nightfall Marcos, Pombo and Pacho returned, the latter far behind and tired. Marcos asked me to take Pacho out of the vanguard if he did not improve. I recorded the path to the new cave on Sketch II. I told them the most important tasks to carry out during their stay. Miguel will remain with them, and we shall return tomorrow.

December 9

We returned slowly in the morning, arriving at noon. Pacho was ordered to stay when the group returned. We tried to make contact with Camp II, but it was not possible. Nothing else is new.

December 10

An uneventful day. For the first time, bread was baked in the house. I spoke with Jorge and Inti about some urgent tasks. There was no news from La Paz.

December 11

The day passed without incident, but in the evening Coco arrived with Papi. He brought Alejandro, Arturo and a Bolivian named Carlos. The second jeep was left on the road as usual. Then they brought in the doctor, Moro, Benigno, and two Bolivians, both *"cambas"* from the farm at Caranavi. We spent the night, in the usual talk about the trip and the absence of Antonio and Felix, who should have reached here by now. We talked with Papi, finally deciding that he would have to make two more trips to bring in Renán and Tania. We settled our financial affairs, and that of the stocks, and I gave $1,000 to aid Sanchez. He will keep the truck and we will sell one jeep to Tania and keep the second one for ourselves. There is still a gun-running trip to make, and I ordered him to put everything in one jeep, to avoid switching loads which might be more easily detected. Chino left for Cuba, apparently very enthusiastic; he plans to return here when he gets back. Coco remained here to go to Camiri to get food. Papi returned to La Paz.

["Camba" is the nickname of the inhabitants of the Santa Cruz region. One of the guerrillas used it as a *nom de guerre*.]

A dangerous incident took place: the Vallegrandino [inhabitant of nearby Vallegrande], a hunter, discovered a footprint made by us, and some paths, apparently saw one of us, found a glove lost by Pombo. That changes our plans and we must be very careful. The Vallegrandino will go out tomorrow with Antonio to show him where he set his traps for tapir.

Inti told me his reservations about the student Carlos who, upon his arrival here brought up the subject of Cuban participation and previously had said that he would not rebel without the participation of the Party. Rodolfo sent him because he said it was all due to a misinterpretation.

December 12

I spoke to the entire group, giving them "the facts of life" on the realities of war. I emphasized the one-man command system of discipline and warned the Bolivians of the responsibility they took in violating the discipline of their party in adopting another line. I assigned duties: Joaquín, as second military chief; Rolando and Inti, as commissars; Alejandro, as chief of operations; Pombo, services; Inti, finances; Nato, supplies and armament for the time being; Moro, medical services.

Rolando and Braulio left to warn the group to be quiet while waiting for the Vallegrandino to put down his traps and explore with Antonio. In the evening they all returned; the trap line was not very far away. The men got the Vallegrandino drunk, and he left during the night, very content with a bottle of liquor in his belly. Coco returned from Caranavi where he purchased the necessary provisions but was seen by some Lagunillas people who were astonished by the quantity he was buying.

Later, Pombo arrived with Marcos who had cut himself on his superciliary arch while chopping wood; he was given two stitches.

December 13

Joaquín, Carlos and the doctor left to join Rolando and Braulio. Pombo accompanied them with orders to return the same day. I gave an order to cover the path and to make a second one; the second one was to start in the same place as the first but lead to the river. This was so successfully done that Pombo, Miguel and Pacho got lost on their return and they followed it.

I talked with Apolinar, who will go to his home in Viacha for a few days. I gave him money for his family, and recommended absolute secrecy. Coco left at nightfall, but at 3 the alarm was sounded when whistles and noises were heard and a bitch barked. It was Coco himself, lost in the woods.

December 14

An uneventful day. The Vallegrandino passed by the house to inspect the trap which he set yesterday, contradicting what he said previously. Antonio was told of the path opened in the jungle so that he might guide the Vallegrandino along it, to avoid suspicion.

December 15

Nothing new. Eight men transported the provision to Camp No. 2 where we shall settle down for good.

December 16

In the morning, Pombo, Urbano, Tuma, Alejandro, Moro, Arturo, Inti and I set out for the camp to stay; we were heavily laden. The trip took 3 hours. Rolando stayed with us and Joaquin, Braulio, Carlos and the doctor returned. Carlos has proved to be a good traveler and a good worker. Moro and Tuma discovered a bend in the river with rather big fish and they caught 17, which gives us a good meal. Moro cut his hand with a hook. We found a spot to make the second cave now that the first one is completed, and suspended our activities until tomorrow. Moro and Inti left to spend the night in ambush, trying themselves at tapir-hunting.

December 17

Moro and Inti caught only a turkey hen. Tuma, Rolando and I concentrated on digging the second cave which might be finished by tomorrow. Arturo and Pombo looked for a place to set up the radio. Then they set to fixing the access path, which is in bad shape. In the afternoon it began to rain and it did not stop until morning.

December 18

It continued to rain but work on the cave did not stop, so that we are only a little short of the required 2.5 meters. We inspected a hill to install the generator for the radio. It seems good enough but the tests will tell.

December 19

This day was also rainy and did not invite one to walk but at about 11 Braulio and Nato came with the news that the river was passable although deep. As we set out we met Marcos and his vanguard who were coming to stay. He will be in charge and I told him to dispatch three to five men, according to the possibilities. We made the trip in a little more than three hours.

At midnight, Ricardo and Coco arrived, bringing with them Antonio, El Rubio (they were not able to obtain passage last Thursday) and Apolinar who is joining us as a permanent member of the group. Ivan arrived also, to discuss a whole series of subjects. The night was spent with hardly any sleep.

December 20

Various points were discussed and everything was being organized when the Camp II group, led by Alejandro, arrived with word that there was a dead deer on the path near the camp. It had been shot and a ribbon was tied to its leg. Joaquín had passed the place an hour earlier and had said nothing. We presumed that the Vallegrandino had carried the deer to that point and for some unknown reason dropped it and fled. A guard was posted at the rear and two men sent to catch the hunter, if he turned up. In a short while we were told that the deer had been dead for some time and was full of maggots. Later, Joaquín, returning, confirmed the fact and also that he had seen the deer. Coco and Loro brought the Vallegrandino to see the little animal; he said that it was an animal he had wounded several days ago. Thus the incident was closed.

It was decided to speed up the contacts with the man in Information whom Coco has neglected and to get Mejía to serve as an intermediary between Ivan and the man in Information who will maintain contact with Mejía, Sanchez, Tania, and the Party member who has not been designated yet. There is a possibility that he may be from Villamontes, but this has not been confirmed.

A telegram received from Manila says that Monje is coming via the south. A system for contact is indicated but it does not satisfy me because there is a clear distrust of Monje shown by his own comrades. At 1 in the morning La Paz reported someone had gone to get Monje.

Ivan has some chances to do business but his false passport prevents it. The thing to do is to improve the document and he should write to Manila so that the friends can fix it up.

Tania will come soon to receive instructions. I shall probably send her to Buenos Aires. It is finally decided that Ricardo, Ivan and Coco will leave Camiri by plane and the jeep will stay here. When they return they will talk to Lagunillas by telephone and report that they are there. Jorge will go at night to seek news and will look for them if there is something positive. At 1 a.m. it was not possible to hear anything from La Paz. At dawn they left for Camiri.

December 21

Loro had not left me the sketches made by the scout, so that I was in the dark as to the type of road to Yaqui. We left in the morning and made the trip with no trouble. Efforts will be made to have everything here by the 24th, on which day a celebration is scheduled. We ran across Pacho, Miguel, Benigno and Camba, who were going to fetch the generator. At 5 in the afternoon Pacho and Camba returned without the generator; they left it hidden in the jungle because it was too heavy. Tomorrow five men from here will go get it. The cave for the provisions is finished; tomorrow we shall begin on the cave for the radio.

December 22

We began the cave for the radio operator. At first we were very successful in the soft soil but we soon hit upon very hard flagstone, which stopped us. They brought in the generator, which is rather heavy. It has not been tested, for lack of gasoline. Loro sent word that he cannot forward maps; the report he got was verbal and he will come tomorrow to give it.

December 23

I went out with Pombo and Alejandro to explore the hard ground to the left. We shall have to clear the way, but it seems that we can walk on it comfortably. Joaquín arrived with two comrades, and said that Loro did not come because a pig had escaped and he was trying to catch it. There is no word on the trip of the Lagunillero [man from Lagunillas].

In the afternoon the pig, a big one, was brought in. But we still have no drinks. Loro is incapable of getting these things: he is very disorganized.

December 24

A day devoted to Christmas Eve. Some people made two trips and arrived late but we were all finally united and the evening went well, with some of us rather high. Loro explained that the Lagunillero's trip had not been fruitful; the only small result was some notes which are very vague.

December 25

Back to work. No trips were made to the start-out camp, baptized "C-26" at the suggestion of the Bolivian doctor. Marcos, Benigno and Camba went out to make a path along the hard ground to our right. They came back in the afternoon with the news that they had spotted a sort of treeless pampa about two hours' march away. Tomorrow they will reach it. Camba returned with a fever. Miguel and Pacho made two false paths along the left bank, and an access footpath to the radio cave. Inti, Antonio, Tuma and I continued digging the radio cave; this is very difficult because the ground is solid rock.

The rearguard took over making another camp and finding

a look-out high enough to cover both ends of the access path. The place is very good.

December 26

Inti and Carlos went off to explore the area up to the point called Yaki [Yaqui; Ché consistently uses the "k" spelling] on the map, an estimated 2-day trip. Rolando, Alejandro and Pombo continued work on the cave; it is very difficult. Pacho and I went out to inspect the paths made by Miguel; the one on the hard ground is not worth continuing. The path leading to the cave is pretty good, and hard to find. We killed two snakes today and another one yesterday. There seem to be quite a few. Tuma, Arturo, Rubio and Antonio went hunting and Braulio and Nato did sentry duty in the other camp. They came with news that Loro had had a spill, and the explanatory note announcing the arrival of Monje. Marcos, Miguel and Benigno left to improve the path on the hard ground but they did not return at all during the night.

December 27

I went out with Tuma to look for Marcos; we walked for some hours until we reached the source of a small stream which came down on the left side, to the west. We followed his tracks through this area, descending along fairly steep slopes. I thought we would reach the camp this way, but hours passed and we were still not in our area. After 5:00 p.m. we arrived at the Nancahuazú, some 5 kilometers below Camp No. 1; at 7:00 p.m. we reached the camp. We then found out that Marcos had spent the night there. I sent no one to report this because I thought Marcos would have told them of a possible route. We saw the jeep, rather beat up; Loro had gone to Camiri to look for some spare parts. According to Nato, he had fallen asleep at the wheel.

December 28

When we were leaving for the camp, Urbano and Antonio came looking for me. Marcos had gone on with Miguel to make a path to the camp along the hard ground and had not arrived. Benigno and Pombo went looking for me along the route we had followed. When I got to the camp I found Marcos and Miguel, who had slept on the ground because they could not reach the camp. Marcos complained to me of the way the others had treated me. Apparently he meant Joaquín, Alejandro and the doctor. Inti and Carlos had returned without discovering any inhabited houses; they only found an abandoned one which, it seems, is not the place marked Yaki on the map.

December 29

With Marcos, Miguel and Alejandro I went to Loma Pelada to get a better perspective of the situation. It looks like the beginning of the Pampa del Tigre; it is a mountain range of even height, and bare hills, about 1,500 meters high. We must forget the high ground on the left because it forms a semicircle toward the Nancahuazú. We started down and arrived at the camp in an hour and 20 minutes. Eight men were sent to get provisions, and they did not bring the entire load. Rubio and the doctor replaced Braulio and Nato. The latter made a new path before coming back; this path comes out on the river on some rocks and leads to the hill from the other side again on rocks; thus no tracks are left. There was no work done on the cave. Loro left for Camiri.

December 30

In spite of the rain, which caused the river to rise, four men went to wind up things at Camp No. 1. It is now cleaned up. There was no news from the farm. Six men went to the cave and in two trips cached away all the things that belonged there. The oven could not be finished because the clay was soft.

December 31

At 7:30 a.m. the doctor arrived with the news that Monje was here. I went with Inti, Tuma, Urbano and Arturo. The meeting was cordial but strained. In the background was the question: What are we here for? Accompanying Monje were Pan Divino, the new recruit, Tania, who came to receive instructions, and Ricardo, who came to stay.

The conversation with Monje began with generalities but he quickly came down to his fundamental premise, stated in three basic conditions:

1) He would resign as party leader but would obtain its neutrality, and cadres would be brought for the struggle.

2) He would be the political and military leader of the struggle as long as the revolution was taking place in Bolivia.

3) He would handle relations with other South American parties, trying to persuade them to support liberation movements (he mentioned Douglas Bravo as an example.).

I answered that the first point was a matter for his own judgment as Party Secretary, although I considered his position to be a great mistake. It was vacillating, accommodating, and would protect the good name in history of those who should be condemned for their crookedness. Time would prove me right.

On the third point, I told him I had no objection to his trying but that he would fail. To ask Codovilla to support Douglas Bravo was equivalent to asking him to support an insurrection within his own Party. Time will tell again.

[Douglas Bravo was at the time the leader of the Castro-oriented guerrillas of the Venezuelan Armed Forces of National Liberation; Vittorio Codovilla the perennial chief of the Moscow-lining Argentine Communist Party. Hence Che's sarcastic remark.]

As for the second point, I could not accept it under any conditions. I was to be the military chief and I would not accept any ambiguities on this matter. Here the discussion stalled into a vicious circle.

We agreed I would think it over and talk to the Bolivian comrades. We went over to the new camp. There he spoke to everybody, laying down the alternative of remaining with us or supporting the party. Everyone stayed, and this seemed to be a blow to him.

At noon we drank a toast in which he noted the historic importance of this date. I responded in support of his words, and calling this moment the new "battle cry" of Murillo of the continental revolution, went on to say that our lives count for nothing before the fact of the revolution.

Fidel sent me the attached messages.

ANALYSIS OF THE MONTH

The formation of the Cuban team has been successfully accomplished, the people's morale is good, and there are only small problems. The Bolivians are good, although there are few of them. Monje's attitude can hamper progress on the one hand, but can be helpful on the other by freeing me from political commitments. The next few steps, in addition to waiting for the arrival of more Bolivians, consist of talking with Guevara and with the Argentines: Mauricio, Jozamy (Masetti and the dissident party).

Too ill to withstand the rigors of guerrilla life, Ché often had to ride rather than walk toward the final days of his campaign. In one of his last photographs, taken by Pombo in mid-September in the area between the Masicurí and Pesca Rivers, he poses with his mule, Chico.

The photographs on this and the following pages are taken from the passports of the Cuban guerrillas which they used to enter Bolivia. The descriptions from a statement by Ciro Roberto Bustos, a visitor to the camp at Nancahuazu, who was a trained artist.

Joaquín. "An older man, more than 40 years old, approximately 5 feet, 9 inches tall, slightly stooped, thin arms, average half-closed eyes, a wide thin mouth, a big and somewhat hooked nose, a thin beard, an average chin, it has been said that he looks like the man who was one of the first peasants who joined Castro in the Sierra Maestre and became a major."

Marcos. "An older white man, more than 40 years old, not very tall, about 5 feet, 5 inches, face furrowed with wrinkles, a grey beard most like a goatee, curly grey hair, a somewhat prominent nose, very bright dark eyes, very nervous and uses a lot of slang as a Spanish speaker, thin, he used to be very fat and this is why he is wrinkled; he is always smoking a pipe, even when he is walking."

Alejandro. "White skin, a long thin nose (somewhat hooked), rather large clear eyes, a very long beard, straight, long, reddish-brown hair; clear small freckles, approximately 5 feet, 8 inches tall, thin, more than 30 years old, and has a high forehead."

Pacho. "White, a heavy beard, and very curly black hair, a straight average size nose, big eyes with long eyelashes and thick eyebrows, approximately 5 feet, 5 inches tall, thin but strong, and around 28 years old."

Urbano. Bustos compares him with Pombo. "Also Negro, about 5 feet, 5 inches tall, robust; he was the best walker and strongest man of all; he has never been sick; more typically Negro face, large nose with the lower lip protruding; heavy curly beard, long thick hair, skin which is more chocolate color; he uses a dental plate (two upper teeth I think); and he is about 26 to 28 years old."

Tuma. "A mulatto, olive-colored skin, angular cheekbones, an average nose, an average forehead, a lot of black frizzled hair, a long beard on the sides and under the chin, average height of about 5 feet, 4 inches, legs bowed like a horse man, a quiet man of 26 to 30 years old; a strong man, although exhausted like the two aforementioned one [Pombo and Urbano] who were always around Ramon and carrying part of his many things (books, valises, lamps, etc.)."

Pombo. This picture is from a roll taken at the Nancahuazu camp. "He is Negro, tall, approximately 5 feet, 9 inches, thin, a face with fine features, a sharp straight nose, large dark eyes, very smooth skin, well formed lips which are not very large; it is what we call a classic face, but Negro; a salt and pepper beard which is full and broad, very thick black hair, long arms and legs, 28 to 30 years old, and he does not smoke."

Braulio. "Negro, 5 feet, 9 inches to 6 feet tall, noisy with a typically Negro voice, a square head, a flat chin, a broad and relatively high forehead, very tightly curled hair, a flat average size nose, average black eyes, an average beard under his chin, and 30 years old."

Rolando. "White, an egg-shaped head, large goggle eyes, a rather prominent average nose, almost beardless with a thin goatee, a fleshy sensuous mouth, an almost boyish face which is very ordinary at the same time, very tangled hair which falls in shocks everywhere and onto his forehead, it gives the impression that he has a very big head and a very small face, a rather small build, approximately 5 feet, 4 inches tall, very thin, yellowish skin, and about 26 years old."

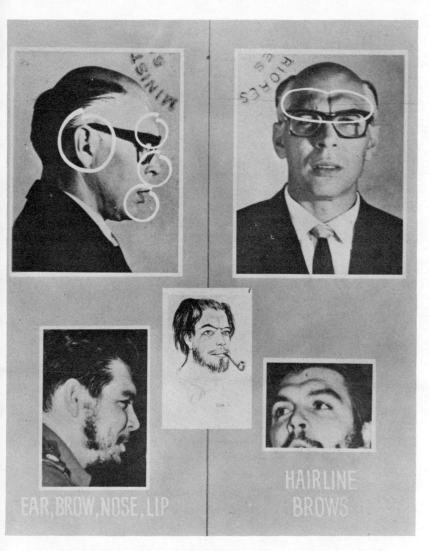

EAR, BROW, NOSE, LIP

HAIRLINE BROWS

A comparison of the photographs on the Uruguayan passports with an older photo of Ché reveals significant similarities which led to Ché's identification. The drawing in the center is one of many portraits of the guerrillas done by Bustos during the early campaign. It shows Ramón (Ché) with his shaven hair beginning to grow back. Fingerprints taken from Ché's corpse were matched with those on the passports and others on record to conclusively confirm his identity.

Sitting among his guerrillas at Nancahuazú, Ché still resembles his passport photographs. Bolivian officials later used this picture as evidence before the OAS in charging that Ché was organizing a guerrilla movement in their country. By November 12, 1966, Ché was able to write in his diary, "My hair is growing, although very sparsely, and the grey hair is turning blond and beginning to disappear. My beard is growing and in two months I [will] start looking like myself again."

...nde el observatorio. informaron que había vendido un
jeep con 2 o tres tripulantes. Resultaron ser de un servicio de lucha contra el paludismo, se fueron, inmedia-
tamente que supieron nuestros de ropa. Pacho y
Rolando llegaron por la noche, muy tarde. Encon-
traron el arroyo del mapa y lo exploraron, además si-
guieron por el curso principal del río hasta encontrar
campos abandonados

26

Por ser sábado, todos quedamos desentonados. Pedí
a Jorge que hiciera una exploración a caballo por el
cauce del río para ver hasta dónde llegaba; el caballo
no estaba y salió a pie a pedir uno a don Remi-
berto (20 a 25 Km.). A la noche no había regresado.
Sin novedad de La Paz.

27

Jorge seguía sin aparecer. Di órden de traer provista toda
la noche pero a las 9 llegó el primer jeep de La Paz. Con
el Coco venían Joaquín y Urbano y un boliviano a
quedarse: Ernesto, estudiante de medicina. Vino el Coco y
trajo a Ricardo con Braulio y después y otro boliviano
Inti, también a quedarse. Ahora somos doce alzados
y Jorge que funge de dueño; Coco y Rodolfo se en-
cargaron de los contactos. Ricardo trajo una noticia...

Ché's entry in his diary for November 27, 1966. On the following pages
are copies of a message he drafted to Fidel Castro on that day and the message he actually sent. His note to Cuba comments on the arrival of more
men; the diary states that "... at 9 the first jeep arrived from La Paz. ...
We are now 12 insurrectionists, plus Jorge, who acts as the householder."

① Leche.

    Esto está bueno llegue sus contratiempos
② Somos 4 en el ③ Refugio y parece que podrán ④ llegar
los demás sin dificultades. Uno de los hombres de
⑤ Entanislao sabe el asunto y está de acuerdo en
⑥ seguir por lo que paga. La ⑦ zona es muy ⑧ despoblada
pero ⑨ está cerca de ⑩ núcleos de población. Hay indicios
de que los ⑪ mejores cuadros se le ⑫ iban a Estanislao
y este no se ⑬ decide. Va para ⑭ Ella. Deben llevar le
la ⑮ cabeza de ajos de gloria pero ⑯ no darle plata ni
soltar la ⑰ prenda principal, salvo que sea absolutamente necesario. Los próximos pasos eran de ⑱ exploración de las ⑲ condiciones del lugar

    La ⑳ escodofa salió ahora. Es necesario prevenir que
los ㉑ certificados de vacuna ㉒ necesitan un ㉓ sello
㉔ En Sao Paolo me la ㉔ quitaron y tuve que ㉔ sacar otra
allí. El mejor ㉕ documento es ㉖ la tarjeta de tus-
ta, trátase de conseguir para ㉗ ...las, pues es
mejor que reproducirla ㉘ ya que el ㉙ número puede coin-
cidir con otra.

    Un abrazo
      to

1.

    Esto está bueno 2 en el 3 y parece que podrán
4. Uno de los hombres de 5. sabe el asunto y esta de
acuerdo en 6. La 7 es muy 8 pero 9 de 10. Hay
indicios de que los 11 se le 12 este 13. Va para
14, deben llevar 6 la 15 pero 16 soltar la 17, salvo
que sea absolutamente necesario. Los próximos pasos se-
son de 18 los 19.

    La escodofa salió ahora. Es necesario prevenir que
los 20 necesitan un 21. 22 me la 23, tuve que 24. El
mejor 25 es 26, trataré de conseguir para 27, pues
es mejor que 28 ya que el 29 con otra

Ché drafted this message to Fidel Castro on November 27, 1966. The underlined words were eliminated from the message he actually sent and code numbers, also indicated in the draft, were substituted. The message reads:

(1) Leche

All is well. ~~I arrived without trouble.~~ (2) We are 4 in (3) the refuge and it seems that (4) the others will be able to arrive without difficulty. One of the men of (5) Estanislao knows of the deal and agrees to (6) continue no matter what. The (7) zone is quite (8) uninhabited but (9) relatively close to (10) populated places. There are indications that the (11) best cadres will (12) go to Estanislao if (13) he does not make up his mind. He is going (14) over there. You must (15) fill his head with glory talk but do not (16) give him any money nor let the (17) cat out of the bag, unless its absolutely necessary. The next steps will be (18) to explore the (19) conditions around us.

The Ecodofa [pseudonym?] has just left. It is necessary to be aware that the (20) Uruguayan Vaccination Certificates require a (21) stamp. (22) In São Paulo they (23) took it away from me and I had to (24) get another one there. The best (25) document is (26) a tourist card, I will try to get some for (27) you, since this is better than (28) reproducing one since its (29) number might coincide with another.

~~Un abrazo~~

~~Jo~~

Ché's message is now encoded. It reads:
1:

All is well. 2 in 3 and it seems that 4. One of the men of 5 knows of the deal and agrees to 6. The 7 is quite 8 but 9 to 10. There are indications that the 11 will 12 if 13. He is going 14. You must 15 but do not 16 nor let the 17, unless it is absolutely necessary. The next steps will be 18 the 19.

The Ecodofa [pseudonym?] has just left. It is necessary to be aware that the 20 require a 21. 22 they 23 and I had to 24. The best 25 is 26. I will try to get some for 27, since this is better than 28 since its 29 with another.

Ché kept an address book with the names and addresses of his followers and sympathizers.

Ché and an unknown guerrilla.

The pictures on this and the following pages were taken at the guerrilla camp at Nancahuazú. The captions and numbers that appear on some of the pictures were put on by the Bolivian Armed Forces in their efforts to identify the members of the guerrilla band.

Two vital problems of guerrilla life are shown here; lack of communications and lack of food were to plague Ché's men continually. In the top picture, a guerrilla listens to the transistor radio; in the bottom one, Ché is shown by the campfire.

Drawn by Bustos at Nancahuazú, Urbano (top), Benigno (left), and Pombo were the three guerrillas who finally escaped to Chile and reached Cuba in March of 1968.

Ché evaluated the members of his band in his notebooks, as well as keeping a record of their true names. He also kept notes on the backgrounds of his sympathizers; one of these evaluations comments:

"Víctor Collazo, law student (University of La Paz). Has qualifications for work in the city. Belongs to the FLIN (president of the FLIN in the University). He has had a year, more or less, of revolutionary activity. He is very active and a partisan of the armed struggle and action. He may be reached through Loyola."

This photograph of Ché with an automatic rifle is another of the group presented by the Bolivians to the OAS.

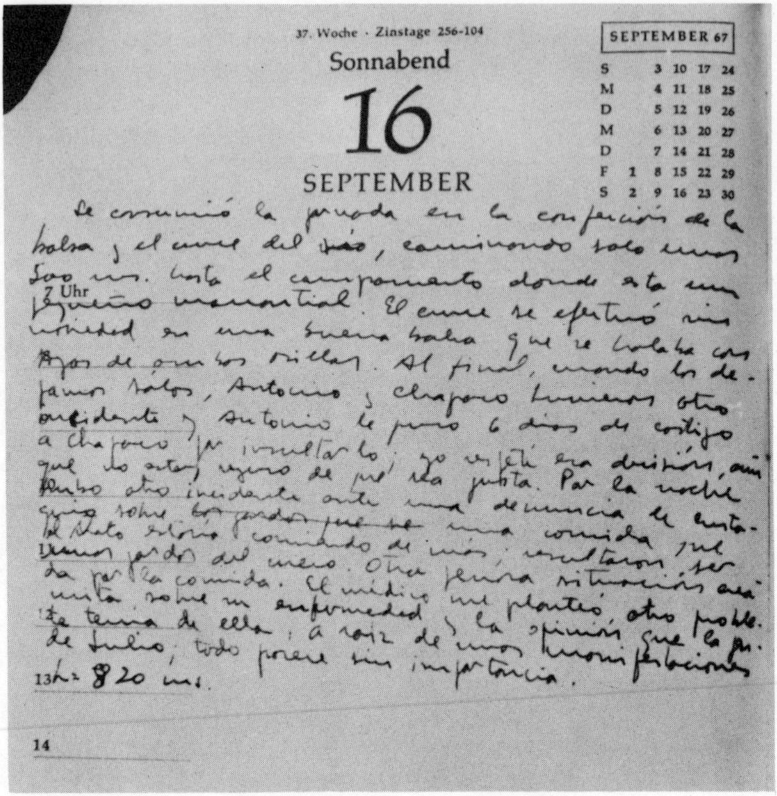

37. Woche · Zinstage 256-104

Sonnabend

16

SEPTEMBER

SEPTEMBER 67

S		3	10	17	24
M		4	11	18	25
D		5	12	19	26
M		6	13	20	27
D		7	14	21	28
F	1	8	15	22	29
S	2	9	16	23	30

Se consumió la jornada en la confección de la
balsa y el cruce del río, caminando solo unos
500 ms. hasta el campamento donde está un
7 Uhr pequeño manantial. El cruce se efectuó sin
novedad en una buena balsa que se halaba con
sogas de ambas orillas. Al final, cuando los de-
jamos solos, Antonio y Chapaco tuvieron otro
incidente y Antonio le puso 6 días de castigo
a Chapaco por insultarlo; yo respeté esa decisión, aun-
que no estoy seguro de que sea justa. Por la noche
hubo otro incidente ante una denuncia de Eustaquio sobre [illegible] una comida
del Ñato [illegible] comiendo de más; resultaron ser
los gordos del medio. Otra penosa situación creada
por la comida. El médico me planteó otros proble-
[illegible] sobre su enfermedad y la opinión que la gente
tenía de ella, a raíz de unas manifestaciones
de Julio; todo parece sin importancia.
13 h = 820 ms.

14

Ché's diary entry for September 16, 1967 comments: "The day was spent in making the raft and crossing the river. We walked only 500 meters to the camp where there is a small spring. The crossing was effected without incident on a good raft pulled by ropes from either bank." *(see the photographs following)*

Crossing the Río Grande River in one of a series of similar desperate maneuvers are (in order) Julio, Moro on muleback, Ché walking with the aid of a pole and not carrying his fieldpack, Pacho, Urbano and Pombo.

Julio is seated on a raft ready to cross the Río Grande; the man with the rifle is Aniceto and Darío is holding the raft in tow with a rope (top). The bottom picture shows Julio in the middle of his crossing. Two men were killed in river crossings during the campaign.

In perhaps the last photograph taken of Ché alive, he examines
a map of the Pesca River region with Adalino.

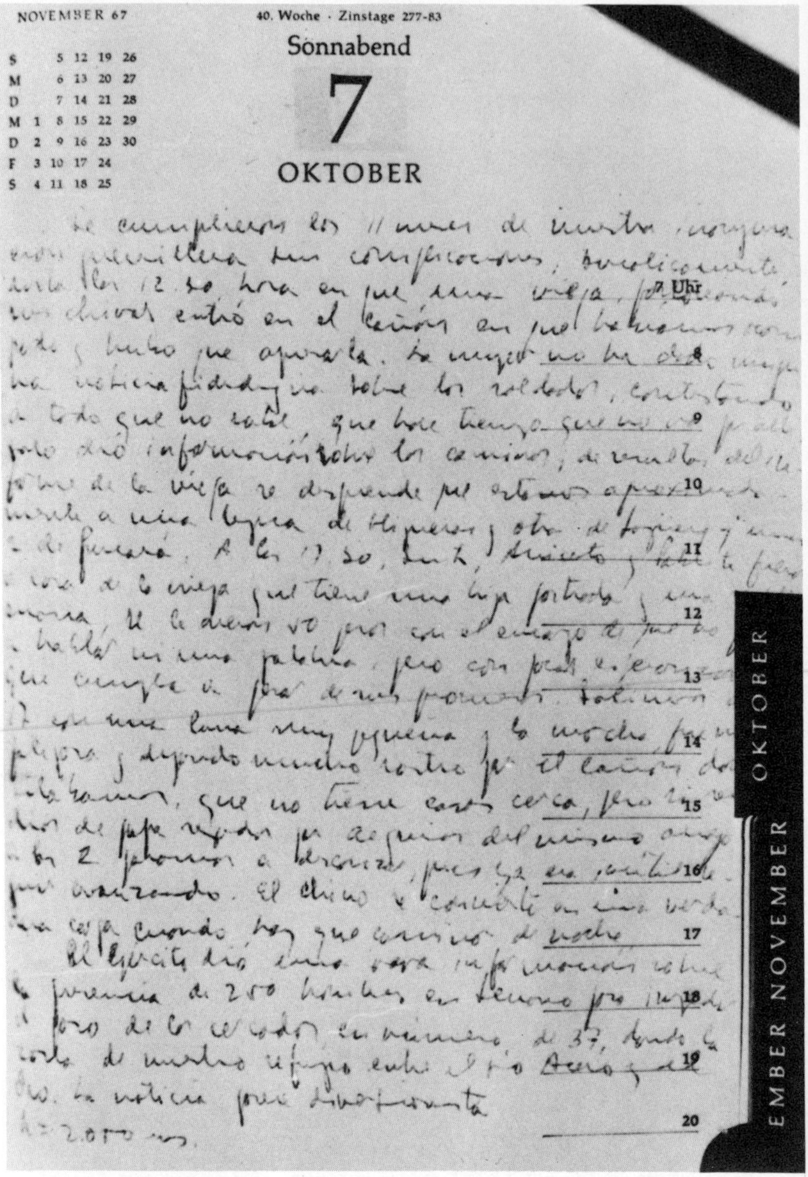
NOVEMBER 67
40. Woche · Zinstage 277-83
Sonnabend
7
OKTOBER
S 5 12 19 26
M 6 13 20 27
D 7 14 21 28
M 1 8 15 22 29
D 2 9 16 23 30
F 3 10 17 24
S 4 11 18 25
7 Uhr
8
9
10
11
12
13
14
15
16
17
18
19
20
OKTOBER
EMBER NOVEMBER

In Ché's last entry in his diary, he comments: "The Army issued an unusual report concerning the presence of 250 men in Serrano to keep the encircled group, numbering 37, from getting out. They report we are hiding between the Acero and Oro Rivers. The news seems to be a diversionary tactic."

1967

Sunday, January 1

In the morning, without discussing it with me, Monje informed me that he was pulling out and would present his resignation to the party leadership on January 8. His mission was all washed up, according to him. He left looking like a man heading for the gallows. My impression is that on learning from Coco of my decision not to yield on strategic matters, he seized on that point to force the rupture, because his arguments are inconsistent.

In the afternoon I got everybody together and explained Monje's attitude, announcing that we would unite with all those who wanted to make the revolution. I prophesied difficult moments and days of moral anguish for the Bolivians; we would try to solve our problems by means of collective discussion or through the commissars.

I arranged for Tania's trip to Argentina to have her see Mauricio and Lozenio and to summon them here. As for Sanchez, we assigned his responsibilities and resolved to leave Rodolfo, Loyola and Humberto in La Paz for now, and to leave one of Loyola's sisters in Camiri and Calvimonte in Santa Cruz. Mito will travel through the Sucre zone to see where he might set himself up. Loyola will be the one in charge of controlling the funds and she will be sent 80 thousand of which 20 are for the purchase of a truck which should be bought by Calvimonte. Sánchez will contact Guevara to have a talk with him. Coco will go to Santa Cruz to talk with a brother of Carlos and put him in charge of receiving the 3 who are coming from Havana. I wrote a message to Fidel which is in documents CZO #2.

Monday, January 2

I spent the morning coding the letter. The others (Sánchez, Coco and Tania) left in the afternoon when Fidel's speech was over. He referred to us in terms that obligate us even more, if that is possible. In the camp, the only work done was on the cave; the rest of the men went to look for the things from the first camp. Marcos, Miguel and Benigno went scouting northward. Inti and Carlos explored the Nancahuazú River until they found some

people, presumably in Yaki. Joaquin and El Médico must explore
the Yaki River until there are signs of or they run into people.
They all have 5 days, maximum. People arrived from the camp
with the news that Loro had not returned after leaving Monje.

Tuesday, January 3

We worked on roofing the cave, without succeeding; we should
finish it tomorrow. Only two men went to pick up cargo and they
brought word that everybody had left during the night. The rest
of the comrades worked at putting the roof on the kitchen; it is
now ready.

Wednesday, January 4

A day without important news; the men went to pick up
cargo. We finished the roof of the radio operator's cave. Shooting
practice was postponed on account of rain.

Thursday, January 5

We continue transporting cargo. There are still several trips
to be made. The cave was finished with its addition (a smaller
cave for the power plant). The rifles of the rearguard were
checked, as were some of the center group; all are O.K. except
Apolinario's rifle. All the scouts returned. Inti and Carlos traveled
down the Nancahuazú River until they met some people; among
them two owners of medium-sized farms, one of whom owns 150
cows and lives in Lagunillas. There is a small town called Ibi from
which a market road leads to Lagunillas. From there the scouts
went to Ticucha, linked by a truck road to Vaca Guzmán [Muyu-
pampa]. They returned by a trail leading to the Iquiri River, which
we have been calling the Yaki River. The place called Yuqui is a
cattle ranch near our camp, abandoned by its owners due to a
plague suffered by the cattle. Joaquín and El Médico followed the
Iquiri until they came to some impassable rocks. They did not
find people but they did see signs of their presence. Marcos,
Miguel and Benigno walked through the area until they came to
an inaccessible place, cut off by a cliff.

We have a new recruit: a little female turkey caught by Inti.

Friday, January 6

In the morning Marcos, Joaquín, Alejandro, Inti and I went to
the barren hard ground. There I made the following plans:
Marcos, with Camba and Pacho, will attempt to go to the Nancahuazu on the right, avoiding any encounters. Miguel, with Braulio

and Aniceto, will look for a land route suitable for the main road. Joaquín, with Benigno and Inti, will look for a route to the Frias River which, according to the map, runs parallel to the Nancahuazú on the other side of the hard ground, which is probably the Pampa del Tigre.

Loro arrived in the afternoon with two mules he bought for 2,000 pesos; a good buy. The animals are tame and strong. Supplies were sent to Braulio and Pedro so that they can leave tomorrow; Carlos and El Médico will replace them.

After class, I gave a talk on the qualities of a guerrilla and the need for greater discipline. I explained that our mission, above all, was to form an exemplary nucleus made of steel, and in that way I pointed out the importance of study as imperative for the future. Next I got the leaders together: Joaquín, Marcos, Alejandro, Inti, Rolando, Pombo, El Médico, Nato and Ricardo. I explained why I had decided to make Joaquín second-in-command, because of certain errors of Marcos's which he repeated constantly. I criticized Joaquín's attitude during the incident with Miguel on New Year's Day and I followed up with explaining some of the tasks that must be accomplished to improve our organization. Ricardo told me of an incident which took place with Ivan in Tania's presence, in which they were continually using foul language to one another and Ricardo ordered Ivan out of the jeep. The disagreements breaking out among the comrades are hindering our work.

Saturday, January 7

The scouts left. The *góndola* was composed of only Alejandro and Nato. The rest busied themselves with tasks around the camp. The power plant and all of Arturo's things were removed and an additional little roof was made for the cave; the well was repaired and a little bridge was built over the *arroyo*.

[The word *"góndola"* is a Bolivianism for a work gang, men sent out to perform such labor as transporting supplies (with or without animals), hacking a path through undergrowth, or cutting logs. All the guerrillas were on gondola duty at one time or another whatever their rank.]

Sunday, January 8

Sunday. The *góndola* was expanded to 8. Everything has been brought in. Loro announced an unscheduled trip to Santa Cruz, apparently to get hobbles for the mules.

There were no classes nor any other activity. I withdrew the outside guard, largely because of the inclemency of the weather.

Monday, January 9

Rain. Everything is wet; the river is swollen and cannot be crossed, so I could not relieve the guard at the old camp. Nothing else happened today.

Tuesday, January 10

The guard was changed at the fixed post of the old camp. Rubio and Apolinar relieved Carlos and El Médico. The river is still high although it has gone down some. Loro went to Santa Cruz and has not returned.

With El Médico (Moro), Tuma and Antonio, who is to be in charge of the camp, I went up to the Pampa del Tigre. There I explained to Antonio that his job for tomorrow will be the exploration of the *arroyo* that might be located to the west of our camp. From there we will look for a connection with Marcos's old road, which will be relatively easy to do.

At dusk, six of the scouts returned: Miguel, with Braulio and Aniceto; Joaquín, with Benigno and Inti. Miguel and Braulio found a route to the river which crosses the plain and they ended up discovering another one, which seems to be the Nancahuazú. Joaquín was able to go down to the river, which must be the Frias, and followed it for a short distance. It seems to be the same one the other group followed. This proves that our maps are very inaccurate since both rivers appear to be separated by a massif and to empty separately into the Río Grande. Marcos still has not returned.

A message was received from Havana which said that El Chino will leave on the 12th with the physician and the radio technician; and Rea [sic; Rhea] on the 14th. It does not say anything about our two other comrades.

Wednesday, January 11

Antonio left to explore the adjacent *arroyo* with Carlos and Arturo. He returned at nightfall and the only concrete news he brought was that the *arroyo* ran down to the Nacahuazú, opposite the pasture where we hunt.

Alejandro and Pombo were making maps in Arturo's cave and they came to report that my books had gotten wet. Some had come apart and the radio sets were wet and rusted. In short, it means that the two radios are out of order; a sad reflection on Arturo's abilities.

Marcos left tonight. He had followed the Nacahuazú River way upstream and still didn't reach the confluence of that river with the presumed Frias River. I am not very sure of the maps nor of the identity of this latter river.

We are starting to learn Quechua. Aniceto and Pedro are teaching us.

Boron day: larvae of flies removed from Marcos, Carlos, Pombo, Antonio, Moro and Joaquín.

Thursday, January 12

The *góndola* was sent to bring the last things. Loro has not returned yet. We did some mountain-climbing practice going up the banks of our *arroyo*. It took more than two hours to cover the distance along the sides and only seven minutes to the center. Our defense must be set up here.

Joaquín told me that Marcos had been hurt by the reference to his errors made at the meeting the other day. I must talk to him.

Friday, January 13

I talked to Marcos. His complaint was that he had been criticized in front of the Bolivians. His complaint was senseless; except for his emotional state, which merits attention, all the rest was despicable. He referred to contemptuous statements that Alejandro had made against him. This was checked with the latter and it seems it had never happened; it was just a bit of gossip. Marcos felt relieved.

Inti and Moro went hunting but they caught nothing. Working teams went up hills to make a cave in a place that could be reached by mules; but nothing could be done in that regard and instead it was decided to make a small cabin above ground.

Alejandro and Pombo made a study of the defense of the entrance and laid out some trenches. Tomorrow they will continue.

Rubio and Apolinario returned, and Braulio and Pedro went to the old camp. There is no news of Loro.

Saturday, January 14

Marcos and his advance guard, except Benigno, went down river to build a shack on the land. He intended to return by night, but came back at midday on account of the rain, without finishing the shack.

Joaquín led a group which began digging the trenches.

Moro, Inti, Urbano and I went out to make a road which would border our position on the plain on the right side of the *arroyo*. We made a bad start and we had to go around some large, broken rocks. At midday it began to rain and activities were suspended. No news of Loro.

Sunday, January 15

I stayed at the camp drafting instructions for the cadres in the city. Because it was Sunday, we worked only half a day: Marcos with the advance guard building the shack on the land; the rear guard and the center group working on the trenches; Ricardo, Urbano and Antonio trying to improve the road we built yesterday, but unable to because there is a big pit between the hill facing the river and the plain.

No trip was made to the old camp.

Monday, January 16

The work on the unfinished trenches was continued. Marcos finished his job, building a very nice little house. El Médico and Carlos relieved Braulio and Pedro, who came back with the news that Loro had arrived with the mules. But Loro did not come even though Aniceto went to get him.

Alejandro shows symptoms of malaria.

Tuesday, January 17

Little activity today. The trenches of the first line were finished, and so was the shack on the land. Loro came to me to report on his trip. When I asked him why he had gone, he answered that he thought he had permission to go. He confessed he had gone to see a woman he had there. He brought the hobbles for the mules but he couldn't make them walk in the river.

There is no news of Coco. By now it is somewhat alarming.

Wednesday, January 18

It was a cloudy morning, so I did not inspect the trenches. Urbano, Nato, El Médico (Moro), Inti, Aniceto, Braulio left as a *góndola*. Alejandro did not work because he felt ill.

It soon began to rain hard. Loro arrived in the rain to report that Arganaraz had talked to Antonio saying he was aware of many things and offering to collaborate with us in cocaine or whatever it might be, thus indicating that he suspects something more. I gave instructions to Loro to make a deal with him without offering him too much money, only payment for anything that he might transport in his jeep, and to threaten him with death if he betrays us. Due to the heavy rain, Loro left immediately to avoid being cut off by the river.

The *góndola* did not arrive at 8 and carte blanche was given over the meal of the *gondoleros,* who were late. A few minutes later Braulio and Nato arrived, reporting how the swollen river had surprised them on the way back. They tried to keep on but Inti had fallen in the water and lost his rifle and was bruised. The others decided to spend the night there, and the two of them returned with much difficulty.

Thursday, January 19

The day began as usual, working on the defense and improving the camp. Miguel came down with a high fever that has all the characteristics of malaria. I felt "achey" all day but my illness did not get worse.

At 8 in the morning the four stragglers arrived with a good supply of *choclos* [corn]. They had spent the night huddled around a fire. We hope the river will go down so that we can try to find Inti's rifle.

About 4 in the afternoon, when Rubio and Pedro had already left to relieve the guards at the other camp, El Médico arrived to tell me the police had been at the other camp. Lt. Fernandez and four policemen, dressed in civilian clothes, came in a rented jeep looking for the cocaine factory. They only checked the house, and some strange things attracted their attention such as the carbide for our lamps, which had not been transferred to the cave. They took Loro's pistol away from him, but they left him the Mauser and the .22. They made a "big deal" about taking away a .22 from Algañaraz, which they showed to Loro, and they left making the remark that they knew everything and that they [Loro, et al.] would have to deal with them. The pistol could be claimed by Loro in Camiri "without too much fanfare, by talking with me," said Lt. Fernandez. He asked for "El Brasilero" ["the Brazilian"].

Loro was instructed to act coldly toward the Vallegrande man and Algañaraz, who must be responsible for the espionage and stooling, and to go to Camiri on the pretext of looking for the gun and try to make contact with Coco. (I have my doubts that he is free.) They should live in the brush as much as possible.

Friday, January 20

I inspected the positions and gave the orders for carrying out the plan of defense, which I explained last night. It is based on the rapid defense of a zone bordering the river, and depend on it. The counterattack will be made by some men of the advance guard via the roads paralleling the river that lead to the rearguard.

We were thinking of making several practice runs but the situation continues to be dangerous at the old camp since a gringo showed up with an M-2 firing bursts of shots. He is a "friend" or Algañaraz and came to spend 10 days' vacation at his house. Scouting parties will be sent out. We will move the camp closer to Algañaraz's house. If this works, before we leave the zone we will make that individual feel our influence.

Miguel still has a high fever.

[NOTE: A passport-type photo of Benigno appears on this page.]

Saturday, January 21

A sham battle was carried out which resulted in disappointment on certain points; but, in general, it went well. We must do some more work on retreat, which was the weakest point of the exercise. Afterwards, the teams left: One, under Braulio, to make a road parallel to the river toward the west; and the other one, under Rolando, to build a road to the east. Pacho went to the barren hill to test the radio transmitter and Marcos went with Aniceto to try to find a way which will enable them to watch Algañaraz adequately. Everybody but Marcos was supposed to return before 2. The roads were made, the radio tested, and the results were positive. Marcos returned early because the rain made visibility impossible.

In the middle of the rain, Pedro arrived leading Coco and three more recruits: Benjamín, Eusebio and Walter. The first, who comes from Cuba, will be assigned to the vanguard because he has more knowledge of arms, and the other two will go to the rearguard. Mario Monje talked with 3 men who came from Cuba and dissuaded them from joining the guerrillas. Not only did he not submit his resignation to the party leaders, but he also sent Fidel the attached document, D-IV. I received a note from Tania telling me about her departure and about Ivan's illness; and another one from him which is attached as D-V.

At night I got the group together and read them the document, pointing out the inaccuracies contained in points a) and b) of the statements and I also gave an additional lecture. They seemed to respond adequately. Of the three new men, two seem determined and fully aware. The youngest is an Aymara peasant who looks very healthy.

Sunday, January 22

A *góndola* of 13 persons went out, also Braulio and Walter who went to relieve Pedro and Rubio. They returned in the afternoon without having finished the job. Everything is tranquil over there. On their way back Rubio fell down; he suffered no serious injury but was quite shaken up.

I am writing Fidel a document, No. 3, to explain the situation and to test the letter drop. I will send it to La Paz with Guevara, if he shows up at the appointment on the 25th in Camiri.

I am writing instructions for the urban cadres, D-III.

Due to the *góndola,* there was no activity in the camp. Miguel is getting better, but today Carlos came down with a high fever. The tuberculine test was made today. Today we killed two turkeys. One little animal was caught in the trap, but the trap cut off its foot and it was able to escape.

[Note: Message D-4 appears at bottom of this sheet.]

Monday, January 23

I assigned tasks in camp and some patrols: Inti, Rolando, and Arturo to look for a future hiding place for El Médico and the wounded. Marcos, Urbano and I went to explore the hill ahead and to look for a place from which Algañarez's house can be observed. We succeeded, and it can be seen very well.

Carlos still has fever; typical of malaria.

Tuesday, January 24

The *góndola* left with 7 men returning early with all the cargo and some corn. This time it was Joaquín who fell in the water, losing his Garand but recovering it. Loro is back and hiding. Coco and Antonio are still out. They should return tomorrow or the day after with Guevara.

One of the roads was improved to enable us to surround the police in any future defense of this position. At night I gave a critique of the exercises which took place the other day, correcting some mistakes.

Wednesday, January 25

We went with Marcos to explore the path that would lead to the rearguard of the attackers. It took us nearly one hour to get there, but the site is very good. Aniceto and Benjamín went to test the transmitter from the hill overlooking the Algañaraz' house, but they lost their way and no communication was made; practice must be repeated. Another cave was started for storing personal effects. Loro arrived and joined the advance guard. He spoke with Algañaraz, telling him what I had indicated. The latter admitted that he had sent the Vallegrandino to spy but denied having been the source of the denunciation. Coco confronted him regarding the matter since Algañaraz said he had sent him to spy.

A message from Manila was received, saying that everything had been received well and that Kolle is going to where Simón Reyes is awaiting him. Leche advises that he will listen and will be firm with them.

Thursday, January 26

We had hardly begun working on the new cave when we got the news that Guevara and Loyola had arrived. We left for the small house of the intermediate camp and they got there at 12.

I stated my conditions to Guevara: dissolution of the group; there are to be no ranks for anybody; there is no political organization yet, and polemics on the international or national discrepancies must be avoided. He agreed to everything straightforwardly and, after a cool start, relations with the Bolivians became cordial.

I was highly impressed by Loyola. She is very young and gentle, but one notes a firm determination. She is about to be expelled from the youth movement, but they are trying to get her to resign. I gave the cadres their instructions and other documents. In addition, I replaced the money spent, which amounts to 70 thousand. We are running short of funds.

Dr. Pareja will be named chief of the network and Rodolfo will come to join us within 15 days.

I am sending a letter to Ivan (D-VI) with instructions. I instructed Coco to sell the jeep, but to insure some means of communication with the farm.

At approximately 7, as night was falling, we parted. They will leave tomorrow night and Guevara will come with the first group of four on February 14. He said he could not come sooner because of the communications and that the men are taking off because of the carnival.

More powerful radios for transmitting will be coming.

Friday, January 27

A strong *góndola* was sent out, which brought back practically everything, but there is still some cargo. At night, Coco and the men sent with him had to leave. The latter will stay in Camiri, and Coco will go on to Santa Cruz to arrange for the sale of the jeep some time after the 15th.

We are continuing to work on the cave. An armadillo was caught in the traps. Preparation of provisions for the trip is almost completed. In principle we shall leave when Coco returns.

Saturday, January 28

The *góndola* is cleaning out the old camp on the information that the Vallegrandino was caught prowling around the corn field, but he escaped. This means that the time for making a decision about the farm is drawing near. Supplies for a ten-day march are now ready, and the date has been decided: about two days after Coco returns.

Sunday, January 29

Day of complete leisure except for the cooks, hunters and guards.

Coco returned in the afternoon; he had not gone to Santa Cruz but to Camiri. He left Loyola to return by plane to La Paz, and Moisés to go on *góndola* to Sucre. They established Sunday as the day for contacts.

February 1 was set as the date for departure.

Monday, January 30

The *góndola* was made up of 12 men and they carried in the greater part of the supplies; there remains a load for 5 men. The cave for personal effects was completed. It did not come out well.

Tuesday, January 31

Last day at camp. The *góndola* cleaned out the old camp and the men mounting guard were relieved. Antonio, Nato, Camba, and Arturo remained behind; their instructions are: make contact at least every three days; as long as there are four, two will be armed; the guard post must not be unoccupied for one moment; the new recruits will be instructed on general norms, but they may not learn more than what is absolutely necessary; the camp will be cleared of all personal items and the weapons will be hidden in the woods, covered with a canvas. The money reserves will remain constantly at camp, on someone's body. The paths will be patrolled and the *arroyos* checked. In case of a sudden withdrawal, two will go to the cave of Arturo: himself and Antonio; Nato and Camba will leave via the *arroyo* and one of them will run to leave a warning at a site to be selected tomorrow. If there should be more than four men, one group will guard the supply cave.

I talked to the troops, giving them last-minute instructions regarding the march. I also gave Coco last-minute instructions (D VII).

ANALYSIS OF THE MONTH

As was to be expected, Monje's attitude was evasive since the first moment and treacherous after. Now the party is up in arms against us and I don't know how far they will go, but this does not scare us, and maybe, it will benefit us in the long run. (I'm almost certain of that.) The finest and most combative people will be on our side; they always go through crisis of conscience more or less serious.

Guevara, so far, has responded well. We shall see how he and his people conduct themselves in the future.

Tania has left, but the Argentinians have not given any signs of life, neither has she. Now begins the real guerrilla phase and we will test the troops; time will show what will happen and what the perspectives of the Bolivian Revolution are.

Of all the things foreseen, the one that is going slowest is the recruitment of Bolivian combatants.

February 1

The first stage is completed. The men arrived rather tired, but generally everything went well. Antonio and Nato came up to decide on the password. They carried my knapsack and Moro's. Moro is recuperating from malaria.

A warning system was established, using a bottle under a plant near the path. In the rearguard Joaquín slackened under his burden and the entire group was held back.

February 2

Laborious and slow day. El Médico slowed down the march somewhat, but the general pace is slow. At 4 we arrived at the last site with water and camped. The vanguard had instructions to go as far as the river, (possibly the Rio Frias) it, too, was not travelling at a very good pace. At night it rained.

February 3

It was raining in the morning, so we postponed our departure until 8. As we started to leave, Aniceto arrived with the rope to help us in the difficult places; shortly thereafter it began to rain again. We arrived, soaking wet, at the brook at 10 and decided not to continue for the day. The stream cannot be the Frias River; it is simply not on the map.

Tomorrow, the vanguard will leave with Pacho bringing up the rear, and we shall communicate every hour.

February 4

We walked from morning until 4 in the afternoon with a two-hour stop at midday for soup. The road following the Nancahuasú was fairly good but fatal for shoes, and there are already several men almost barefoot. The band is tired but all have responded quite well. I have been relieved of almost 15 pounds and can walk with agility even though the pain in my shoulders is at times unbearable.

We have not found any signs of people's passage along the river but we should come across inhabited zones shortly, according to the map.

February 5

Unexpectedly, after a fve-hour walk in the morning (12-14 kilometers), the vanguard informed us that they had encountered some animals which turned out to be a mare and colt. We stopped and I ordered a reconnaissance to avoid the nearby village. The discussion was whether we were on the Iripiti or at the fork with the Saladillo marked on the map.

Pacho returned with the news that there was a big river,

several times larger than the Nancahuazú and that he could not cross. We moved on and encountered the authentic Rio Grande, which, moreover, was swollen. There are signs of life, but rather old and the paths that we followed faded into the undergrowth where there are no signs of traffic.

We camped in a bad spot, near the Nancahuazú, to get a supply of water. Tomorrow we will investigate both sides of the river (east and west) to get to know the crossing points, and the other group will try to cross it.

February 6

A day of calm and of recovering strength. Joaquín left with Walter and the doctor to explore the Rio Grande downstream; they walked 8 kilometers without finding any fords, only a saltwater brook. Marcos went upstream and did not reach the Frias; he was accompanied by Aniceto and Loro. Alejandro, Inti, and Pacho tried to cross the river but were unable to make it. We moved back about one kilometer looking for a better location. Pombo is somewhat sick. Tomorrow we shall begin construction of the raft to try to get across.

February 7

The raft was made under the direction of Marcos; it was too big and not very maneuverable, At 1:30 p.m. we began moving toward the crossing point and at 2:30 we began going across. The vanguard made it in two trips and on the third trip half of the people of the center group had crossed, along with my clothes but not my knapsack. On the next trip to transport the remainder of the center group, Rubio miscalculated and the raft was carried downstream; we were unable to recover it. Joaquín started making another one which was completed by 9:00 p.m, but it was not necessary to cross at night since it did not rain and the river continued to recede. Of the center group Tuma, Urbano, Inti, Alejandro, and I remained. Tuma and I slept on the ground.

February 8

The rest of the center group began crossing at 6:30 a.m. At 6:00 a.m. the head of the vanguard left and when the center arrived they all went together. The center left at 8:30 when the entire rearguard was on the other side. They were instructed to hide the raft and follow us. The journey was difficult and the path had to be hacked open. At 6:00 p.m., tired and hungry, we arrived at a brook with a small waterhole, where we decided to camp. There are many boar tracks here.

Braulio, Aniceto, and Benigno went up to the river, some 3 kilometers away, and returned with the news that they had seen sandal prints and the tracks of three animals, one of them wounded; all were fresh.

February 9

After walking over a half-hour it occurred to me to leave the path we were following and continue along the arroyo; shortly thereafter we came upon a corn field. I sent Inti and Ricardo to explore. Everything became pandemonium; the signs that we had left for those behind were not seen by them and they thought I was lost. They were going back and forth; the vanguard had seen the house and was awaiting my arrival. Inti and Ricardo met some boys and went to the house of a young peasant who had six children, he gave them a good welcome and a lot of information. In a second meeting Inti told him that he was the leader of the guerrillas and bought two pigs, thus making friends. We remained in the same place eating corn and pork; the big one was ready in the early dawn but we left it for the next day.

February 10

Posing as Inti's assistant, I went to talk with the peasants. I do not think the comedy was very successful because of Inti's timidity. This peasant is typical: capable of helping us, but incapable of foreseeing the dangers involved and therefore potentially dangerous. He told us numerous things about the peasants but was not willing to join us because of a certain insecurity. The doctor treated the children, who had worms, and another who had been kicked by a mare, and we left. (The peasant's name is Rojas.)

The afternoon and evening were spent in making *huminta* (not good at all). At night I made certain comments to all the comrades about the coming 10 days.

As of now, I intend to walk 10 days more toward Masicurí and have the comrades get a first-hand look at the soldiers; we shall then try to come back along the Frias to leave another path explored.

February 11
    The old man's birthday (67)

["The old man" is Che's father, Ernesto Guevara, Sr., who had just
turned 67.]

    We followed a clearly-marked path along the bank of the
river until it became difficult to follow and sometimes vanished,
indicating that no one had used it for a long time. At noon we
arrived at a point where the path was completely closed, near a
large river, which suddenly brought doubt to our minds as to
whether or not it was the Masicurí. We stopped at an *arroyo*
while Marcos and Miguel went to explore upstream. Inti, Carlos,
and Pedro did the same thing downstream in an effort to locate
the river mouth. They found it and confirmed that this is the
Masicurí, whose first ford must be further down. There they
saw at a distance several peasants who were loading horses. They
probably saw our footprints; from now on more precautions
must be taken. We are about one or two leagues from Arenales,
according to information from the peasant.
                                                    Altitude 760 meters

February 12
    The 2 kilometers walked by the vanguard yesterday were
covered quite rapidly. After that the pace was very slow. At
4:00 p.m. we came upon a road which seemed to be the one
we were looking for. On the other side of the river, facing us,
was a house which we decided to bypass and we looked for
another one on our side which should be Montaño's. Montaño
was recommended by Rojas. Inti and Loro went there but found
no one, although indications were that it was the house.
    At 7:30 p.m. we started out on a night march which helped
to show how much there is to learn. At approximately 9:00 p.m.
Inti and Loro went back to the house, bringing not very good
news: the man was drunk and not very receptive. All he has
is corn. He had gotten drunk at Caballero's house on the other
side of the river, where the ford is. We decided to sleep in a
nearby wood. I was extremely tired because the *humintas* had
upset my stomach and I had not eaten for a day.

February 13
    At dawn it began to rain heavily. It lasted all morning,
causing the river to swell. We received better news: Montaño is
the son of the owner, he is about 16 years old. His father was

not home and will not be back for a week. He gave us quite a bit of precise information, as far as Los Lagos, about one league away. A part of the road is on the left shore but it is small. On this bank lives only a brother of Pérez, a middle-class peasant whose daughter is the girl friend of an Army man.

We moved to a new camp next to the arroyo and a corn field. Marcos and Miguel made a short cut to the main road. Altitude 350 meters (stormy weather)

[Occasionally Che notes the altitude in meters, here 350 meters, by map calculations.]

February 14

A peaceful day, spent at the same camp. The boy from the house came three times, once to tell us that some people had crossed over from the other side of the river to look for some pigs, but they did not go any further. He was paid more for the damage done to the corn field.

The macheteros spent the entire day chopping without finding anything; they figure they have prepared some 6 kilometers which will be one half of tomorrow's job.

A long message from Havana is deciphered, dealing mainly with news about the interview with Kolle. He said that he had not been informed of the continent-wide magnitude of the task, but this being the case they would be willing to collaborate at a certain level, the details of which they wanted to discuss with me; Kolle, Simón Rodríguez [sic; Reyes intended], and Ramírez would come. I was also informed that Simón has indicated his decision to help us regardless of what the party decides. They also advise that the Frenchman, traveling with his passport, will arrive at La Paz on the 23d and will stay at Pareja's or Rhea's house. Part of the message is still undecipherable. We shall see how this new conciliatory offensive can be confronted.

Other news: Merci arrived without the money claiming that it had been stolen; we suspect misappropriation although it could be something more serious. Lechín is going to ask for money and training.

February 15

Hildita's birthday (11)

[Hildita is Che's oldest child, named after his first wife, Hilda Gadea Acosta.]

Day of uneventful marching. At 10 a.m. we had arrived at the point which the trailblazers had reached. After that everything went slowly. At 5 p.m. they advised they had found a cultivated field and at 6:00 p.m. it was confirmed. We sent Inti, Loro, and Aniceto to talk to the peasant. He turned out to be Miguel Pérez, brother of Nicolás, a rich peasant, but he is poor and exploited by his brother, so he was willing to collaborate. We did not eat because it was so late.

February 16

We walked a few meters to protect ourselves from the brother's curiosity and camped on a hill facing the river some 50 meters below. The location is good insofar as protecting us from surprises is concerned, but somewhat uncomfortable. We began the task of preparing a good quantity of food for the journey we shall make crossing the range toward the Rosita.

In the afternoon it rained violently and continued all night without stopping; it delayed our plans, made the river rise, and left us isolated again. We lent the peasant 1,000 [bolivianos] to purchase and fatten pigs; he has capitalistic ambitions.

February 17

It continued to rain all morning; 18 hours of rain. Everything is wet and the river is swollen. I sent Marcos with Miguel and Braulio to look for a road to go to the Rosita. He returned in the afternoon after making a path of 4 kilometers. He reported that there is a barren plain similar to what we call the Pampa del Tigre. Inti does not feel well, the result of overeating.

Atmospheric conditions are abnormal.

Altitude 720 meters

February 18

Josefina's birthday (33)

A partial failure, We walked slowly following the pace of the macheteros but at 2:00 p.m. they had arrived at a clear plain where the machetes were not needed. We took a little longer and at 3:00 p.m. we arrived at a watering spot where we camped, hoping to cross the ridge in the morning. Marcos and Tuma set out to explore but came back with very bad news; the entire area is cut off by sharp cliffs which are impossible to descend. There is nothing else to do but go back.

Altitude 980 meters

February 19

A lost day. We went down the hill until we found the arroyo

and tried to go up along it, but it was impossible. I sent Miguel and Aniceto to climb the abutment and they tried unsuccessfully to get to the other side. We waited all day for them and they returned saying that the cliffs were of the same type, impossible to climb. Tomorrow we shall try to go up to the last ridge past the arroyo which lies toward the west (the others will do it towards the south where the hill ends).

Altitude 760 meters

February 20

A day of little progress and with obstacles. Miguel and Braulio set out on the old path to the small arroyo by the corn field, from where they lost their way and returned to the arroyo at nightfall. On arriving at the next arroyo I sent Rolando and Pombo to explore it until they found the cliff, but they did not return until 3:00 p.m., so we followed the path Marcos was making, leaving Pedro and Rubio to explore. At 4:30 we arrived at the arroyo by the corn field where we camped. The explorers did not return.

February 21

A slow walk upstream. Pombo and Rolando returned to report that the other arroyo had a passageway, but Marcos explored it and it looked the same. We left at 11:00 a.m. but at 1:30 p.m. we came to some pools of very cold water which we were unable to cross. Loro went to explore but he took too long, so I sent Braulio and Joaquín to the rearguard. Loro returned saying that the arroyo widened further up and (the crossing) was more feasible, We therefore decided to continue without waiting for Joaquín's report. When we camped at 6 he came to report that it was possible to climb the ridge and that a good part of the path was practicable. Inti is not well; "bloated" [with gas] for the second time this week.
Altitude 860 meters.

February 22

We spent the entire day climbing difficult ridges which were full of mosquitoes. After a hard day the time came to set up camp before we reached the summit. I sent Joaquín and Pedro to try to do so alone and they returned at 7:00 p.m. with the news that they still had 3 hours more of ground clearing to do. We are at the head of an arroyo which flows into the Masicurí, but toward the south.

February 23

A black day for me; I made it by sheer guts, for I am very exhausted. Marcos, Braulio, and Tuma left in the morning to prepare the path while we waited in the camp. There we deciphered a new message announcing that mine had been received at the French letterdrop. At 12:00 a.m. we left under a sun that melted the stones and shortly thereafter I had a fainting spell as we reached the top of the highest hill; from then on I walked by forcing myself. The highest point of that area has an altitude of 1,420 meters and overlooks a vast area including the Río Grande, the mouth of the Nacahuasu, and part of the Rosita. The topography is different from that which is marked on the map. From a clear dividing line it descends abruptly to what looks like a wooded plateau 8 to 10 kilometers wide, at the end of which flows the Rosita; then there rises another ridge with altitudes equivalent to those of this chain. We decided to go down through a practical but very steep path in order to follow a stream which leads to the Río Grande and from there to the Rosita. Contrary to what the map indicates, there appear to be no houses along the banks. We camped at 900 meters after a hellish journey, without water, and the night falling upon us. Yesterday morning I heard Marcos cursing at a comrade and today at another one. I will have to talk to him.

February 24

Ernestico's birthday (2)

[Ernestico (the diminutive, Cuban style, of Ernesto) is Che's son by his second wife, Aleida March.]

A hard and discouraging day. Very little progress was made. We had no water since this arroyo is dry. At noon the macheteros were relieved; they were exhausted. At 2:00 p.m. it rained a little and the canteens were filled. A short while later we found a small water hole and at 5:00 p.m. we camped at a level spot near the water. Marcos and Urbano continued to explore and Marcos returned saying that the river was a couple of kilometers away but that the path by the arroyo was very bad because it became a marsh.

Altitude 680 meters

February 25

A difficult day. Little progress was made, and to make things worse Marcos missed the route and the morning was lost. He had gone out with Miguel and Loro. At noon he reported [that he was lost] and asked for help and communication. Braulio, Tuma and Pacho went. Pacho returned 2 hours later saying that Marcos had sent him because reception was no longer good. At 4:30 p.m. I sent Benigno to tell Marcos that if by 6:00 p.m. he had not found the river he should return. After Benigno left Pacho called me to say that he and Marcos had had an argument and that Marcos had given him peremptory orders, threatening him with a machete and hitting him on the face with the handle. When Pacho told him to stop, Marcos threatened him again with the machete, shaking him and tearing his clothes. Because of the seriousness of the incident, I called Inti and Rolando, who confirmed the dissension existing in the vanguard because of Marcos' bad temper, but they also mentioned some of Pacho's shortcomings.

February 26

In the morning I had a talk with Marcos and Pacho, which convinced me that Marcos was guilty of the alleged insults and mistreatment and possibly of threatening Pacho with the machete, but not of the beating; that Pacho had made offensive remarks and has an innate tendency to be quarrelsome (there have been other instances). I waited until all the men were together and talked about the significance of our effort to reach the Rosita, explaining how this type of privation was an introduction to the hardships we would suffer in the future, and that their failure to adapt themselves to the situation would produce shameful incidents such as this one between two Cubans. I reprimanded Marcos for his attitude and told Pacho that another incident like this would result in his dishonorable demotion in the guerrilla unit. In addition to his refusal to remain with the communications man, Pacho had returned without mentioning the incident to me, and then in all probability had lied to me when he said that Marcos hit him.

I told the Bolivians that anyone who felt too weak to continue should not resort to sneaky methods, but should tell me and he would be quietly dismissed.

We continued walking trying to reach the Río Grande in order to follow it. We succeeded and were able to travel for slightly over one kilometer; however, we had to return because we could not get past a cliff. Benjamin fell behind because he was having trouble with his knapsack and was physically exhausted. When he reached us I instructed him to continue and he did so. He walked about 50 meters and lost the footpath. He began to look for it from a rock. As I was telling Urbano to show him the way, he [Benjamin] moved abruptly and fell in the water. He could not swim, The current was strong and it carried him away as he touched bottom. We ran to try to hold him and when we took off our clothes he disappeared in a pool. Rolando swam toward the place and tried to dive but the current pulled him far out. Minutes later all hope was lost. He was a weak and absolutely inept fellow, but he had a tremendous desire to succeed, The test was too much for him; his physical strength did not match his will, and so we have our baptism of death in an absurd manner on the shores of the Rio Grande. We camped at 5 in the afternoon without having reached the Rosita. We ate our last ration of black beans.

February 27

After another exhausting day walking along the river edge and climbing cliffs we arrived at the Rosita river. It is larger than the Nacahuasu and smaller than the Masicurí, and its waters are reddish. We ate the last rations held in reserve. There were no signs of life in the area, despite the fact that we are near roads and inhabited areas.

Altitude 600 meters

February 28

A day of partial rest. After breakfast (tea) I gave a brief talk analyzing Benigno's [sic; actually, Benjamin's] death, and told some anecdotes about the Sierra Maestra. Afterwards the explorers, Miguel, Inti and Loro, went upstream along the Rosita with the intention of walking 3½ hours which I believed was the time it would take to reach the Abapocito River, but it did not work out that way for lack of a path. They found no recent signs of life. Joaquín and Pedro went up into the woods but saw nothing and found no road or path leading to one. Alejandro and Rubio crossed the river but found no road, although their exploration was superficial. Marcos directed construction of the raft, and as soon as it was finished we began crossing at a bend in the river where the Rosita ends. They took across the knapsacks of five men, and Miguel's passed over but not Benigno's, which was left behind [some words blotted out by ink or water] and Benigno also left his shoes.

The raft could not be recovered and the second one was not finished, so that we postponed the crossing until tomorrow.

ANALYSIS OF THE MONTH

Even though I have no news of the happenings at camp, everything has gone fairly well, with the usual exceptions, which were fatal in this case.

From the outside, no news has been received regarding the two men that were to be sent to complete the unit. The Frenchman should now be in La Paz and should arrive at the camp any day. I have no news of the Argentines nor of Chino. The messages are received well in both directions. The Party's attitude continues to be vacillating and two-faced which is the least that can be said about it, although one point, which may be decisive, remains to be clarified when I talk to the new delegation.

The march was accomplished fairly well but was clouded by the accident which took Benjamin's life. The men are still weak and not all the Bolivians will hold out. The last days of hunger have caused a weakening of their enthusiasm, which becomes more evident now that they are divided. Of the Cubans, Pacho and Rubio, who are among those with little experience, have yet to respond; Alejandro has done so to the fullest. Of the older ones, Marcos is a continuous problem, and Ricardo is not performing properly. The rest are behaving well.

The next stage will be of fighting and decision.

March 1

It began to rain at 6:00 a.m. We postponed the crossing until it would stop raining, but the rain got worse and continued until 3:00 p.m. The flood waters came and it became unwise to make the crossing. The river is now swollen and looks like it will not recede rapidly.

I moved to an abandoned *tapera* to get away from the rain, and there I set up a new camp. Joaquín remained in the same place. At night I was informed that Polo had consumed his can of milk and Eusebio the milk and sardines for now. As punishment they will not be permitted to eat these when [illegible].

March 2

The day started rainy and the people listless, beginning with me. The river is even more swollen. It was decided to leave the camp as soon as the rain stops, and continue parallel to the river on the path we came on. We left at 12 and got a good supply of sprouts of palm. At 4:30 we stopped because we had left our path to take advantage of an old path and lost it. We have no news from the vanguard.

March 3

We started out with enthusiasm, walking well, but the time wore us down and we had to walk a straighter path through the hard ground, as I was afraid that some accident might occur in the area where Benjamín fell. It took us 4 hours to cover the distance which took half an hour on the lower level. At 6:00 p.m. we arrived at the edge of the *arroyo* where we set up camp but, since we only had two sprouts of palm, Miguel, Urbano, and later Braulio went to find some farther away. They returned at 9:00 p.m. We ate around midnight. The sprouts of palm (*"totoi"* in Bolivia) are saving the situation.
Altitude 600 meters.

March 4

Miguel and Urbano left in the morning and they were out all day, cutting a path with their *machetes;* they returned 6 p.m. They advanced about 5 km and saw a plain that should allow advancing but there is no room for a camp and it was decided to remain there until the footpath is lengthened. The hunters got two monkeys, a parrot, and a dove which was our food, together with sprouts of palm, abundant in this arroyo.

March 5

Joaquín and Braulio left in the rain to continue to work with their *machetes* but both are weak and did not advance much. Twelve palm sprouts were collected and some birds were caught, which permits our saving the canned food one more day and put away a 2-day reserve supply of sprouts.

March 6

A day of intermittent walking until 1700 hours. Miguel, Urbano, and Tuma are the *macheteros*. Some advance is made and some higher stretches can be seen in the distance which might be those of the Nacahuasu. Only one parrot is caught and de-

livered to the rearguard. Today we ate palm sprouts with meat. We have three scanty meals left.
Altitude 600 meters.

March 7

Four months. The men are getting increasingly discouraged at seeing the approaching end of the provisions but not of the distance to be covered. Today we advanced about 4 or 5 kilometers following the bank of the river and we finally came upon a promising foot-path. The meal: 6½ small birds and the rest of the palm sprouts. Starting tomorrow, canned food alone, one can for each three persons, for 2 days; after that the milk, which will be the last. It must be about 2 or 3 marching days to the Nacahuasu.
Altitude 610 meters.

March 8

A day of little walking, of surprises and tensions. At 10 a.m. we left the camp without waiting for Rolando, who was out hunting, we walked for only 1½ hours and we met with the *macheteros* (Urbano, Miguel, and Tuma) and the hunters (El Médico and Chinchin). They had a pile of parrots, but they had found a waterhole and stopped. I went to see the place, after giving orders to set up camp, and it appeared to be an oil pumping station. Inti and Ricardo jumped into the water; they had to pretend to be hunters. They dived in with their clothes on to cross in two stages, but Inti had trouble and almost drowned. Ricardo helped him and finally they came out onto the shore, attracting the attention of the whole world. The signal denoting danger was not given, and they disappeared, They started to cross at 12, and at 1515 I left without their giving any sign of life. I waited all afternoon and they did not appear. The last sentry retired at 2100 and no new signal had been given.

I was very worried; two valuable comrades were exposed and we did not know what had happened. It was resolved that Alejandro and Rolando, the best swimmers, would cross tomorrow at dawn. We ate better than on other days, despite the lack of palm sprouts, because of the abundance of parrots and two monkeys that Rolando killed.

March 9

Early in the morning we started the crossing, but we had to

build a raft, and this caused a considerable delay. The lookout announced that he could see people gathering on the other side. It was 0830; we held off crossing. A path had been made which comes out on the other side, but into a clearing where we could be seen. So we have to set out in the early dawn, taking advantage of the bend in the river. Close to 1600 hours, after a worrisome watch which for me had lasted since 1030, the providers (Inti and Chinchu) jumped into the river and came out a considerable distance downstream. They brought back a pig, bread, rice, sugar, coffee, some canned goods, corn, fatback, etc. We had a little banquet of coffee and bread and used up the can of sweetened condensed milk we had in reserve.

They explained that they had come out every other hour in order to be seen, but fruitlessly for ourselves. Marcos and his men went by 3 days ago, and it seems that Marcos acted in his typical fashion and let the weapons be seen. The Yacimientos engineers are not certain how far it is to the Nancahuazú, but they imagine it is 5 days' march. If this is so our supplies will hold out. The pump is part of a pumping station under construction.

["Yacmientos" is short for Yacimientos Petroliferos Fiscales de Bolivia, or YPFB, the Bolivian state-owned oil corporation.]

March 10

We left at 0630 hours, walked for 45 minutes until we overtook the macheteros. At 0800 it started to rain and continued until 1100. We walked for about 3 hours, and camped at 1700, Some hills, that could be the Nacahuasu, can be seen. Braulio left to explore and returned with the news that there is a path and the river follows straight toward the west.

Altitude 600 meters

March 11

The day started well. We walked for more than one hour on a perfect path but then it ended suddenly. Braulio picked up a machete and worked hard until he found a beach. We gave him and Urbano time to open a path and when we were going to follow, the flood cut us off. It was a lightning flood; the river rose a couple of meters. We were isolated from the macheteros and forced to hack our way through the woods. At 1330 we stopped and I sent Miguel and Tuma with orders to contact the vanguard and give the order to return if it does not [expect?] to arrive at the Nicahuasu or at a good place. At 1800 they returned; they had walked about 3 kilometers and arrived at a vertical cliff. It would appear that we are close but the last few marches will be very tough if the river does not go down, which appears to be very improbable. We walked 4 or 5 kilometers.

A disagreeable incident occurred because of lack of order in the rearguard and there are suspicions about either short rations or certain liberties Braulio takes. He must be spoken to.

Altitude 610 meters

March 12

In one hour and 10 minutes we walked the distance we had made yesterday. When we arrived, Miguel and Tuma, who had gone ahead, were already scouting for a way to pass a vertical cliff. The entire day was spent on this; our only activity was to shoot four little birds which we ate as a complement to the rice and mussels. We have two meals left. Miguel stayed on the other side and it would appear that he was able to cross over to the Nacahuazú. We walked some 3 or 4 kilometers.

March 13

From 0630 through 1200 we were on the backs of fearful cliffs, following the path made by Miguel by cyclopean effort. We thought that we were at the Nacahuasu but then we ran into some bad stretches and in 5 hours we advanced very little. We camped under moderate rain shower at 1700. The people are pretty tired and a bit demoralized again. We have only one meal left. We walked some 6 kilometers but little [illegible word].

March 14

Almost without realizing it, we arrived at the Nacahuasu. I was (and am) so tired I feel as though a boulder had fallen on top of me. The river is very rough and we do not dare to attempt the crossing but Rolando volunteered and crossed easily, starting for the base at 1520 sharp. I hope he arrives in 2 days. We ate our last meal, cooked corn and meat, and now we are dependent on our hunting. At the time these notes were made we have one small bird and have heard three shots (El Médico and Inti are the hunters).

Altitude 600 meters

We heard part of the speech in which Fidel castigates with utter bluntness the Venezuelan Communists and with harshness the attitude of the USSR with respect to the American puppets.

[The "Venezuelan Communists" are the Venezuelan Communist Party. Fidel bitterly attacked it for withdrawing support from the Venezuelan guerrillas known as the Armed Forces of National Liberation.]

March 15

We crossed the river, but only with Rubio and El Médico to help us. We thought we would arrive at the mouth of the Nacahuazú but we had three men who could not swim and one passenger. The current pulled us close to one kilometer and now the raft could not cross it, as was our intention. The 11 of us are still on this side and tomorrow El Médico and Rubio will cross over again. We hunted four hawks and made a meal of them, not as bad as might be expected. Everything got wet and the weather continues to be water. The morale of the men is low; Miguel has swollen feet, and there are several others in that condition. Altitude 580 meters.

March 16

We decided to eat the horse because the swelling was getting to be alarming. Miguel, Inti, and Alejandro displayed various symptoms, and I an extreme weakness. We made an error in our calculation inasmuch as we believed that Joaquin would cross, but this was not the case. El Médico and Rubio tried to cross to help us, but they were impelled down river and lost from sight. Joaquin requested permission to cross and I gave it to him; they were [sic] lost down river also. I sent Pombo and Tuma to look for them but they did not find them, returning at night. From 1700 hours we glutted on horsemeat. Tomorrow we will probably suffer the consequences. I estimate that Rolando must be arriving at the camp today.

Message #32 is deciphered completely; it announces the arrival of a Bolivian to join the group, with shipment of Glucantime, an anti-parasite (Bismonio). Up to this time we have none of those things.

March 17

Once again a tragedy before getting a taste of combat. Joaquin showed up in midmorning; Miguel and Tuma had left to catch up with him with good pieces of meat. The odyssey had been serious. They could not control the raft and it went down the

Nacahuasu until it was caught in a whirlpool and tumbled several times, according to them. The final result was the loss of several haversacks, nearly all the bullets, 6 rifles, and one man: Carlos. He let go in the quiet area together with Braulio but with different luck. Braulio reached the bank of the river and could observe Carlos being washed down without resistance. Joaquín had already come out with all of the people, further down, and did not see him pass. Up to this moment he had been considered the best of the Bolivians in the rearguard, because of his seriousness, discipline, and enthusiasm,

The weapons lost were: one Brno, belonging to Braulio; two M-1 rifles, to Carlos and Pedro; and three Mausers, to Abel, Eusebio, and Polo.

Joaquín reported that he had seen Rubio and El Médico in the other group and he had already instructed them to make another small raft and return. They appeared at 1600 with their story of adventures and misfortunes; both nude and Rubio barefoot. Their raft was wrecked in the first whirlpool. They came out onto the bank of the river almost on the same spot we did. Our departure is scheduled for early tomorrow and Joaquin will leave around noon. Hope to find some news sometime tomorrow. The morale of Joaquin's people appears to be good.

March 18

We left early, leaving Joaquin to digest and finish garnishing his half a horse, and with instructions to leave as soon as he felt strong. I had a struggle to keep some meat in reserve, against the opinion of the men, who wanted to wolf it all. By mid-morning Ricardo, Luis, and Urbano had fallen back and we had to wait for them, which was contrary to my intentions to rest at the camp from which we had started on our way out. In any event we had a poor march. At 1430 hours Urbano appeared with a *urina* caught by Ricardo, which gave us some variety and a reserve of horse shortribs. At 1630 hours we arrived at the intended half-way point, and there we slept. Several men are grumbling and ill-humored: Chinchu, Urbano, and Alejandro.

March 19

During the morning those of us up front walked well and we stopped at 1100 hours, as agreed, but once again Ricardo and Urbano and this time Alejandro fell back. They arrived at 1300 hours, but with another *urina*, also caught by Ricardo, and Joaquin arrived with them. There was an incident, arising from a quarrel between Joaquin and Rubio, in which I had to speak harshly to the latter without conviction that he was at fault.

In any event I decided to continue up to the arroyo. A small plane was circling, not at all a good omen; in addition I was worried by the lack of news from the base. I thought that it would be a long haul, but despite the lackadaisical mood of the men we arrived at 1730. We were met there by the Peruvian doctor, Negro, who had arrived with Chino and the telegraph operator with the news that Benigno was awaiting us with food and that two of Guevara's men had deserted and the police had raided the farm. Benigno explained that he had left to meet us with food and that he came across Rolando 3 days ago. He has been here 2 days but had not dared return because the Army might advance on the river: the small plane had been circling for 3 days. Negro witnessed the attack on the farm by six men. Neither Antonio nor Coco were there. Coco had gone to Camiri to get another group of Guevara's men, and Antonio left immediately to tell him what had happened. I received a long report from Marcos (Document VIII) in which he explains his adventures in his own way (he went to the farm contrary to my express orders) and two reports from Antonio explaining the situation (Documents IX and X).

The men at the base now are the Frenchman, Chino, my comrades, Pelado, Tania and Guevara with 2, the first part of his group. After a sumptuous meal of rice and beans with *visna,* Miguel left to look for Joaquin, who had not arrived, and to locate Chinchu, who was lagging again. He returned with Ricardo, and at dawn Joaquin showed up, and we were all together.

March 20

We left at 10, at a good pace. Benigno and Negro were going ahead of us with a message for Marcos in which he was ordered to take charge of the defense and leave administrative affairs to Antonio. Joaquin left after erasing all traces of having entered the arroyo but without haste. Three of his men are barefoot. At 1300, during a long stop, Pacho appeared with a message from Marcos; the information expanded upon the first one from Benigno but now it was more complicated because 60 guards had entered the Vallegrandino's road and captured Salustio, a messenger to us from Guevara's people. They took a mule from us and we lost the jeep. There was no news from Loro, who had remained at the sentry post at the little house. We decided by whatever means to get to Bear Camp, so called now because a bear was killed there. We sent Benigno, Miguel, and Urbano ahead to prepare food for the hungry men, and we got there at nightfall. In the camp were Danton, Pelao, Chino, as well as Tania and a group of Bolivians who had come by supply trucks to bring food and then leave. Rolando had been sent to organize the withdrawal of everything; there was a mood of defeat. Soon afterwards a Bolivian doctor, just recently enrolled, arrived with a message for Rolando which stated that Marcos and Antonio were at La Aguada, and that he should go there for a talk. I answered by the same messenger that war is won with gunfire, that they should withdraw immediately to the camp and wait for me. Everything appears to be in complete chaos; nobody knows what to do.

I talked first with Chino. He wants $5,000 a month for 10 months, and Havana told him to discuss it with me. He is also bringing a message that was too long for Arturo to decipher. I told him that I agreed on the basis that they would go to the mountains in six months. He planned to go to the region of Ayacucho—himself as chief, with 15 men. Besides, it was agreed that he would get five men now and 15 more a short while later, along with weapons, after being trained in combat. He is to send me a couple of medium-range (40-mile) transmitters and we shall work on setting up a code for our use and to be in permanent contact. He seems very enthusiastic. He also brought some very old reports about Leche. Loro appeared and announced that he had killed a soldier.

March 21

I spent the day in conversations and discussions with Chino, clearing up a few points, the Frenchman, Pelao, and Tania. The Frenchman brought news, already known, about Monje, Kolle, Simon Reyes, etc. He came to stay but I asked him to return to organize a network of assistance in France and go to Cuba en route, an idea which coincides with his desires to marry and have a child with his woman. I must write letters to Sartre and B. Russell requesting them to organize an international fund in support of the Bolivian Liberation Movement. He should, moreover, speak to a friend and get him to organize every means of assistance, especially money, medicine, and electronics in the form of an engineer and equipment.

Pelao, of course, is ready to accept my orders, and I proposed that he be a kind of coordinator of the groups of Jozamy, Gelman and Stamponi, and send me five men to begin training. He is to convey my regards to Maria Rosa Oliver and the old man. He will be given 500 pesos to send and 1,000 more to operate with. If they accept, they should begin exploratory work in Northern Argentina and send me their reports.

Tania made the contacts and the people came, but, according to her, they made her travel here by jeep. She had expected to stay one day, but things became complicated. Jozamy could not stay the first time and the second he did not even make contact because Tania was here. He refers to Iván with considerable scorn; I do not know what is at the bottom of all this. An accounting was received from La Loyola up to 9 February (1,500 dollars)*. Two reports were received from Iván, one uninteresting on a military school with photographs, the other making some points, also without great importance. The important thing is that we cannot decipher the writing (D XIII). A report was received from Antonio (D XII), in which he tries to justify his attitude. A radio report heard announces one death, and this is later denied, which indicates that that about Loro was true.

March 22

A [blotted out by water] departed leaving the field abandoned with some food, precariously . . . We reached bottom at 1200, a group of 47 men, counting visitors and all.

Upon arriving, Inti presented a number of instances of disrespect by Marcos. I exploded. I told Marcos that if this were so, he would be expelled from the guerrilla band, and he replied that [blotted out words] shot before.

Orders had been given for an ambush of 5 men down the river and a scouting expedition by three men, headed by Antonio and with Miguel and Loro. Pacho took up observation on the barren hill that overlooks Algaranaz's house, but saw nothing. At night the scouts returned and I let them have it. Polo reacted very emotionally and denied the charges. The meeting was explosive and did not end well. It is not clear what Marcos said. I sent for Rolando to settle once for all the problem of new recruits;

---

* And she reports that she has been separated from the youth leadership.

their numbers and distribution, since we were more than 30 men from the center going hungry.

March 23

A day of warlike events. Pombo wanted to organize an expedition up ahead to recover provisions, but I objected to it until the substitution of Marcos was cleared up. At a little after 0800 Coco ran in to report that a section of the Army had fallen into the ambush. The final result, up till now: three mortars, 60-mm. 16 Mausers, two BZ (Bazookas), three 130 UZIs, two radios, boots, etc.; 7 dead, 14 uninjured prisoners and four wounded ones, but we failed to capture food supplies. We captured the plan of operation, which was to advance along both ends of the Nacahuasú and make contact at mid-point. We hurriedly transferred some people to the other side and I put Marcos with the whole vanguard at the end of the maneuver route while the center and part of the rearguard remain on the defense and Braulio sets an ambush at the other maneuver routes. Thus we shall spend the night to see if the famous Rangers will come tomorow. A major and a captain, prisoners, talked like parrots.

The message sent with Chino was deciphered. It deals with Debré's [sic] trip, the sending of the $60,000, Chino's requests, and an explanation of why they do not write to Iván.

I also received a communication from Sánchez which reports about the possibilities of establishing Mito at some points.

March 24

The complete booty is as follows: 16 Mausers, 3 mortars with 64 shells, 2 BZ, 2,000 Mauser rounds, 3 UZIs with 8 magazines each, one 30 with 2 belts. There are 7 dead and 14 prisoners, including 4 wounded. I sent Marcos out to reconnoiter; the results were negative, but the planes bombed close to our house.

I sent Inti to talk to the prisoners for the last time and set them free after having them remove all their clothes we could use, but not from the two officers, whom we spoke with separately and they left dressed. We told the major that we were giving him until 1200 on the 27th to remove his dead and we offered a truce for the entire zone of Lagunillas if he remained here but he replied that he was leaving the Army. The captain stated that he had reentered the Army a year ago at the request of the Party and that he had a brother studying in Cuba. In addition he gave the names of two other officers willing to collaborate. When the planes commenced to bomb they gave him a terrible scare, but two of our men also were frightened: Raul and Walter; the latter was weak in the ambush.

Marcos did some scouting but found nothing in his area. Nato and Coco left with the goldbricks foraging upstream but had to send them back because they did not want to walk. We will have to discharge them.

March 25

The day went by uneventfully. León, Urbano, and Arturo were sent to an observation point overlooking the entrances of the river on both sides. At 1200 hours Marcos left his position at ambush and all the people remained concentrated at the principal ambush. At 1830 with practically all of the personnel present I made an analysis of the trip and its significance, and I expounded on the mistakes made by Marcos and took away his command and named Miguel chief of the vanguard. At the same time I announced the discharge of Paco, Pepe, Chino, and Eusebic. They were told that they will not eat if they do not work. I suspended their tobacco ration, and redistributed their personal things and gear among other, needier comrades. I referred to Kolle's coming to discuss what to do, simultaneously with the expulsion of the members of the Youth present here. We are interested in deeds; words that do not match the deeds are not important. I announced the search for the cow and the resumption of classes.

I spoke to Pedro and El Médico, telling them that they have almost graduated as full-fledged guerrillas and with Apolinar, whom I encouraged. I criticized Walter for weakening during the trip, for his attitude in combat and for the fear he showed of the planes; he did not respond well.

I gave details to Chino and Pelado and gave the Frenchman a long oral report on the situation.

During the meeting this group was given the name Ejército de Liberación Nacional de Bolivia and a report will be prepared on the encounter.

March 26

Inti departed early with Antonio, Raúl and Pedro to find a cow in the area of Ticucha, but they came upon troops after

3 hours and they returned, apparently without being seen. They reported that the soldiers had a sentry post on a treeless hill and a kind of house with a shining roof from which about 8 men emerged. They are in the immediate area of the river we called Yaki. I spoke with Marcos and I sent him to the rearguard; I do not believe that his conduct will improve much.

A small foraging expedition was conducted and the usual sentries were posted; from the observation point at the Algaranaz lookout 30 to 40 soldiers were seen. A helicopter landed.

March 27

Today the news exploded, monopolizing all the space on the radio and producing a multitude of communiques including the Barrientos press conference. The official report includes one more dead than we do and it reports them as wounded and later executed and they assign to us 15 dead and 4 prisoners, two of these foreigners; but there is also talk about a foreigner who eliminated himself, and of the composition of the guerrilla force. Obviously the deserters or the prisoner talked, but we do not know exactly how much they told and how they told it. Everything appears to indicate that Tania is spotted, whereby two years of good and patient work are lost. The departure of the people is difficult now; I received the impression that Danton was not very happy when I told him that. We shall see what happens.

Benigno, Loro, and Julio left to find the path to Pirirenda; it should take them 2 or 3 days, and their instructions are to arrive without being seen at Pirirenda, then to effect an expedition to Gutiérrez. The reconnaissance plane dropped some parachutes that the lookout said fell in the hunting area. Antonio and two others were sent to investigate and endeavor to take prisoners but there was nothing there.

At night we had a staff meeting to make plans for the following days. For tomorrow a foraging expedition to our little house to pick up some corn; later, another to effect some purchases in Gutiérrez, and finally, a small diversion attack perhaps in the woods between Pincal and Lagunilla against the vehicles that travel through there.

Communiqué No. 1 is being prepared, which we will endeavor to deliver to the newspapermen at Camiri (D XVII).

March 28

The radio reports continue to be full of news about the

guerrillas. We are surrounded by 2,000 men within a radius of 120 kilometers, and the ring is closing, complemented by napalm bombing; we have 10-15 casualties.

I sent Braulio at the head of a group of nine men to try to find corn. They returned at night with a list of crazy news: 1) Coco, who had set out ahead to warn us, has disappeared. 2) At 1000 hours they reached the farm; they find that the cave had been searched; they spread out to begin collecting, when seven Red Cross men show up, two doctors and several military men, unarmed. They take them prisoners, explaining to them that the truce has expired, but authorizing them to go on. 3) A truck full of soldiers arrives and, instead of firing, they make them promise to withdraw. 4) The soldiers retreat in good order and our men escort the medics where the rotting corpses are, but they cannot carry the latter and say they will return tomorrow to burn them. Two of Algaranaz's horses are taken from them and they move on. Antonio, Rubio, and Aniceto stay where the animals cannot follow. Just as we were about to look for Coco, he showed up; it seems that he had been asleep. No sign of Benigno yet.

The Frenchman stated too vehemently how useful he could be on the outside.

March 29

A day of little action but of extreme excitement in the news; the Army provides much information which, if true, can be very valuable to us. Radio Havana has given the news that the Government has announced that it will support Venezuela's action in presenting the case of Cuba before the OAS. Among the news items there is one which worries me: that there was an encounter in the Tirabay ravine where two guerrillas died. That place is on the way to Pirirenda, where Benigno should be scouting around and today he should be returning if he can make it. They were ordered not to pass the ravine but these last few days they have repeatedly disobeyed the orders I gave.

Guevara is advancing very slowly. They were given dynamite but they could not set it off all day. A horse was killed and plenty of meat eaten, although it has to last four days. We shall try to bring the other one here although it may be difficult. Judging by the birds of prey they still have not burned the bodies. As soon as the cave is ready we can make the transfer of this camp which is uncomfortable and very well known.

I notified Alejandro that he would remain here together with the doctor and Joaquin (probably in Bear Camp). Rolando also is very worn out. I spoke with Urbano and Tuma; with the latter I could not even make myself understood about the reason for my criticisms.

March 30

All is quiet again. In mid-morning, Benigno and his companions return. Actually, they had crossed Piribay ravine but they found nothing but evidence that two people had gone by. They reached their destination, although they were seen by the peasants, and returned. Their report says that it takes about 4 hours to reach Pirirenda, and that apparently there is no danger. The planes fired constantly on the little house.

I sent Antonio with two others to explore the river upstream and the report is that the guards remain in one place although there are footprints indicating an exploration along the river. They have dug trenches.

The missing mare returned, so that, if worst comes to worst, we have meat for four days. Tomorrow we shall rest and day after tomorrow the vanguard will set out for the next two operations: to take Gutierrez and to set up an ambush on the Algaranaz-Lagunillas road.

March 31

No important events. Guevara announced that the cave would be completed tomorrow. Inti and Ricardo reported that the soldiers had again taken over our small farm, after a preliminary assault with artillery (mortars) aircraft, etc. This hampers our plans to go to Pirirenda and get provisions; nonetheless, I gave Manuel instructions to advance with his men as far as the little house. If the little house was empty, Manuel was to take it over and send two men back to tell me so that we could get going tomorrow or the day after tomorrow; if the little house has been taken and he could not mount a surprise attack, return and explore the possibilities of flanking Algaranaz to set up an ambush between Pincal and Lagunillas.

The radio is keeping up its racket, and the reports are interspersed with semiofficial communiques on the fighting. They have established our position with pinpoint accuracy between the Yaki and the Nancahuasu and I fear that they will try to surround us.

I spoke with Benigno about his error in not going to look for us and explained Marcos' situation to him; he reacted well.

During the evening I spoke with Loro and Aniceto. The conversation went very badly; Loro even said that we were rotten, and when I pressed him to specify, he left that to Marcos and Benigno. Aniceto partially agreed with him but later confessed to Coco that they had been accomplices in stealing some canned goods, and to Inti that he was not in agreement with Loro's comments about Benigno and another comment about Pombo and on the "general disorganization in the guerrilla unit," more or less.

ANALYSIS OF THE MONTH

This month was full of events, but the general pattern has the following characteristics: the consolidation and purification phase for the guerrillas, which was fully accomplished; a slow state of development with the incorporation of some elements who came from Cuba, who do not appear bad, and Guevara's men who have turned out to be of generally low grade: two deserters, one "talkative" prisoner, three quitters, and two slackers. The beginning of the struggle phase characterized by a precise and spectacular attack but studded with glaring indecisions before and after the combat (Marcos' retreat, Braulio's action). Beginning phase of enemy counteroffensive, marked until now by: a) tendency to establish controls which will isolate us, b) clamoring at the national and international level, c) total ineffectiveness until now, d) mobilization of peasants.

Evidently we will have to get going before I had thought and [expected?], leaving a group inactive for now and with the deadweight of four potential informers. The situation is not good but today begins a phase to test the guerrillas, which should do them much good once they get over it.

Composition: Vanguard—Chief, Miguel; Benigno, Pacho, Loro, Aniceto, Camba, Coco, Darío, Julio, Pablo, Raúl. Rearguard—Chief: Joaquín; second-in-command: Braulio; Rubio, Marcos, Pedro, Médico, Polo, Walter, Victor (Pepe, Paco, Eusebio, Chingolo). Center—Myself, Alejandro, Rolando, Inti, Pombo, Ñato, Tuma, Urbano, Moro, Negro, Ricardo, Arturo, Eustaquio, Guevara, Willy, Luis, Antonio, León (Tania, Pelado, Dantón, Chino—visitors; Serapio—refugee).

April 1

The vanguard left at 0700 hours, with considerable delay. Camba is missing. He did not return from the expedition with

Nato to hide the weapons at El Oso cave. At 1000 hours Tuma arrived from the lookout point reporting he had seen three or four soldiers on the small hunting plain. We took our positions and from the lookout point Walter said he had seen three men and a mule or burro and that they were setting up something. He pointed them out to me but I saw nothing. At 1600 hours, I left, judging that, in any case, it was not necessary to remain because they would not attack, but I think it was an optical illusion that Walter saw.

I decided to evacuate everything tomorrow and put Rolando in charge of the rearguard in the absence of Joaquin. Nato and Camba arrived at 2100. They had hidden everything away except some food for the six who were to remain. They were: Joaquín Alejandro, Moro, Serapio, Eustaquio and Polo, the three Cubans protesting. The other mare was killed to leave *charqui* [dried meat] for the six. At 2300 Antonio arrived with a sack of corn and the news that everything had gone without incident.

At 0400 hours Rolando left, taking with him the impediment of the four slack ones (Chingolo, Eusebio, Paco, and Pepe). Pepe wants to be given a weapon, and that he would stay. Camba went with him.

At 5, Coco arrived with a new message indicating that they had killed a cow and were waiting for us. I gave him as a meeting place the *arroyo* that comes out in the woods below the farm, the day after tomorrow at 12:00 noon.

April 2

The incredible amount of things we had accumulated made it necessary for us to spend the whole day storing them in their respective caves, finishing this at 1700 hours. We posted four men to watch, but the day was dead calm; not even planes flew over the area. The radio reports speak of the "narrowing of the circle" and that the guerrillas are preparing defensive positions in a canyon of the Nacahuasu. They say that Don Remberto has been arrested and tell how he sold the farm to Coco.

Because it was so late, we decided not to set out today but to wait until 3:00 a.m. and spend the day going directly through the Nacahuasu despite the fact that the meeting place is behind it.

I spoke with Moro, explaining to him that I did not name him in the group of the best because he has certain weaknesses with respect to food and a tendency to exasperate his companions with his pranks. We discussed the subject for awhile.

April 3

We followed the schedule without problems. We set out at 3:30 a.m. and walked slowly until we passed the bend in the shortcut at 6:30 and reached the edge of the farm at 8:30. We passed in front of the ambush site. There were only a few perfectly clean skeletons left of the seven bodies. The birds of prey had done their job quite efficiently. I sent two men (Urbano and Nato) to make contact with Rolando and in the afternoon we moved to the Piriboy ravine, where we slept, our bellies full of cow meat and corn.

I spoke with Danton and Carlos, outlining three alternatives: To go along with us; to leave by themselves; or to go to Gutiérrez and from there try their luck the best way they could. They chose the third. Tomorrow we shall try our luck.

April 4

Almost total failure. At 1830 we arrived at a point where there were tracks of police and even a paratrooper's beret and some evidence of North American food (individual rations). I decided to take the first house, belonging to [name omitted] by assault and so we did at 1830. There were only two Guaraní peasants who reported that the Army, close to 150 men, had left yesterday and that the owner of the house had gone out to take his cattle far away. A pork and yucca meal was ordered while we went to occupy the second house of [name omitted]. Loro, Coco, Aniceto, and then Inti went to the second house accompanied by another of the peasants. The couple were not there but when they arrived the little laborer escaped in the confusion. At last it was possible to establish that approximately a company of the 2nd Bolivar Regimen had been there, having left that morning. They had instructions to go down by way of the Tiraboi ravine, but they elected to go over another terrain and that is the reason we did not run into them. There are no guards in Gutiérrez, but they will return tomorrow so it is not advisable to stay.

In the first house we found military objects such as dinner plates, canteens, even bullets and miscellaneous equipment. We confiscated everything.

After eating well but without overdoing it, the rearguard left at 0300 and we left at 0330. The vanguard was to leave when they ate their last portions. We got lost and ended up further down from the ambush site provoking a confusion that lasted until morning.

April 5

Uneventful day, but with certain tension in the air. At 10 we were all together, and a little later Miguel left with his knapsacks to occupy the head of the ravine with the order to send back the three men of the rearguard who were standing guard at that point so that they could pick up their knapsacks. To speed up the movement, I assigned Urbano, Nato, León to the task of replacing the three men of the rearguard. At 1530 I stopped at the center group to organize the ambush to hold back the forces which might come down the ravine. The vanguard and rearguard would defend the banks of the little arroyo at its mouth. At 1400 I sent Tuma to see about the three men, and at 1700 he returned with no information. We moved to the camp we had before and I repeated the order. At 1815, Rolando arrived. Since the men had not arrived, he and the others brought the three knapsacks.

Braulio made an exposition that casts very serious doubts on Marcos's present fighting capability.

I was thinking of going down river at dawn but soldiers were seen bathing 300 meters from our position. Then we decided to cross the river without leaving tracks and to walk on the other side to "our" arroyo.

April 6

A very tense day. We crossed the Nacahuasu River at 0400 and stopped to await the dawn before proceeding. Later Miguel started to scout but he had to return twice due to some mistakes that placed us very close to the guards. At 0800 Rolando reported that ten soldiers were in front of the ravine we had just left. We departed slowly and at 1100 we were out of danger on solid ground. Rolando arrived with the news that there were more than 100 men posted at the ravine.

At night before we had arrived at the arroyo we heard voices of cowboys in the river. We went out and picked up four campesinos and a group of a Algaranaz's cows. They had an Army safe-conduct for 12 head of cattle. Some of the cattle had already passed by and it was not possible to catch them. We kept two cows for ourselves and took them along the river to our arroyo. The four civilians turned out to be the contractor and his son, a peasant from Chuquisaca, and another from Camiri, who proved to be receptive and to whom we gave the document and promised to publicize it.

We held them for a while and later let them go with the request that they say nothing, and they promised.

We spent the night eating.

April 7

We went into the arroyo taking the remaining cow with us. We killed it to make jerked beef. Rolando stayed at the ambush at the river with orders to shoot at anything that appeared; nothing happened the whole day. Benigno and Camba followed the path that is to take us to Pirirenda, and reported having heard a noise as of a sawmill in a canyon close to our arroyo.

I sent Urbano and Julio with a message for Joaquin and they did not return all day.

April 8

An uneventful day. Benigno went and returned to his work without completing it and says that he will not do it tomorrow either. Miguel left to look for a canyon which Benigno saw from the hill, but he did not return. Urbano and Julio returned with Polo. The police have taken over the camp and are scouting in the hills. They passed by the "elevator" on their way up. Joaquin reports on this and other problems in the attached document (D. XIX).

April 9

Polo, Luis, and Willy departed with orders to deliver a note to Joaquin and help them to return in order to install them in a secure place up the arroyo which Nato and Guevara will select. According to Nato, there are good locations, which, though near the *arroyo,* are slightly over an hour's journey from where we are. Miguel returned. According to his explorations, the ravine leads to Pirirenda and it takes one day to travel through it with a knapsack. Therefore, instructions were given for Benigno to suspend work on the path he was making, which would take at least one more day to complete.

April 10

It dawned, and the morning wore on with no promise of

new events while we prepared to leave the *arroyo* and proceed through Quebrada de Miguel up to the Pirirenda or Gutiérrez. In midmorning Negro came up, very excited, and said that 15 soldiers were coming down river; Inti had left to advise Rolando at the ambush. There was nothing left to do but to wait, and this we did; I sent Tuma so that he would be ready to inform me. Soon the first news arrived, and it was unpleasant. Rubio, Jesús Suárez Gayol, was mortally wounded; he was dead on arrival at our camp, a bullet in his head. It was like this: the ambush was composed of nine men, six rearguardsmen and a reinforcement of three vanguardsmen, distributed on both sides of the river. Upon reporting on the arrival of the 15 soldiers, Inti went to the area where Rubio was and observed that he was in a very bad position since he was clearly visible from the river. The soldiers advanced without major precautions but they explored the banks looking for paths; they entered one of these and clashed with Braulio and Pedro before they entered the ambush. The gunfire lasted a few seconds, resulting in one dead and three wounded in addition to six prisoners. Shortly thereafter a noncommissioned officer also fell and four escaped. Rubio was found next to a wounded man; he was already in his death throes; his Garand was jammed, and a grenade was beside him, its pin pulled but unexploded. The prisoner could not be interrogated because of his serious condition; he died shortly thereafter, and so did the lieutenant who commanded them. I got the following picture from the interrogation of the prisoners: These 15 men belonged to the company that was higher up the Nacahuasú River; it had crossed through the canyon and picked up the skeletons, and later had taken the camp. According to the soldiers they did not find anything there although the radio spoke of photos and documents found there. The company consisted of 100 men, of whom 15 accompanied a group of newspapermen to our camp. These left to conduct an exploration and return at 1700. The major forces are at Pincal; at Lagunillas there are about 30 and it is assumed that the group that went past Piraboi was sent to Gutiérrez. They told the story of this group, which had been lost in the mountains without water, and therefore it was necessary to rescue them. Estimating that the fugitives would arrive late, I decided to leave in place the ambush that Rolando had advanced some 500 meters, but counting now on the help of the entire vanguard. At first I had ordered the withdrawal, but it seemed to me logical to leave it that way. Near 1700 hours the news came that the Army was advancing with heavy forces. The only thing to do is wait. I sent Pombo to give me a clear idea of the situation. Scattered gunfire is heard for quite a while, and Pombo returned announcing that they had again fallen into the ambush, that there are several dead and that a major had been taken prisoner. This time things occurred as follows: the troops advanced down the river but without taking precautions and fell [illegible words] completely. This time there were seven dead, five wounded, and a total of 22 prisoners. The following is the final outcome: (total) (It cannot be done for lack of data.)

April 11

During the morning we started to transfer all the implements and buried Rubio in a small shallow grave, owing to the lack of materials. Inti was left with the rearguard to accompany the prisoners and let them go free, in addition to looking for more scattered weapons. The only result obtained in the search was the capture of two more prisoners with their Garands. The major was given two copies of [communique] No. 1, under his promise to give them to the newspapermen. The total of casualties was as follows: 10 dead, including two lieutenants; 30 prisoners: one major and a few NCO's, and the rest soldiers. Six are wounded, one in the first battle and the rest in the second, They are under the 4th division but with elements from various mixed regiments. There are Rangers, paratroopers, and local soldiers, almost children.

Only in the afternoon we finished the moving and located the cave where we were to leave the impediments; but without putting it in shape yet. In the last stretch the cows ran off and all we have left is one calf.

Early, just as we arrived at the new camp, we met with Joaquin and Alejandro who were coming down with all their people. The report indicates that the soldiers seen were only imagined by Eustaquio and the transfer was a useless effort.

The radio announced "a new and bloody clash" and spoke of nine Army dead and four of ours "confirmed" dead. One Chilean newspaperman made a commentary on our camp from memory and decribed a photo of me, beardless and with a pipe. We must investigate further to ascertain how it was obtained. There is no proof that the upper cave has been located, although there are some indications.

April 12

At 6:30 I called together all the combatants, except the four "dregs," to conduct a small memorial service for Rubio and to point out that the first blood drawn was Cuban. I brought to their attention the tendency observed in the vanguard to look down on the Cubans, which jelled yesterday with Camba's statement that he had less and less confidence in the Cubans, after an incident with Ricardo. I called their attention again to the need to unite as the only possibility to develop our army, which is increasing in fire power and fighting prowess but not in numbers; on the contrary, it has grown smaller in the last few days.

After concealing all the booty in a cave, very well prepared by Nato, we left at 1400 hours at a slow pace. It was so slow that we hardly made progress, and had to sleep at a small water hole, a short distance from our starting point.

Now that the Army has admitted that 11 are dead, it would appear that they found another one of the wounded had died. I started a short course on Debray's book.

Part of a message has been deciphered; it does not appear to be very important.

April 13

We divided the group in 2 to make faster progress. In spite of that, we went slowly, arriving at 1600 hours at the camp, the last ones coming at 1830. Miguel had arrived that morning. The caves have not been discovered and nothing has been touched; the benches, the stoves, the oven and the seedbeds are intact.

Aniceto and Raul went scouting but they did not do it right; tomorrow we must repeat, up to the Ikira River.

The Americans announce that the sending of advisers to Bolivia accords with an old plan and has nothing to do with the guerrillas. We may be witnessing the first episode of a new Vietnam.

[The "old plan" refers to the Military Assistance Program in existence since 1958 when Bolivia and the United States signed a bilateral military aid agreement.]

April 14

A monotonous day. Some things are brought from the shelter of the sick, which gives us food for 5 days. Cans of milk are procured from the lower cave, and we find that 23 cans are unaccountably missing, since Moro left 48 and it would appear that no one had the time to remove them. Milk is part of our survival items. From the special cave we got a mortar and the machine gun to reinforce the position until Joaquin arrives.

It is not clear how the operation is to be effected, but it would appear to me that it would be best for everybody to go out and operate for a while around the Muyupampa area, in order to fall back toward the north later. If it is possible, Dantón and Carlos should continue toward Sucre-Cochabamba, depending on the circumstances.

We are writing Communiqué No. 2 (Document XXI) for the Bolivian people and Report No. 4 for Manila, which is to be carried by the Frenchman.

April 15

Joaquin arrived with the entire rearguard and it was decided to leave tomorrow. He reported flights over the area and bombardment of the woods. The day was uneventful. The armament of the group was completed; the .30 caliber machine gun was assigned to the rearguard (Marcos), with the "dregs" as assistants.

In the evening I made some remarks on the trip and admonished them with regards to the missing cans of milk, giving them a severe warning.

Part of a long message from Cuba was deciphered; briefly, Lechín knows about what I am doing and he will write a declaration of support, returning to the country clandestinely in another 20 days.

A letter is written to Fidel (No. 4), informing him of the latest events. It is being sent in code and put in invisible writing.

April 16

The vanguard left at 6:15 and we at 7:15, marching well up to the Ikira River, but Tania and Alejandro fell behind. When their temperatures were taken, Tania's was more than 39 degrees and Alejandro's 38 degrees [Centigrade]. Moreover, the delay prevented us from marching according to schedule. We left the two, with Negro and Serapio, one kilometer upriver from the Ikira and went on, taking the settlement called Bella Vista; more precisely, four peasants who sold us potatoes, a pig, and some corn. The peasants are very poor and frightened by our presence here. We spent the night cooking and eating and did not stir from the place, awaiting the morrow to go on to Ticucha without being recognized.

April 17

The news kept varying and with it our decisions. Ticucha is a waste of time according to the peasants, and there is a road directly to Muyupampa (Vaca Guzmán) which is shorter and on the last portion of which vehicles can travel. So we decided to go on directly to Muyupampa, after much hesitation on my part. I sent for the stay-behinds so that they would remain with Joaquin and I told him to make a demonstration in the zone to avoid any excessive movement; and to wait 3 days, at the end of which they should remain around the area, but without head-on fighting, and await our return.

At night we found out that one of the sons of a peasant had disappeared and he could have gone to inform on us, but we decided to go on anyway, to try to get the Frenchman and Carlos out once and for all. Moisés joined the group of stragglers, because he had a bad attack of colic in the bile ducts.

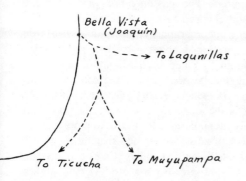

This is a sketch of our position. If we return by the same road we are exposing ourselves to an encounter with the Army troops alerted in Lagunillas or some column coming from Ticucha; nevertheless we must, so as not to lose touch with the rearguard.

We started out at 2200 hours, walking very quickly until 0430, at which time we stopped to sleep a little, We advanced 10 kilometers.

Of all the peasants we have seen, there is one, Limón, who appears to be cooperative, but with fear, and another one, Vides, who could be dangerous; he is the "rich one" of the area. Besides, we must remember that the son of Carlos Rodas disappeared; he could be an informer (although under the influence of Vides, who is the economic boss of the area).

April 18

We marched until dawn, dozing during the last hour of the night in a considerable chill. In the morning, the vanguard went to explore, finding a house of Guaraní Indians who gave very little information. Our sentry detained a horseman who proved to be the son of Carlos Rodas (another one) who was going to Yacunda and we took him prisoner. The march was continued at a slow pace and at 1500 hours we were able to reach Matajal, the house of A. Padilla, the poor brother of another who lives a league away from there, and whose house we also passed. The man was afraid and tried every way he could to get us to go away, but to make thing worse it began to rain and we had to take shelter in his house.

April 19

We remained in the place all day, capturing peasants who were coming from the crossing in both directions by which we gained a wide assortment of prisoners. At 1300 hours the sentry brought us a Greek-style gift, an English newspaperman surnamed Roth who, following our tracks, was being guided by some children from Lagunillas. His documents were in order but there were some suspicious things. The passport had the occupation of student crossed out and changed to that of newspaperman (actually he claims to be a photographer); he had a visa from Puerto Rico and when questioned about a card of an organizer in Buenos Aires, he admitted he had been a Spanish teacher for a student body. He said that he had been at the camp and they had shown him a diary in which Braulio described his experiences and his trips. It is the same story as ever: Lack of discipline and irresponsibility dominating all. From a report of the children who guided the journalist, we learned that the very night of our arrival here was known in Lagunillas, thanks to a report brought by someone, We put pressure on Rodas's son and he confessed that his brother and one of Vides's laborers had gone to earn the reward of between 500 and 1,000 [Bolivian pesos]. We confiscated his horse in reprisal and told the detained peasants of it.

The Frenchman asked to present the problem to the Englishman, and as a test of his good faith, to help get them out. Carlos agreed reluctantly and I washed my hands of it. We arrived at 2100 hours at [blank space] and we continued on the trip to Muyupampa, where, according to reports from the peasants, everything was quiet. The Englishman accepted the conditions which Inti proposed, including a small account I had written and at 2345, after handshakes for those departing, the march to take the town was initiated. I stayed behind, with Pombo, Tuma, and Urbano. The cold was intense and we made a small fire. At 0100, Nato arrived to report that the town was in a state of alert, with Army troops billeted in units of 20 and self-defense patrols. One of these, with two M-3s and two revolvers, surprised our outposts, but they surrendered without fighting. They asked me for instructions, and I told them to withdraw because of the late hour, permitting the Englishman, the Frenchman and Carlos take whatever decision they deemed advisable. At four, we began to return, without having accomplished our objective, but Carlos decided to stay and the Frenchman followed suit, this time unwillingly.

April 20

It was around 7 when we arrived at the house of Nemesio Caraballo, whom we had met during the night and who had offered us some coffee. The man had gone, leaving the house locked, with only some scared servants remaining. We prepared our meal there, buying corn and squash from the laborers. At about 1300 a station wagon arrived carrying a white flag, bringing the subprefect, the doctor, and the Muyupampa priest, a German. Inti spoke with them. They came on a peace mission, a nation-wide peace for which they offered to act as middlemen. Inti offered peace for Muyupampa in return for a list of supplies which they were to deliver to us before 1830. They did not accept this commitment because, according to them, the Army had taken over the town; however, they asked that the time be extended until 6 in the morning, but we refused.

They brought, as a token of good will, two cartons of cigarettes and the news that the three outbound ones had been captured in Muyupampa and two were compromised for carrying false documents, It looks bad for Carlos. Danton should come out all right.

At 1730, three AT-6's did a little bombing over the very house where we were cooking. One fell 15 meters away and Ricardo was wounded slightly by a splinter. That was the Army's reply. The proclamations have to be made known in order to achieve the complete demoralization of the soldiers who, judging from the emissaries, are frightened.

We left at 2330 with two horses, the one we confiscated and the one that belonged to the newspaperman, walking toward Ticucha until 0130, when we stopped to sleep,

April 21

We walked a short distance to the house of Roco Carrasco, who treated us well, selling us what we needed. At night we walked up to the crossing of the Muyupampa-Monteagudo road at a place called Taperillas. The idea was to stay at a watering place and make an exploration to place the ambush. There was another reason, which was the news given by the radio of the death of three mercenaries: a Frenchman, an Englishman, and an Argentine. This uncertainty must be clarified to make an exemplary punishment,

Before crossing we passed by the house of the veteran Rodas, who was the stepfather of Vargas, the one who died at Nacahuasu. We gave him an explanation which seemed to satisfy him.

The vanguard did not understand and continued down the road, waking up some dogs that barked excessively.

April 22

The errors started in the morning; Rolando, Miguel and Antonio went out scouting to set up an ambush, after we withdrew, going back into the woods, They surprised some men in a small truck of the YPFB who were studying our tracks while the peasant was telling them of our presence there at night, and they decided to capture everybody. That upset all our plans, but we decided to wait in ambush during the day and capture the trucks loaded with merchandise which might come along, and to ambush the Army if it came.

A truck with some merchandise and a great many bananas, as well as a considerable group of *campesinos,* was captured, but we let go others which came along looking at the tracks and, especially, other small trucks belonging to Yacimientos. The food, together with the temptation of the bread offered, which was never coming caused us delay.

My intention was to load the small Yacimientos truck with all the provisions and advance with the vanguard to the crossroads where the road to Ticucha began, 4 kilometers away. At nightfall, the small plane began to circle over our position and the barking of the dogs in the nearby houses became more insistent. At 2000 hours we were ready to leave, in spite of the evidence that our presence had been detected, when a short combat began and then we heard voices calling for our surrender. We were all careless and had no idea about what was going on. Fortunately, our belongings and the provisions were in the small truck. In a short while everything was organized; only Loro was missing, but for the moment there was no indication that anything had happened to him, since the clash was between Ricardo and the policemen's guide, when he surprised them as they came up on a ridge to surround us. The guide may have been shot. We left with the small truck and all the available horses, six altogether; we walked part of the time on foot and on horseback, alternating; finally the group all climbed into the small truck and six from the vanguard riding horseback. We reached Ticucha at 3:30, and El Mesón, the priest's property, at 6:30 after we got stuck in a hole.

The net result of the action is a negative one: On the one hand, a lack of discipline and foresight; on the other, the loss (I hope temporary) of men; provisions for which we paid and did not take along with us, and, finally, the loss of a package of dollars, which fell from Pombo's bag, were the results of the skirmish. Not counting that we were attacked by surprise and forced to withdraw by a group which, of necessity, had to be small. It will take a good deal to transform this into a fighting force although the morale is rather high.

April 23

Day of rest and little news. At noon the small airplane (AT 6) flew over the zone; the watch returned, but there was nothing to report. At night I gave instructions for tomorrow: Benigno and Aniceto will go search for Joaquin: 4 days; Coco and Camba will explore the path to the Rio Grande and prepare it to make it practicable: 4 days; we ourselves shall stay near the corn, waiting to see if the Army comes until we have recovered Joaquin. The order is to bring everyone, only leaving there one of the dregs, if ill.

The question of Danton, Pelao and the English journalist still exists. There is press censorship and now they have announced the capture of 5 or 6 prisoners.

April 24

The scouts set out. We stopped at a small ridge one kilometer up the arroyo. It is possible to see as far as the house of the last peasant some 500 ms. before reaching the priest's farm. (We found marijuana in the fields.) The peasant came again and snooped around; in the afternoon an AT-6 fired two bursts at the small house. Pacho disappeared mysteriously. He was sick and stayed behind. Antonio told him the way and he went in the direction by which it should have taken him 5 hours to arrive, but he did not return. Tomorrow we shall look for him.

April 25

A black day. At 10 in the morning Pombo returned from the observation post advising that 30 police were going toward the little house. Antonio remained at the observation point. While we were getting ready, he came with the news that there were 60 men and that they were preparing to proceed. The observation point was proving ineffectual in giving advance warning. We decided to improvise an ambush on the road of access to the camp; we hastily chose a small road along the arroyo, which allowed a 50-meter field of vision. I posted myself there with Urbano and Miguel with the automatic rifle; the Doctor, Arturo, and Raul occupied the position on the right to cut off any escape or advance that way. Rolando, Pombo, Antonio, Ricardo, Julio, Pablito, Darío, Willy, Luis and León occupied the lateral position on the other side of the *arroyo,* to take them completely by surprise. Inti remained in the bed of the arroyo to attack any who tried to look for cover there. Nato and Eustaquio went scouting with instructions to withdraw to the rear when the shooting began. Chino remained in the rear to guard the camp. My scant force was reduced by three men: Pacho, who was lost, and Tuma and Luis, who were looking for him.

A short while later the vanguard appeared. To our surprise, it consisted of three German dogs with their handler. The animals were restless, but I did not think they had raised us; however, they continued to advance and I shot the first dog; when I was going to shoot the guide, my M-2 jammed. Miguel killed another dog, as far as I could see, and no one else walked into the ambush. On the Army side, intermittent firing began. When the firing ceased, I sent Urbano to order the withdrawal, but he came with the news that Rolando had been wounded. They brought him a short while later, dying from loss of blood, and he died when we began to administer plasma. A bullet had fractured the femur and the whole nervous vascular bundle, and he had lost too much blood before any action could be taken. We have lost the best man in the guerrilla band and, naturally, one of its pillars, my comrade since the time, still practically a child, he was a messenger for Column 4, until the invasion and now this new revolutionary adventure. Of his unknown and unheralded death for a hypothetical future that may materialize, one can only say: "Your little corpse, valiant captain, has extended into immensity its metallic form."

[Presumably the "invasion" Che refers to is that at the Bay of Pigs in April 1961.

Column 4 was the famous Rebel force Che led to the decisive victory at Las Villas, Cuba, in December 1958, after which he entered Havana in triumph.]

The rest was the slow operation of withdrawal, recovering everything and the body of Rolando (San Luis). Pacho joined us later. He had made a mistake and caught up with Coco; nightfall overtook him on his return. At 0300 hours we buried the body under a thin layer of earth. Benigno and Aniceto arrived at 1000 saying that they had run into an Army ambush (or rather, a clash) losing the knapsacks but coming out unscathed. According to Benigno's calculation, this happened at a place not far from the Nacahuasu. Now the two natural exits are blocked and we will have to climb mountains, since the way out to the Rio Grande is not a wise one to take for two reasons: it is a natural exit and it would separate us from Joaquin, of whom we have no news. At night we will arrive at the place where the two roads meet, the one leading to the Nacahuasu and the other to the Rio Grande. We will sleep there and will wait for Coco and Camba to concentrate our little troop.

The results of the operation are extremely poor: Rolando dies, but not only that; the Army casualties cannot be more than two and the dog, at most, since we had not planned nor prepared our position and our riflemen could not see the enemy. Lastly, our warning system was very poor, for which reason we did not have time to get ready.

A helicopter landed twice at the priest's house, perhaps to remove some wounded men, the planes bombed our old position, which indicates that they did not advance at all.

April 26

We walked a few meters and I ordered Miguel to find a

place in which to make camp while we sent someone to look for Coco and Camba, but he returned at noon with both men. According to them, they had worked for four hours on the road, and there were possibilities for attempting to climb the ridge. Nevertheless, I sent Benigno and Urbano to explore a possible route of ascent near the canyon of the *arroyo* that joins the Nacahuasu, but they returned at nightfall with the news that it was all very difficult. We decided to continue along the path opened by Coco to try to find another one which leads to the Iquiri.

We have a mascot called Lola. It is a darling baby *visna*. We shall see if it survives.

April 27

Coco's 4 hours turned out to be 2½. We thought we recognized in a place where many sour orange bushes grow the place marked on the map, as Matico. Urbano and Benigno continued clearing the way and prepared a path for another hour's march, It is extremely cold at night.

The Bolivian radio broadcast Army reports announcing the death of a civilian guide, the handler of the dogs, and the dog Royo. Our losses as announced are two killed, one supposedly Cuban, knicknamed Rubio, and the other a Bolivian. It is confirmed that Danton is in a jail near Camiri. The others surely are alive and with him.

Altitude 950 meters

April 28

We walked slowly until 1500 hours. At that time the arroyo had dried up and took another course, for which reason we stopped. It was already too late to do any scouting, and we returned to camp near the water. We have food for only 4 days. Tomorrow we will attempt to reach the Nacahuasu through the Iquiri and we will have to cross mountains.

April 29

Another attempt was made through some short cuts which ended in negative results. At this point, at least, we are in an unbroken canyon. Coco thinks he has seen a transversal canyon which he did not explore. Tomorrow we will do it with the entire troop.

It took a long time to decipher message No. 35 completely. It had a paragraph requesting my authorization to add my name on an appeal in favor of Vietnam, with Bertrand Russell as the first signatory.

April 30

We initiated the attack on the hill. This canyon ends in some cliffs but we managed to find a rib whereby we could climb. The night came upon us when we were close to the peak and we slept there; it was not too cold.

Lola died a victim of Urbano's temper: he threw a rifle at its head.

Radio Havana transmitted some information by Chilean reporters indicating that the guerrillas were so strong that they endanger the cities and recently they had taken some military trucks filled with food, The magazine *Siempre* interviewed Barrientos, who, among other things, admitted that there were Yankee military advisers present and that the guerrilla warfare is due to the social conditons in Bolivia.

ANALYSIS OF THE MONTH

Things are normal, although we suffered two great losses: Rubio and Rolando. The death of the latter is a severe blow since I planned to leave him in charge of the eventual second front. We had four additional actions, all of these with positive results in general and one very good: the ambush in which Rubio died.

On another plane: the isolation continues to be complete, sicknesses have undermined the health of some comrades, forcing us to divide forces, which has greatly diminished our effectiveness. As yet we have been unable to establish contact with Joaquin. The peasant base has not yet been developed although it appears that through planned terror we can neutralize some of them; support will come later. Not one enlistment has been obtained, and apart from the dead we have lost Loro, who disappeared after the action at Taperillas.

Concerning the points noted regarding the military strategy, it can be emphasized: a) the controls have not been effective to date and they cause us some annoyance but they allow us to move around because of their slight mobility and their weakness. In addition, following the last ambush against the dogs and their handler, they can be expected to be very careful not to enter the woods. b) The clamor continues but now on both sides, and after the publication of my article in Havana there must not be any doubt about my presence here. It appears certain that the Americans will intervene here strongly and they are already sending helicopters and, apparently, Green Berets, although they have not been seen around here. c) The Army (at least one company or two) has improved its technique; they surprised us at Taperillas and did not become demoralized on Mesón. d) Peasant mobilization is nonexistent, except in regard to intelligence tasks, which are rather bothersome to us. But they are not very fast or efficient; they can be neutralized.

The status of Chino has changed and he will be a combatant until a second or third front is formed.

Dantón and Carlos fell victim to their own haste, their near desperation to leave, and of my lack of energy to stop them, so that communication with Cuba (Dantón) has been cut and the plan of action in Argentina (Carlos) is lost.

In short: A month in which everything resolved itself in the normal manner, considering the necessary hazards of guerrilla warfare. The morale is good among all the combatants who have passed their preliminary test as guerrillas.

May 1

We spent this day breaking trail, but walking very little. We still have not reached the water dividing line.

In Havana, Almeida spoke on the radio, applauding me and the famous Bolivian guerrillas. The speech was a little long, but good. We have sufficient food for 3 days. Today, Nato killed a bird with a slingshot. We are in the age of the bird.

[Juan Almeida, whose speech lauding the guerrillas Che mentions approvingly, was then Chief of the Revolutionary Armed Forces of Cuba.]

May 2

A day of slow progress and much confusion about our geographic position. We walked approximately two hours because of the difficulty of the brush. From a height, we could make out a point near the Nacahuasu, which indicates that we are very far north, but there are no signs of the Iquiri.

I ordered Miguel and Benigno to hack away all day in order

to try to get to the Iquiri, or at least to some body of water because we are running out of it.

We have food for 5 days, but there is very little of it.

Radio Havana continues its exaggerated propaganda offensive about Bolivia.

Altitude attained, 1760 meters. We turned in for the night at 1730 hours.

May 3

After a day of continuous hacking away through the brush, covering the equivalent of about a two-hour walk, we arrived at an arroyo with plenty of water, which seemed to be flowing north. Tomorrow we will simultaneously explore the route of the brook and continue with the cutting. We now have food for only two days, and it is running out. We are at an altitude of 1080 meters, 200 above the level of the Nacahuazú. In the distance we can hear a noise of motors, but cannot tell where it is coming from.

May 4

In the morning, we continued our trek, while Coco and Aniceto explored the arroyo. They returned about 1300, stating that the arroyo ran south and east into what seemed to be the Iquiri. I called back the *macheteros* and we continued down the arroyo. We started out at 1330 and stopped at 1700, because now the general direction was east by northeast, which cannot be the Iquiri unless it has changed its route. The macheteros told us they had not found any water, but that they would keep on. We decide to go ahead on the theory that we were heading toward the Rio Grande. We caught only a *cacare* [a black bird inhabiting the Bolivian highlands], which we divided up with the macheteros. Because of its small size, it will provide food for only two days.

The radio told us of the arrest of Loro, who had been wounded in the leg. The news about him is good so far. Everything seems to indicate that he was not shot from the front but from behind, presumably trying to escape.

Altitude 980 meters

May 5

We walked for five hours, about 12-14 kms, reaching a camp that Inti and Benigno made. We are now in the Congri arroyo, which does not appear on the map, and very far north of where we thought we were. This gives rise to several questions. Where is the Iquiri? Could this not be the camp where Benigno and Aniceto were surprised? Could the captives have been Joaquín's people? At the present time we are thinking of going towards the Oro, where there ought to be rations for two days, and from there to our old camp. Today we killed two big birds and a *cacaré,* as a result of which we had a good meal and still have a reserve for two days: envelopes of dried soups and canned meat. Inti, Coco and El Médico are first class hunters.

The news said that Debray would be tried by a military tribunal in Camiri as a presumed leader of the guerrilla organization. His mother arrives tomorrow and there is plenty of fear because of the matter. No news of Loro.

Altitude 840 meters

May 6

Our calculations on reaching the Oro River turned out to be wrong, as the distance to the little house at the arroyo was further than expected and the trail was blocked, so we had to cut our way through. We arrived at the little house at 1630 hours, after climbing to an altitude of 1400 meters with the group exhausted from walking. We ate our penultimate poor meal. We had caught only a partridge, which we gave to the machetero, Benigno, and the two who followed behind him in the order of march.

The news centered around the Debray case.

Altitude 1400 meters

May 7

We arrived at the Oro River campsite early and there found 8 cans of milk waiting for us on which we made a good breakfast. We took several things from the nearby cave, among them a Mauser for Nato, who will be our "bazooka-man" and get five anti-tank shells. Nato is quite ill, having had a spell of vomiting. We had barely arrived at the campsite when Benigno, Urbano, Leon, Aniceto, and Pablito set out to explore the small farm. We ate the last of the soups and meats, but we have a supply of lard in the cave. Footprints were seen, and there was some minor destruction, indicating that soldiers had been here. The scouts returned at daybreak with empty hands: soldiers are at the little farm and have stolen the corn. (Today marks just six months of the official beginning of guerrilla activities, which started with my arrival.)

Altitude 880 meters

May 8

Early in the morning I insisted that the caves be put in order and the other can of lard be taken down and put into bottles, for this is all we have left to eat. About 10:30, scattered shots were heard from the direction of the ambush; two unarmed soldiers were working their way up the Nacahuazú. Pacho believed that they were the vanguard and wounded them, one in the leg, and the other in the belly. He said that he had fired because they did not stop when challenged. They, naturally, heard nothing. The ambush was badly coordinated, and Pacho did what he did because he was very nervous. The ambush was improved by sending Antonio and some others to the right side. The soldiers' statements indicate that they are camped near the Iquiri; but, actually, they are lying. At 12, two more who were hurrying down the Nacahuasu, were captured. They said that they had gone out hunting and, returning by way of the Iquiri, discovered that their company had disappeared and they were running around in search of it, They lied, too. Actually, they had been sent out to hunt but had run off instead to search for food on our *finca* because their helicopter had not come to supply them. From them we captured raw and roasted corn, four cans of onions, and sugar and coffee. This solved the day's food problem for us, with the help of the lard which we ate in great amounts. Some of the men became ill from this.

Later, the guardpost informed us of the repeated explorations by soldiers, who reached the corner of the river, then turned back. Everyone was nervous when there arrived, at the worst, some 27 *guardias*. They had seen something unusual, and the group, led by 2nd Lieutenant Loredo, advanced. He opened fire, and was killed at once, together with two other soldiers. Night had already fallen and our men advanced, capturing 6 soldiers; the rest withdrew.

The total result was: three dead and ten prisoners, two of them wounded; seven M-1's, four Mausers, personal gear, ammo clips, and a small amount of food, which with the lard helped to relieve our hunger. We slept there.

May 9

We arose at 4 (I did not sleep) and freed the prisoners after first interrogating them. We took away their shoes and exchanged clothes with them—but the liars were sent off in their shorts. They left, heading toward the small *finca,* carrying the wounded man. At 6:30 we completed our withdrawal, in the direction of Arroyo de los Monos by way of the cave where we left our booty, The only food left was the lard. I felt faint and had to sleep for two hours before I could continue, at a slow and vacillating pace. In general, this was the tenor of the whole march. We ate "lard soup" at the first waterhole. The men are weak, and some of them are suffering from edema.

At nightfall the Army broadcast a report on the action, naming their dead and wounded, but not mentioning the prisoners. They announced a great battle, with big losses on our side.

May 10

We continued advancing slowly. On reaching the camp where Antonio's grave is, we found dried beef (*charqui*) which we had left in bad state and condition. We reorganized everything. There were no signs of the police, We crossed the Nacahuazú cautiously and started out toward Pirienda through an arroyo which Miguel had scouted, but whose trail is not completed. We stopped at 1700 and ate the piece of dried beef and the lard.

May 11

The vanguard left first. I remained to listen to the news. In a short while, Urbano came to inform me that Benigno had killed a wild pig and asked permission to make a fire and skin it. We decided to stop and eat the animal while Benigno, Urbano and Miguel went on cutting a path towards the lake. At 1400 we resumed the march, making camp at 1800. Miguel and the others went on ahead.

I must speak seriously with Benigno and Urbano, for the former ate a tin of fish on the day of the fighting but denied it, and I knew that Urbano had eaten a part of the *charqui* from Rubio's camp.

The news mentioned the promotion of Colonel Rocha, chief of the 4th Division which operates in the zone.

Altitude 1050 meters

May 12

We walked slowly. Urbano and Benigno opened the trail. At 1500 hours, we saw the lake about 5 kms. away, and soon after we found an old trail. Within the hour we came upon a tremendous field of calabash, but there was no water. We prepared a little roast and salted meat with lard and we also had some corn. We also prepared some roasted corn. The scouts arrived with the news that they had stumbled on Chico's house. The same one who is named in the newspaper as being a good friend of Lt. Henry Loredo. He was not home, but there were 4 peons there and a servant girl, whose husband came looking for her and was detained. She cooked us a roast pig with rice, and noodles and squash. Pancho, Arturo, Willy and Darío stayed to look after the knapsacks. The worst of it is, we still have not found any water, other than that at the house.

We left at 5:30, at a slow pace and with almost everybody sick. The owner of the house still had not returned and we left a note giving all the details of the expenses incurred. The peons and the servant were paid 10 pesos each for the work.

Altitude 950 meters

May 13

Day of belching, farting, vomiting and diarrhea: a real organ concert. We remained completely immobilized, trying to digest the pork. We have two cans of water. I was very sick until I vomited, and then I felt better. At night we ate some corn and roasted calabash, and the rest of the banquet from the day before; that is, those who were able to eat. All the radios were insistently broadcasting news about a landing of Cubans in Venezuela which had been frustrated. Leoni's government showed two men, giving their names and ranks. I don't know them, but obviously something went wrong.

May 14

We left early, but reluctantly, for Lake Pirirenda, by way of a trail that Benigno and Camba had found while scouting. Before leaving I called everyone together, and gave them a talk about the problems facing us; principally about the food situation. I criticized Benigno for having eaten a can of food and then denying it; Urbano for having eaten a *charqui* on the sly; and Aniceto for his eagerness to eat his share of the food, but for not being so willing to do his share in other matters. During the course of the meeting, we heard the sound of some trucks approaching. In a nearby hiding place, we hid some 50 bags of beans, and two hundred kilograms of corn harvested for our future needs.

When we were off the road, busy picking beans, we heard some shots nearby. Shortly after this, we heard planes searching for us, but they were about two or three kilometers from our position. We continued to ascend a little hill, and spotted the lake. Meanwhile, the police continued their shooting. At nightfall we came upon a house, which appeared to have been abandoned recently. It was well provisioned and there was water. We ate a delicious chicken fricasse with rice, and we remained there until 0400 hours.

May 15

An uneventful day.

May 16

When we started on the march I was ill with the most violent colic, vomiting and diarrhea. They stopped it with demerol, and I lost consciousness while they carried me in a hammock. When I awoke I was much relieved but dirtied all over like a nursing baby. They lent me a pair of pants, but without water my stench extends for a league. We spent the whole day there. I drowsed. Coco explored and found a road running south-north. At night we followed it while the moon was up, and then rested. Message No. 36 arrived, from which our total isolation can be inferred.

May 17

We continued marching until 1300, when we came upon a sawmill which bore signs of having been abandoned some three days ago. It had sugar, corn, lard, cornmeal and water in barrels, which apparently had been transported from a long distance off. Raúl has a sore on his knee which is intensely painful and prevents him from walking. He was given a strong antibiotic and tomorrow it will be lanced. We walked about 15 kilometers.

Altitude 920 meters

May 18

We spent the whole day in ambush in case the workers or the troops came. Nothing happened. Miguel went out with Pablito. They found water about two hours away from the camp on a crossroad. We did the operation on Raúl, drawing out 50 cc of purulent liquid. We are giving him general anti-infection treatments. He can hardly walk a step. I extracted my first tooth in this guerrilla band. Unwilling victim: Camba. Everything is going well. We ate some bread made in a small oven and, at night, we had a terrific soup which made me feel great.

May 19

The advance guard went out early, taking up position in the ambush at the crossroads. Later, we went out to relieve part of the advance guard while they returned to look after Raúl; and they carried him as far as the crossroads. The other part of the guard went on to the waterhole to leave the knapsacks, and returned to look after Raúl, who is recovering slowly. Antonio made a small exploration down the arroyo and found an abandoned police camp. Here too were found various supplies. The Nacahuasu cannot be too far away and I figure that we should emerge below the Congri arroyo.

It rained all night, surprising the experts. We have food for 10 days and in the nearby fields there are calabash and corn.

Altitude 780 meters

May 20

No movement today. The center remained in the ambush in the morning; and in the afternoon, the advance guard, which is still commanded by Pombo, who is of the opinion that the position chosen for us by Miguel is very poor. The latter explored downstream and found the Nacahuasu to be a two-hour walk away for a man without a pack. We heard a shot, but didn't know who was shooting. On the banks of the Nacahuasu are traces of another military camp, of probably two platoons. Had an incident with Luis, who protested against my orders not to go near the ambush. However, I think he took it well.

In a news conference, Barrientos denied Debray's status as a newspaperman, and announced that he would ask Congress for the death penalty. All the newspapermen and all the foreigners asked him about Debray. He answered with an incredible smokescreen of nonsense, the most ridiculous that one could imagine.

May 21

A quiet Sunday. We continue with the ambush, rotating 10 and 10 until midday. Raúl is slowly recovering. We lanced him again and removed about 40 cc's of pus. He no longer has fever, but he is in pain and can hardly walk. He is my main worry. In the evening, we ate soup, meal, *aporreado* [a Cuban dish], and calabash sprinkled with *mote*.

May 22

As one might expect, at midday Guzmán Robles, who is

in charge of the sawmill, arrived with a chauffeur and his son in a broken-down jeep. At first it appeared there was an Army scouting party checking to see what was happening, but then they passed by and he decided to leave for Gutiérrez that night, leaving his son as hostage; he would return tomorrow. The advance guard remained all night in the ambush, and tomorrow we will wait until 1500 hours, then it will be necessary to pull back, as the situation has become very dangerous. One gets the feeling that the man will not betray us, but we don't know about his ability to conduct himself discreetly without arousing suspicions. We paid him for all we consumed in Batay. He gave us information about the situation in Tatarenda, Limón and Ipita, where there are no police, except a Lieutenant at this last spot. His information about Tatarenda is secondhand, because he has not actually been there.

May 23

A tense day. The man in charge did not return the whole day, and even though there had been no activity we decided to pull out that night with the hostage, a boy of 17 years. We walked along the trail for an hour, by the light of the moon, and we slept on the trail. We left with enough food to last us 10 days.

May 24

In two hours we arrived at the Nacahuasu, which was free. We left, about 0400 hours, down the Congri River arroyo. We walked slowly, our progress determined by Ricardo's slow pace, and we were tense. In another hour, we arrived at the camp that we had used on the first day of our march on the first trip. We left no signs and did not see anyone. The radio announced that the petition of habeas corpus on Debray had been denied. I estimate that we are about one or two hours from the Saladillo; when we reach the top we will decide what to do.

May 25

In an hour and a half, we arived at the Saladillo without leaving tracks. We walked upstream about two hours to its source. We ate there and continued on at 1530 hours, walking another couple of hours until 1800, when we camped at about 1100 meters, still without having reached the plain. According to the boy, we still have a couple of leagues left until we reach his grandfather's shack; or, according to Benigno, a whole day's march to Vargas' house, on the Río Grande. Tomorrow we will make the decision.

May 26

After two hours of walking, reaching the crest at 1200 meters, we reached the hut of the boy's grandfather. There were two peons working there who must have been informed about us because they came walking toward us. They were brothers-in-law of the old man, who was married to a sister of theirs. Their ages: 16-20 years. They told us that the boy's father made the purchases but was arrested and confessed everything. There are 30 police in Ipita and they are patrolling the town. We ate a pig, fried in a kind of stew with lard because there was no water in the region and it is brought in drums from Ipita. After nightfall, we left for the hut which the boys had 8 kms away, four toward Ipita and four to the west. We arrived at dawn.

Altitude 1100 meters

May 27

Day of laziness and, a little, of despair. Of all the marvels that were promised, they only had a bit of old sugarcane and the mill was useless. As was to be expected, the old man who owned the hut came at midday with his cart, bringing water for the pigs. He looked strange as he was passing where the rearguard was lying in ambush, so they took him prisoner together with a peon. They were kept prisoner until 1800 hours when we let them go, together with the younger of the brothers, with orders to stay away from here until Monday and to keep their mouths shut. We marched two hours and slept in a cornfield, now oriented on the road which will take us to Caraguatarenda.

May 28

Sunday. We arose early and began our march. In an hour and a half, we were at the outskirts of the huts of Caraguatarenda and Benigno and Coco were sent to scout. But they were seen by a peasant, and they took him prisoner. In a little while we had a prison colony, with no signs of fear until an old woman began to scream, together with her children, at the top of their lungs, and neither Palo nor Pablo had any desire to take her prisoner. Continuing toward the village, we took it at 1400, taking up posts at both ends of the settlement. We found a jeep belonging to Yacimientos; altogether we seized two jeeps and two trucks, half privately owned and half belonging to Yacimientos. We ate something, drank coffee, and behind 50 men, left at 1930 for Ipitacito. There, we broke into a store and took 500 pesos' worth of merchandise, which we left in the custody of two peasants, issuing a very ceremonious receipt for them. We continued our peregrination, arriving at Italy, where they received us very well at a house where, as it turned out, the lady school teacher who owns the store in Ipitacita happened to be present and we paid the bill. It appears that they recognized me. They had a cheese and a little bread and gave us a cup of coffee, but there was a false note in the reception. We went on toward Espino, on the railroad line to Santa Cruz, but the truck, a Ford from which the front wheel drive had been removed, broke down and it took all morning to make 3 leagues from Espino. The motor of the vehicle burned out and halted altogether two leagues from the place. The vanguard took the ranch and the jeep made trips until all were transported.

Altitude 800 meters

May 29

The road from Espino is relatively new because the old one was washed out by the floods in 1958. It is a Guaraní community whose few interpreters speak, or pretend to speak, very little Spanish. Oilworkers were in the vicinity. We were able to pick up another truck in which we could load everybody, but the opportunity was muffed because Ricardo got it bogged down and it could not be pulled out. The silence was absolute, as though we were in a world apart. Coco was charged with collecting information about the roads, but what he brought was so deficient and contradictory that we were about to start on a rather dangerous day's travel that would take us near the Río Grande when, at the last moment, it was discovered that we should not go that way, but toward Muchiri, a place where there is water. Despite all our problems of organization, we left at 3:30, the vanguard in the jeep (6, 7 men with Coco) and the rest on foot.

The radio brings us the news of the escape of Loro, which took place in Camiri.

May 30

We reached the railroad line in daylight, discovering that the road that we had been told about, which would take us to Muchiri, did not exist. After a search, we found a straight road, 500 meters

from the crossing, which is used by the oilworkers, and the vanguard followed it in the jeep. When Antonio was coming back,
a young boy with a shotgun and a dog came along the railroad
track and, when told to halt, ran away. In view of this news, I
left Antonio in ambush at the entrance to the road, and we
moved away some 500 meters. At 11:45, Miguel appeared with
the news that he had walked 12 km toward the east without
finding houses or water; only a road that went off toward the
north. I gave him orders to scout, with three men in the jeep,
along that road up to 10 km to the north, and to return
before nightfall. At 1500, when I was sleeping placidly, I was
awakened by the sound of gunfire from the ambush. The news
came quickly. The Army had advanced and fallen into the trap.
The outcome appeared to be 3 dead and one wounded. Those
who took part were: Antonio, Arturo, Nato, Luis, Willy, and
Raúl; the last-named a slacker. We retired on foot, marching the
12 km. to the crossing without meeting Miguel. At that point, we
heard that the jeep had stalled for lack of water. We found it
about 7 kms from there; we all got in it together and, with a
canteenful of water, were able to get to the farthest point reached,
where Julio and Pablo were waiting. At 0200, everybody was
reunited there, around a fire over which we roasted 3 turkeys
and fried a piece of pork. We saved one animal in case we
should find water at the waterholes, by any chance.

We are going down from 750 meters. We are now at an
altitude of 650 meters.

May 31

The jeep went on bravely trying with our prayers and an occasional canteenful of water. Two things occured which changed all
this: the road which ran northward came to an end and so
Miguel called a halt to the march; and, on a side road, one of
the security groups detained a peasant named Gregorio Vargas,
who was coming along on his bicycle to set up some traps, which
is his trade. The attitude of the man was not entirely clear, but
he gave us valuable information about the waterholes. One of
them was behind us and I sent a group to find water and cook,
with him as their guide. As they were arriving, they saw two
Army trucks and set up a hasty ambuscade, felling at least two
men, it appeared. Nato, when his first round failed to fire off
his anti-tank grenade, dropped in another round and the device
exploded in his face, without doing him any damage personally

but destroying the weapon. We continued withdrawing, without any harassment from the planes, marching some 15 kms before we found the second waterhole after nightfall. The jeep gave its last stertorous wheezes from want of gasoline and from the overheating. We spent the night eating.

The Army released a communique admitting the ambush and that one soldier was killed yesterday, and attributing losses to us in the form of dead men who "had been seen." For tomorrow, it is my intention to cross the rail line, seeking the mountains.

Altitude 620 meters

ANALYSIS OF THE MONTH

The negative item is the impossibility of making contact with Joaquín, despite our peregrinations through the foothills. There are indications that he has gone toward the north.

From the military point of view, the new combats, causing losses to the Army without suffering any ourselves, in addition to the penetrations of Pirirenda and Caraguatarenda are auguries of success. The dogs have shown themselves to be incompetent and have withdrawn to civilization.

The most important characteristics are:

1) Total lack of contact with Manila, La Paz and Joaquín, which reduces us to the 25 men who comprise the group.

2) Complete lack of peasant recruitment, although they are losing their fear of us and we are beginning to win their admiration. It is a slow and patient task.

3) The party, through Kolle, offers its collaboration, it would appear, without reservations.

4) The clamor over the Debray case has given more belligerency to our movement than 10 victorious battles.

5) The guerrilla movement is acquiring a powerful morale, which, if well administered, is a guarantee of success.

6) The Army continues to fail to get itself organized, and its technique is not substantially improving.

The news of the month is the capture and escape of Loro, who now should be rejoining us or heading for La Paz to make contact. The Army issued a communique announcing the arrest of all the peasants who collaborated with us in the Masicurí zone. Now comes the stage in which terror will be used against the peasants by both sides, although with different objectives. Our triumph will signify the qualitative change that is necessary for a leap in development.

June 1

I sent the vanguard to take up posts on the road and to scout as far as the intersection with the petroleum road, about 8 kms away. In the afternoon, excitement began to stir when we heard the radio report to the effect that bad weather had hindered operations on the preceding days, but that now they would be reinitiated. They gave a strange report of two killed and three wounded; one doesn't know whether this refers to old occurrences or new ones. After we ate, at 1700, we left in the direction of the railroad. We covered 7-8 kms without incident, marched 1½ kms along the railroad and took an abandoned lane which should lead to a hut 7 kms farther on, but by now everybody was tired and we slept half way there. On the whole trip, we heard only one distant gunshot.

Altitude 800 meters

June 2

The seven kms indicated by Gregorio were put behind us and we reached the hut. There, we caught a robust pig. We killed it, but at that moment Braulio Robles's herdsman showed up, with his son and two peons. One of the peons proved to be Symuni, the owner's stepson. We used their horses to transport the quartered hog the 3 kms to the arroyo, and we kept the four men there while we hid Gregorio, whose disappearance was known. As the center group arrived, an Army truck passed, with two little soldiers and some steel drums, an easy mark, but it was a day for laziness and eating pork. We spent the night cooking it and at 0300 we turned the four prisoners loose, paying them 10 pesos each for their day. At 0430 Gregorio departed. He was waiting to eat, and to be paid, and was given him 100 pesos. The water in this arroyo is bitter.

Altitude 800 meters

June 3

We left at 0630, along the left side of the arroyo, marching until 1200, at which time Benigno and Ricardo were sent to scout the road and they found a good place for an ambush. At 1300 we took up positions: Ricardo and I, each one with a group in the center; Pombo at one end; and Miguel, with all the vanguard, at the ideal point. At 1430 a truck loaded with pigs came by, which we let pass; at 1630, a pickup truck with empty bottles; at 1700, an Army truck, the same one that passed us yesterday, with two little soldiers wrapped in blankets in the bed of the vehicle. I did not feel up to shooting them, and my brain didn't work fast enough to take them prisoner, so we let it go by. At 1800, we lifted the ambuscade and continued down the road until we reached the arroyo again. Scarcely had we got there, when four trucks in convoy went by, and then three more, apparently without soldiers.

June 4

We continued marching along the side of the arroyo with the intention of making another ambush if favorable conditions presented, but we came upon a trail which took us westward and we followed it; then it continued through a dry ravine and turned south. At 1445 we stopped to prepare coffee and oatmeal at a little pool of muddy water; but it took so long, we made camp right there. In the night, the *surazo* [cold wind from the south] let loose a steady drizzle all night.

June 5

We left the trail and went on breaking a way through the brush under the constant "zing-zing-zing" of the *surazo*. We marched until 1700; we were 2½ hours breaking through the tangle of wild brush along the slope of the hill in this place. Fire became the great god of the journey. The day was a blank so far as food was concerned. We saved the brackish water in our canteens for tomorrow's breakfast.

Altitude 750 meters

June 6

After a meager breakfast, Miguel, Benigno and Pablito set out to cut a trail and to scout. At approximately 1400, Pablo returned with the news that they had come upon an abandoned hut with cattle around it. We set out and, following the arroyo, passed the hut and went on toward the Río Grande. From there, a scouting party was sent out with instructions to occupy any house that is near and isolated; it was done and the first information obtained indicated that we were about 3 km from Puerto Camacho, where there were about 50 soldiers. They are connected by a road. We spent the whole night cooking pork and *locro*. Today's march was not what we expected, and we set out, exhausted, at dawn.

June 7

We continued along at a dragging pace, leaving behind us

the better pasture lands, until our guide, one of the sons of the owner, announced that he could go no further. We continued along the sandy stretch until we came to another hut, which he had not spoken of, with some jars of cane, bananas and beans. So we took a jar of beans. Here, we made camp. The scout that was leading us began to complain of sharp pains in his chest. We do not know whether he is faking or not.

Altitude 560 meters

June 8

We moved the camp about 300 meters to avoid having to watch both the sandy stretch and the clearing around the hut (*chaco*). However, we later learned that the owner had not cut a trail, but always came by flatboat. Benigno, Pablo, Urbano and Leon went to try to hack a trail around the cliffs, but returned in the afternoon to report that it was impossible. I had to warn Urbano again about taking risks. We will load everything on a raft tomorrow, close to the cliffs.

There is news about the state of siege and the threat from the miners, but it is all hogwash.

June 9

We walked for two hours until we came to the cliffs. Nato was working away furiously at building a raft; but it took him too long and it didn't turn out well. It still hasn't been tested. I sent Miguel to try find another way out, but he failed. We caught a beautiful fish; Benigno did.

Altitude 590 meters

June 10

The raft, as was to be expected, could not handle more than three fieldpacks and this . . . [Che's ellipsis]. The swimmers dived in, but they could not do anything because of the cold; I sent for a flatboat which was at the prisoner's house, and Coco, Pacho, Aniceto and Nato left in it. Shortly thereafter mortar fire was heard and Nato returned with the news that they had clashed with the Army, which was on the other bank. According to all indications, our men were walking incautiously and were spotted. The police began firing, as usual, and Pacho and Coco began to fire without rhyme or reason, thereby alerting them. We decided to stay right where we were, and to begin our withdrawal tomorrow. The situation is a little uncomfortable if they decide to attack us in force because, at best, we would have to fall back through the waterless rocky terrain.

June 11

A very peaceful day. We stayed at the ambush but the Army did not advance; only a small plane flew over the zone for a few minutes. It may be that they will be waiting for us at Rosita. We trekked across the plain, almost to the hill. We'll be out of here by tomorrow. We have food for 5-6 days.

June 12

At first we thought that we could reach Rosita, or at least the Río Grande once more, so we began the trek. Upon reaching a small waterhole, we could see that it was going to be difficult so we stayed there, awaiting news. At 1500 we got another report that stated that there was another, larger waterhole; but it was impossible to go down there yet. We decided to stay here. The day began to get worse and, in the end the *surazo* gave us a cold and wet night.

The radio gives an interesting bit of news: the newspaper *Presencia* announced one man dead and one injured on the Army's side, in Saturday's encounter. This is very good and it is certainly true, insofar as it maintains the balance of encounters and deaths. Another communique announces three dead, and Inti, one of the guerrilla chiefs, among them. It also announced the foreign composition of the guerrilla group: 17 Cubans, 14 Brazilians, 4 Argentines, and 3 Peruvians. The Cuban and Peruvian figures are correct; we have to find out where they obtained the information.

Altitude 900 meters

June 13

We only walked for an hour to the next waterhole, because the scouts got neither to the Rosita nor the river. It is very cold. It is possible we'll get there tomorrow. We have light rations for five days.

The interesting thing is the political convulsion the country is in and the fabulous number of pacts and counterpacts there are. Rarely is the possibility of the guerrillas becoming a catalyst seen so clearly.

Altitude 880 meters

June 14

We spent the day at the cold waterhole, huddled around the

fire, awaiting news from Miguel and Urbano, who were the scouts. At 1500, we were to move out, but Urbano arrived late to tell us that he had come upon an arroyo and that he could see small patrols, and because of this he thought he could reach the Río Grande from there. We stayed there, eating the last of the porridge; we only have one ration of peanuts and three of *mote* [a kind of stewed corn preparation].

I am now 39 and am relentlessly approaching the age when I must think about my future as a guerrilla; in the meantime I am "complete."

Altitude 840 meters

June 15

We walked a little less than three hours in order to get to the banks of the Río Grande, at a place we recognized and which I estimate is about two hours from the Rosita. Nicolas, the peasant, says about three kms. We gave him 150 pesos and the opportunity to leave and he took off like a rocket. We stayed right there. Aniceto scouted and thinks that the river can be crossed. We ate peanut soup and a little *palmito,* boiled and salted, in lard. We have *mote* for only 6 days.

Altitude 610 meters

June 16

We had walked one kilometer when we saw the vanguard on the opposite bank. Pedro had crossed over to scout and had found the ford. We crossed over in icy water up to our waists and a fairly strong current, but found nothing new. An hour later we arrived at the Rosita where there were some old shoe prints, apparently left by the Army. We found that the Rosita River was deeper than we had supposed, and there are no signs of the trail shown on the map. We walked for an hour in the icy water and decided to camp in order to take advantage of the palmito and try to find the beehive that Miguel had found on a previous exploration. We did not find the beehive, and ate only the *mote* and palmito with lard. There is enough food (*mote*) for tomorrow and the day after. We walked about 3 km along the Rosita River and another 3 km along the Rio Grande.

Altitude 610 meters

June 17

We walked about 15 kms along the Rosita River in 5½ hours. On the way we crossed four arroyos, although the map showed only one, the Rio Abapocito. We have found a large amount of recent footprints. Ricardo killed a *hochi,* and with this and the *mote* we passed the day. There is enough *mote* for tomorrow but it is possible that we will find a house.

June 18

This evening we cooked the peanuts, having eaten all the *mote* at breakfast. At 1100, after 2½ hours of walking, we came upon a hut with corn, yucca, sugar cane, a mill to grind the cane, *jocos* and rice. We prepared a meal, without proteins, and sent Benigno and Pablito on ahead to scout. At 1400, Pablo returned with the news that they had come across a peasant whose hut is situated 500 meters from here, and behind him others could be seen who were captured when they came here. At night we changed camp, sleeping in the hut, situated close to the outlet to the road which comes from Abapó, about 7 leagues from here. Its houses are about 10-15 kms away, above the juncture of the Mosquera and Oscura Rivers, located on the latter.

Altitude 680 meters

June 19

We walked rather slowly for about 12 kms, and got to a ranch made up of three houses and with a few other families living there. A Galvez family lives two kilometers downstream, close to the juncture of the woods and the Oscura. The inhabitants have to be hunted down to be able to speak to them for they are like little animals. In general, they received us well, but Calixto, who was appointed Mayor by a military commission that passed by here a month ago, acted reserved and unwilling to sell us little things. At nightfall, pork vendors arrived, armed with a revolver and a Mauser rifle. They were passed by the outpost. Inti, who interrogated them, did not take their weapons away and Antonio, who kept watch over them, did it very carelessly. Calixto assured us that they were peddlers from Postervalle and that he knew them.

Altitude 680 meters

There is another river that flows into the Rosita River, according to my map of the area, and it is called Suspiro. No one lives along this river.

June 20

In the morning, Paulino, one of the boys from the hut downstream, informed us that the three men were not peddlers: one was a Lieutenant, and the other two were not peddlers either. He got the information from Calixto's daughter, who was his girlfriend. Inti went out with several men and gave them until 0900 to make the officer step out; otherwise they would all be shot. The officer stepped out immediately, weeping. He is a 2nd Lt. of the police that was sent with a *carabinero* and the teacher from Postervalle who came as a volunteer. A colonel, who is in Postervalle with 60 men, sent them. His mission entailed a long trip, for which they allowed him four days, including a patrol of other points along the Oscura. We considered killing them, but then I decided to send them back alive, with a severe warning on the rules of the war. Checking on how they could have gotten by, it was ascertained that Aniceto had left his post to go call Julio and they got by in his absence. In addition, Aniceto and Luis were found sleeping on their posts. They were given seven days kitchen duty and one without being allowed to eat the fried pork and stew that is being served until operations begin again. The prisoners will be stripped of all their belongings.

June 21

After two days of profuse dental extractions, in which I made famous my name of "Fernando-the-tooth-puller" (alias "Chaco"), I closed my "office" and we left in the afternoon, walking for a little over an hour. For the first time in this war, I was mounted on a mule. The three prisoners were taken along for an hour on the road to the Mosquera and stripped of all their belongings, including watches and sandals. We thought about taking with us Calixto, the mayor, as a guide along with Paulino; but he was sick, or pretended he was, and we left him with serious warnings that probably won't make much impression on him. Paulino has promised to go to Cochabamba with a message. He will be given a letter for Inti's wife, a coded message for Manila, and the four messages. The fourth details the composition of our guerrilla band, and clears up the unfounded rumor of Inti's death; it is the [space left blank by Ché]. We will try to establish contact with the city. Paulino pretended to come with us as our prisoner.

Altitude 750 meters

June 22

We walked about two hours leaving the Oscura River in order to get to a waterhole at a place named Pasiones. We consulted the map and everything indicated that we were no less than 6 leagues from Florida; or the nearest place where there were houses, Piray, where Paulino's brother-in-law lives. But he does not know the way. We thought we would keep on climbing the hill, but it is not worth it considering how far away we were.

Altitude 950 meters

June 23

We only walked about an hour in terms of real progress, because we lost the trail and we wasted all morning and part of the afternoon in trying to locate it, and the rest of the day in opening the trail for tomorrow. The eve of San Juan was not as cold as one might expect, considering its reputation.

Altitude 1850 meters

My asthma is seriously affecting me and there is little of my medicine left.

June 24

We walked 12 kilometers in all; actually about four hours. At some places the trail was good and could be seen, but at others we had to guess at it. We came down an incredibly steep cliff, following the footprints of some cattlemen who had been driving their herd. We set up camp at a waterhole on the lower slopes of El Duran Mountain (Cerro El Duran). The radio broadcast the news of the battle in the mines; one man had been killed.

Altitude 1200 meters

June 25

We followed the trail made by the cattlemen, without catching up with them. At mid-morning, we saw a pasture on fire and a plane flew over the zone. We didn't find out what the relationship was between these two things, but we continued onward. At 1600 we arrived at Piray, the home of Paulino's sister. Here there are three houses, one of which was abandoned, the second had no inhabitants and the third was the one in which Paulino's sister and her four children lived. Her husband was not there. He had left with Paniagua, the man from the other house, to go to Florida. Everything seemed perfectly normal. Paniagua's daughter lives about one kilometer from here, and we chose her house to set up camp in. We bought a lamb and butchered it immediately. Coco, Julio, Camba and Leon went on horseback to

Florida to do some buying but they have a total of about 120-130 in all. An old man named Favelon Coca owns the house.

The Argentine radio tells of the 87 victims. The Bolivians do not state a figure (Siglo XX). My asthma continues getting worse. Now I cannot sleep well.

Altitude 280 meters

[The Argentine radio referred to a bloody clash between striking miners and the Army at Siglo XX, one of Bolivia's most important mines, in the Potosí region.]

June 26

A black day for me. It seemed as though everything was going along quietly and peacefully and I had sent 5 men to relieve those in the ambush on the road to Florida, when shots were heard. We went quickly on our horses, and came upon a strange spectacle. In the midst of an intense silence, in the hot sun were the bodies of 4 soldiers lying on the sand of the river bank. We couldn't find the weapons as we didn't know the enemy's position. It was 1700 hours and we waited for nightfall to effect the rescue. Miguel sent word that he could hear sporadic firing on his left. It was Antonio and Pacho, but I gave the order not to shoot without being sure. Immediately, one could hear shots that seemed to come from both sides, and I gave the order to retreat as we could lose under those conditions. The retreat was delayed and news arrived that Pombo had been wounded in one leg and Tuma in the stomach. We took them quickly to the house to operate on them with the instruments that we had there. Pombo's wound was superficial and he only had a headache and was still mobile; but Tuma's wound had destroyed his liver and punctured his intestines, and he died during the operation. With his death I lost an inseparable comrade of many years' standing, whose loyalty survived every test, and whose absence I already feel almost like that of a son. When he fell, he asked that his watch be given to me, but since I was attending him he took it off and gave it to Arturo. That signified his desire that it be given to his son, whom he had never seen, as I had done with the watches of other dead comrades. I shall carry it with me through the war. We loaded the body on a pack animal and took it to be buried far from here.

We took two new prisoners: a *carabinero* lieutenant, and a *carabinero*. We gave them a lecture and we let them go in just

their undershorts. Because of a misinterpretation of my orders,
they were stripped of everything they had. We came out of it
with 9 horses.

June 27

After we had completed the painful job of badly burying
Tuma, we continued on our way, arriving at Tejeria strictly speaking, At 1400, the vanguard left on a 15 km trip and the rest of us
set out at 1420. The trip was long for the latter, who were caught
by darkness and had to wait for the moon, arriving at Paulino's
house at 2:30 where the first group had already arrived.

Altitude 850 meters

We returned two animals to the owner of the house in Tejeria,
a nephew of old lady Paniagua, to give to her.

June 28

We succeeded in getting a guide for 40 [pesos] who agreed
to lead us to the intersection of the road that led to Don Lucas'
house, where once before we had stayed in a house that had its
own water supply. We left late but the last ones, Moro and Ricardo,
were terribly late, and we didn't know where they were. We were
going along at an average of one kilometer an hour. The rumors
of the Army continue and some radio station spoke of three
dead and two wounded in a clash with guerrillas in the area
around Mosquera. It must be a reference to our encounter; but
actually there were four dead unless one of them managed to
escape death.

The house, of a certain Zea, was not inhabited, but it did
have some cows whose calves were corraled.

Altitude 110 meters

June 29

I had harsh words with both Moro and Ricardo for their late-
ness, especially with Ricardo. We then left with the packs on
the horses, Coco and Dario in the vanguard with Moro. Nato
took his own knapsack, as he is in charge of the animals. In
addition, Pombo's and mine were carried on a mule. Pombo
could manage very nicely on a mare. We set out for Don Lucas'
house, which is at an altitude of 1800 meters. He lives in this
house with his two children, one of them with a goiter. There
are two other houses, one of a sporadic laborer with hardly any-

thing in it; the other house is well equipped. The night was rainy and cold. The reports say that Barchelón is a half day's walk from here; but, according to the peasants who live along this trail, it is a very poor road. The owner of the house says differently: he says that it can be easily managed. The peasants came to see the people in the other house, and were detained on suspicion.

On the road I had a talk with our troops, which now consist of 24 men. I pointed out Chino as an example to the men, and I also explained to them again what a terrible loss the death of Tuma was for me; I had considered him almost like a son. I criticized the lack of self-discipline of the men, and the slowness of the march; and I promised to give the men more lessons so that what happened in the previous ambushes does not happen again: unnecessary loss of lives due to violation of duty.

June 30

Old man Lucas gave us his impression of some of his neighbors. That is, about those who had left the area because the Army is making its preparation for this area. One of the neighbors, Andulfo Díaz, is the Secretary General of the zone's Peasant Union, alleged to be a pro-Barrientos man; another is an old busybody that can be disregarded as he is a paralytic; another is a coward that might talk, according to his colleagues, wherefore I foresee complications. The old man promised to accompany us and help us to open the road to Barchelon; the two peasants followed us. We rested all day as it was very rainy and disagreeable.

On the political plane, the most important happening is the official statement by Ovando that I am here. He also said that the Army is battling the guerrillas, who are extremely well trained and have among them a Viet Cong commander, who has beaten some of the best U.S. troops. It is based on Debray's declarations, who, it seems, is talking more than necessary, although we cannot know what implications this might have, nor under what circumstances he made the statements. It is also rumored that Loro has been killed. They accuse me of being the instigator of the rebellions in the mines, as well as being responsible for the incident on the Nacahuasu River. Things are looking up, within a short time I will cease to be "Fernando-the-tooth-puller."

We received a message from Cuba in which they explain the

poor progress made by the guerrilla organizations in Peru, where they have hardly any arms nor men; but they put in a lot of money and they speak of a supposed guerrilla organization between Paz Estenssoro, and a Col. Seoane and someone called Ruben Julio, of the Pando area; they would be in [text damaged].

ANALYSIS OF THE MONTH

The negative aspects are: the impossibility of making contact with Joaquín; and the loss of our men, the loss of each of which constitutes a serious defeat, even though the Army does not know this. We have had two small battles during the month, causing the death of 4 Army troops and wounding three others, according to their own reports.

The most important items are:

1) The total lack of contacts, which leaves us with only 24 fighting men, and with Pombo wounded our movements have become very slow.

2) The lack of peasant recruits continues. It is a vicious circle: to get this enlistment we need to settle in a populated area, and for this we need men.

3) The legend of the guerrilla movement continues to grow. Now we are the super-men guerrillas.

4) Our lack of contact extends even to the Party; although we have tried to make a contact here through Paulino, which might work out.

5) Debray continues to be news, but now it is more related to my case. I now appear as the leader of this movement. We shall see what results from this step of the government, whether it will be negative or positive for us.

6) The morale of the guerrilla group continues to be good, and their willingness to fight keeps increasing. All the Cubans are excellent in combat, and we only have two or three lazy Bolivians.

7) Militarily the Army's action has been nil, but they are working on the peasants in a way that we must be very careful of as they can change a whole community into informers, either through fear of our aims or through trickery.

8) The massacre in the mines has cleared the picture for us; and if the proclamation can be spread, it will bring strong endorsements.

Our most urgent task is to establish contact with La Paz and get military supplies and a doctor. Also to enlist 50 or 100 more men from the town, although the number of combatants would be reduced in action to 10 or 25 men.

July 1

Before the day had cleared up completely, we went out toward Barchelon, which is Barcelona on the map. Old Lucas gave us a little help with mapping out the route but, despite our preparations, we found the route quite steep and slippery. The vanguard went out in the morning and we left at noon, spending the entire afternoon climbing up and down the little brook. We had to spend the night in the first clearing, except for the vanguard which was further ahead. I talked with three children surnamed Yepez who were extremely timid.

Barrientos held his press conference, and while admitting my presence in Bolivia predicted that I would be liquidated in a few days. He repeated the usual comments calling us rats and snakes and reiterated his determination to punish Debray.

Altitude 1550 meters

We detained a peasant named Andrés Coca whom we encountered on the road and we took him with us together with the other two: Roque and his son Pedro.

July 2

In the morning we rejoined the vanguard which had camped higher up in Don Nicomedes Arteaga's house; where there is an orange grove and they sold us cigars. The main house was further down, along the Piojera River and we went there; we were fed sumptuously. The Piojera flows along totally enclosed within a deep ravine and it can only be crossed by traveling on foot, descending toward the Angostura gorge; the exit is near Junta, another point along the same river, but across a rather high hill. This is important because it becomes the junction point for several routes. This place is only 950 meters high, and is much milder, weatherwise. Here one exchanges the ticks for the *mórigui*. The hamlet consists of Arteaga's dwelling and the houses of several of his sons; they have a small coffee plantation where men come to work in groups, and arrive from different nearby places. Now there are six peons from the San Juan area.

Pombo's leg is not healing quickly enough, due, probably, to the constant trips on horseback, but there are no complications and so far there is no fear of them.

July 3

We stayed there the entire day, trying to give Pombo's leg the longest possible time to rest. Purchases are becoming much more costly thereby causing the peasants to mix fear with self-interest and they obtain the things for us. I took some photos, which sparked everyone's interest; we shall see how they come out and how we enlarge them and send them to them: problems. An airplane passed over us during the afternoon, and during the evening someone spoke of the danger of a night bombardment, and everyone was going out at night until we stopped them, explaining to them that there was no danger. My asthma continues to be troublesome.

July 4

We walked the two leagues between us and la Junta slowly, arriving there at 1530 hours. A peasant named Manuel Carrillo who lives there received us in panic-stricken terror. We ate sumptuously, as has been customary during these past few days, and slept in an abandoned house. My asthma punished me severely and for the first time prevented me from sleeping.

Altitude 1000 meters

Two days ago seven soldiers passed by, coming from Filo and going in the direction of Bermejo.

July 5

The entire area, the families and their belongings, "mobilized themselves" to escape the Army's reprisals. All of us, with oxen, dogs, chickens, and people walked together toward Lagunillas, away from the Rio Piojera and taking instead its tributary, the Lagunillero, for a kilometer. Our guide was a very unhappy peasant named Ramon, whose family feels the fear which is common to this area. We slept on the edge of the path. Along the way, we met an uncle of Sandoval Moron who lives in San Juan and seems to be much more alert.

Altitude 1160 meters

July 6

We left early, traveling in the direction of Peña Colorada

and crossing an inhabited area which received us with terror. Towards evening, we arrived at Palomino, 1600 meters high, and began the descent toward a spot where there is a small grocery store in which we made some purchases in case of need. By nightfall we ended up on a highway where there is only one little house belonging to an old widow. The vanguard was not very successful in their takeover of the same due to indecision. The plan was to steal a vehicle that might come from Samaipata, ask about existing conditions, go to Samaipata with the driver of the vehicle; take over the DIC [Departamento de Investigaciones Criminales—Department of Criminal Investigation], buy some things at the pharmacy, continue on to the hospital, buy some canned goods, gasoline, and return.

The plan was changed because no vehicles arrived from Samaipata; we learned that they were not detaining vehicles in that area—that is to say, that the barrier was lifted—not down. Ricardo, Coco, Pacho, Aniceto, Julio and Chino were assigned for the action.

They safely stopped a truck that came from Santa Cruz, but another truck came along behind the first one and they had to detain it also; then a "give and take" began with a lady who did not want to let her daughter get out of the truck in which they were traveling; a third truck stopped to see what was happening and finally the road was blocked when a fourth vehicle had to stop because of everyone's indecision. Things were finally settled, and the 4 vehicles were parked along one side of the road. One of the drivers said they were stopping to rest when he was asked what was happening. The men left in a truck, arrived in Samaipata, first capturing two policemen, then Lieutenant Vacaflor, chief of the post. They made him give the password to the Sergeant and then they took over the barracks and ten soldiers in lightning action, after a brief skirmish and crossfire with one soldier who resisted but was shot down by Mausers and a ZB30 [a Czech lightweight submachine gun of 7.29 millimeters]. They then made the 10 prisoners climb into our truck, later leaving them, completely stripped of their clothing, one kilometer from Samaipata. In terms of getting supplies, the action was a failure; El Chino let himself be dominated by Pacho and Julio and bought nothing of any use and when buying medicines he bought nothing of the items necessary for me, even though he did buy the most essential medicines for the guerrillas. The action took place before the whole village and many travelers in such a way that the news will spread like fire. At two o'clock in the morning we were on our way back with the booty.

July 7

We walked without pausing to rest until we reached a sugar-cane field—one league away from Ramón's house—where there was a man who had received us pleasantly the previous time. Fear continues to prevail among the people; the man sold us a pig and was amiable, but he warned us that there were 200 men in Los Ajos and that his brother had just come from San Juan and told him that there were 100 soldiers there. He wanted to have some teeth pulled, but he preferred not to get this done. My asthma is getting worse.

July 8

We walked from the house in the sugar-field to the Piojera River, taking every precaution, but everything was all right; there were not even rumors about soldiers, and people returning from San Juan denied that there were soldiers there. It seems that this was a trick played on us by the man in the sugar-cane field so that we would leave. We walked some two leagues further along the river to the Piray and from there one league more to the cave, which we reached at nightfall. We are near Filo.

I gave myself various injections in order to continue, finally using a solution of adrenalin prepared as an eyewash. If Paulino has not accomplished his mission, we will have to return to Nanca-huasu to get medicine for my asthma.

The Army gave an account of the action, noting that one of their men was dead—this must have happened in the firefight. Ricardo, Coco and Pacho took the little barracks.

July 9

On setting out, we lost the path and spent the morning looking for it. At noon we followed a path that was not very clear; it brought us out to the highest point we had reached so far— 1840 meters—but shortly afterwards it led to an abandoned house where we spent the night. We are not at all certain of the route to Filo.

The radio announced a 14-point agreement between the workers of the Catavi and Siglo XX mines and the Comibol firm; this constitutes a total defeat for the workers.

["Comibol," usually capitalized, is the abbreviation for Corporacion

Minera de Bolivia, the state authority which runs the country's nationalized mines.]

July 10

We left late because we lost a horse which turned up later. We went over the highest altitude, 1900 meters, via a route that was rarely used. At 1500 hours we reached an abandoned house where we decided to spend the night, but a disagreeable surprise awaited us, for the path ended right there. Some abandoned footpaths were explored, but they also led nowhere. Some huts which might make up the village of Filo can be seen in front of us.

The radio announced a skirmish with guerrillas in the El Dorado area, which is not shown on the map but it is located between Samaipata and Río Grande; the Army reported that one of its members was wounded, and attributed two deaths to our force.

On the other hand, the statements made by Debray and El Pelado were not good; above all, they had admitted the intercontinental objective of the guerrilla band, a thing they did not have to do.

July 11

Returning on a rainy day, in deep fog, we lost all the paths, and were completely separated from the vanguard which was descending by reopening an old footpath. We killed a small calf.

July 12

We spent all day waiting for news about Miguel, but it was only at nightfall that Julio arrived with word that Miguel had gone down an arroyo that went in a southerly direction. We remained where we were. My asthma is giving me a pretty rough time.

Now the radio is broadcasting more news which appears to be true in its most important parts; it tells of a fight in the Iquiri, with one death among our forces; his corpse was taken to Lagunillas. The information given about the body indicates that there is something true in the account.

July 13

In the morning we went down a steep hill which was slippery as a result of the bad weather; we found Miguel at 11:30. He had sent Camba and Pacho to explore a bypath branching out from the path following the course of the arroyo, and they returned an hour later with the news that they had seen several small clearings and houses and that they had been in an uninhabited clearing. We went over there and later, following the course of a small arroyo, reached the first house, where we stopped for the night. The owner of the house arrived later and told us that a woman, the mother of the mayor, had seen us, and had undoubtedly already informed the soldiers at Filo's ranch one league away from us. We mounted guard all night.

July 14

It was a night of continuous heavy showers which continued during the entire next day, but at 12 o'clock we went out taking with us two persons who know the area: Pablo, brother-in-law of the mayor, and Aurelio Morilla, the man in the first house. The women continued crying. We reached a point where the path split into two bypaths, one going to Florida and Moroco, the second to Pampas. The guides proposed following the bypath to Pampas where a recently opened shortcut could be taken to El Mosquem, and we accepted this suggestion, but when we had walked some 500 meters a young soldier and a campesino appeared, along with a horse carrying flour; they also carried a message for the second lieutenant in Filo from his colleague in Pampas, where there are 30 soldiers; we decided to change direction to advance along the road to Florida, making camp very shortly afterwards.

The PRA and the PSB withdrew from the revolutionary front and the campesinos warned Barrientos of a possible alliance with the Falange. The government is disintegrating rapidly, it is a shame that we do not have 100 more men at this moment.

[The PRA is the Partido Revolucionario Auténtico, the PSB, Partido Socialista Boliviano, two small parties which were part of the multiparty coalition supporting President Barrientos. The Falange is the Falange Socialista Boliviano, which started out as a Spanish-style Fascist party but in recent years has been veering leftward.]

July 15

We walked very little because the path was so bad, it had been abandoned many years ago. At Aurelio's suggestion, we killed a cow belonging to the magistrate, we ate sumptuously. My asthma is a little better.

Barrientos announced Operation Cynthia to liquidate us in a few hours.

July 16

We began the march very slowly due to the strenuous work of clearing away the shrubs and underbrush; the animals suffered a great deal because of the roughness of the trail, but the journey ended, without any major incidents, when we arrived at a deep canyon which the horses could not descend with their heavy loads. Miguel and four men of the vanguard continued on ahead, and slept apart from us.

There was no news of any importance on the radio. We are at an altitude of 1.600 m., near the peak named El Duran, which is on our left.

July 17

We kept on walking slowly, because the path is so unmarked. We hoped to reach an orange grove that the guide had mentioned but, on arrival, found only dead trees. There is a waterhole, around which we camped. We were not actually able to travel more than three hours. My asthma is much better. It seems that we will arrive at the junction point which we use to reach Piray. We are alongside El Duran.

Altitude 1560 meters

July 18

After walking for one hour the guide lost the route and claimed that he no longer knew the way. Finally, an old footpath was found and, while it was being cleared, Miguel went on ahead cutting through the bush and reached a crossroad, thus finding the route to Piray. On reaching a small arroyo in which we camped, we freed the three campesinos and the young soldier, after giving them a lecture. Coco left with Pablito and Pacho to find out whether Paulino had left anything in the cave; they should return tomorrow night if everything has been properly calculated. The young soldier says that he is going to desert.

Altitude 1300 meters

July 19

We made the short trek to the old campsite and stayed there, reinforcing the guard, while awaiting Coco's return; he arrived sometime after 18:00 hours, announcing that there was no change in the cave; the rifle was in place and there were no traces of Paulino. On the other hand, there were many traces of the passing of troops, who had also left signs along the part of the road where we now are.

The political news indicates a tremendous crisis, and there is no way to determine how it will turn out. In the meantime, the agricultural syndicates of Cochabamba have formed a political party "of Christian inspiration" which supports Barrientos and the latter is asking that "he be allowed to govern for four years"; it is almost a plea. Siles Salinas threatens the opposition that our rise to power will cost them all their heads, he calls for national unity, declaring that the country is on the brink of war. He appears to be imploring on the one hand and ranting on the other; perhaps a replacement is being prepared.

July 20

We walked along with great caution until we reached the first two houses, where we met one of the Paniagua brothers, and Paulino's son-in-law. They knew nothing about Paulino except that the Army was looking for him because he had acted as a guide for us. The tracks which were seen appear to have been made by 100 men who passed by about a week after we did, and continued on to Florida. It seems that the Army suffered three dead and two wounded in the ambush. Coco, Camba, Leon and Julio were sent to explore Florida and to buy what they could find there. At 4 the group returned with some provisions and a certain Melgar, the owner of two of our horses, who offered us his services and gave us some detailed, if somewhat imaginary, information, from which we extracted the following: 4 days after our departure, Tuma's corpse, eaten by animals, was discovered; the Army began advancing one day after the fight, after the reappearance of the nude lieutenant; everything, down to minute details and extra-added ones, is known about the action at Samaipata, and is the subject of jokes among the peasants; Tuma's pipe and some scattered belongings were found. A Major named Soperna seems to be either semi-sympathetic to us, or an admirer of ours; the Army arrived at Coco's house, where Tuma had died, and from there went on to Tejeria returning to Florida. Coco was thinking of using the man to deliver a letter but it seemed to me more prudent to test him first by sending him to buy some medicines. This Melgar told us of a group that was coming towards us, there was a woman in the group, and he had learned this in a letter from the mayor of Río Grande to the mayor in this place; as the man could possibly mean the messenger carrying the letter mentioned was on the way to Florida, we told Inti, Coco, and Julio to interview him. He denied having news of any other groups but confirmed, in general, the statements of the other. We spent a "bitch of a night," because of the rain. The radio announced the identification of the body of the dead guerrilla, as Moisés Guevara, but during a press conference, Ovando had very little to say about this, and put the responsibility for the identification of the corpse on the Ministry of the Interior. It may be possible that the supposed identification is a farce, or even invented.

July 21

We spent a calm day. We talked to the old man Coca, about the cow he had sold us that did not belong to him; later the old man said he had not been paid for it, and emphatically denied the fact. We ordered him to pay for it. In the evening we went to Tejeria, buying a big pig and some *chancaca* [similar to molasses]. Inti, Benigno, and Aniceto, who were the ones who had gone there, were very well received by the people.

July 22

We left early with great numbers of men and animals and the intention of alerting everybody to the reality of our presence. We left the road that leads to Moroco and took the one along the lagoon about one or two kilometers to the northwest. We did not know exactly the rest of the way and sent Pombo. In the meantime Mancilla and the Paniagua boy appeared around the lagoon grazing cattle. They were warned not to say anything but now the situation is very different. We walked for a couple of hours sleeping at the edge of a creek that has one path towards the northwest, following the stream's course, and another, less marked path towards the south.

The radio reports the news that the wife of Bustos (Pelao) confirmed that he saw me here, but says that he came with other intentions.

Altitude 640 meters

July 23

We remained at the same camp while the two possible roads were being explored. One of them leads to the Rio Seco at a point where it gets water from the Piray which is not yet absorbed by the sand, that is, between our ambush site and Florida; the other one leads to an abandoned house some 2-3 hours away, and according to Miguel who did the exploring, from there it is possible to reach the Rosita. Tomorrow we shall take that road, which may be one of Melgar's paths, according to information he gave Coco and Julio.

July 24

We walked some 3 hours following the explored path which led us over altitudes of 1,000 ms., camping at 940 ms. at the edge of a creek. Here the paths ended and tomorrow the whole day has to be spent in search of the best way out. There is a series of clearings in succession which indicates their relation to Florida; this could be the place called Canalones. We are trying to decode a long message from Manila.

Raul spoke to the graduating officers of the Maximo Gomez School and, among other things, refuted the arguments of the Czechs about the article on the Vietnams. The friends call me a new Bakunin and deplore the blood that has been shed and that which will be shed if there are 3 or 4 Vietnams.

July 25

We spent the day resting, having sent three groups to explore different areas; Coco, Benigno and Miguel were in charge of doing this. Coco and Benigno came out at the same place and from there the road to Moroco can be taken. Miguel reported that the creek definitely leads to the Rosita and that it is possible to walk along it although the way has to be cleared with *machetes*.

Two actions were reported, one in Taperillas and another in San Juan del Potrero, which could not have been carried out by the same group, and doubt continues as to whether this really happened and what the true facts are.

July 26

Benigno, Camba and Urbano were commissioned to make a path along the creek, avoiding Moroco, the rest of the personnel stayed at the camp and the center lay back in ambush. Nothing happened.

The news of the action at San Juan del Potrero was broadcast by foreign radio in great detail: the capture of 15 soldiers and one colonel, despoiled and set free: our technique. That point is on the other side of the Cochabamba—Santa Cruz highway.

In the evening I gave a short lecture on the meaning of the

July 26th rebellion against the oligarchies and against the revolutionary dogmas. Fidel made some mention of Bolivia.

July 27

We had everything ready to leave and the people in ambush had received instructions to carry it out promptly at 11, when a few minutes before that time Willy arrived saying that the Army was there, Willy, Ricardo, Inti, Chino, Leon and Eustaquio went there, and together with Antonio, Arturo and Chaparo, took action, which developed as follows: 8 soldiers appeared on the hill, walked toward the south following a blind road and returning lifting some mortars, making signals with a rag. At one point we heard one Melgar being called. He could be the one from Florida. After resting for a while the 8 soldiers began walking toward the ambush. Only four fell in it because the others were proceeding apart. Three were surely killed and the fourth one if not killed was at least wounded. We withdrew without taking their weapons and equipment because it became difficult to take them, and we left down stream. Where the stream met another little canyon, we laid a new ambush; the horses went as far as the road.

My asthma hit me hard and the supply of sedatives is getting low.

Altitude 800 meters

July 28

I sent Coco with Pombo, Raul and Aniceto to cover the mouth of the river which we believe is the Suspiro. We walked a little, opening the path through a rather narrow canyon. We camped apart from the vanguard because Miguel had gone too fast for the horses whose legs sank in the sand or were hurt by the rocks.

July 29

We kept on walking through a canyon which goes down toward the south with good shelter along the sides in an area with plenty of water. At approximately 16 hours we met Pablito who told us that we were at the mouth of the Suspiro; for a moment I thought that canyon could not be the Suspiro because of its southernly direction, but on the last bend it turned westward and led to the Rosita. The rearguard arrived at approximately 16:30 and I decided to continue the journey to get away

from the mouth of the Suspiro River. At night I let Chino have
the floor so that he could talk about the independence of his
country (28 July) and after that I explained why the camp was
poorly located, giving instructions to rise at 5 and leave to follow
Paulino's clearing.

Radio Havana reported an ambush in which the Army suffered some casualties which were rescued by helicopter, but
radio reception was not good.

July 30

My asthma kept me awake all night. At 4:30 as Moro was
making coffee he reported seeing a lantern across the river. Miguel,
who was awake because he had changed guards, and Moro
went to detain the wanderers. From the kitchen I heard:

"Who goes there?"

Trinidad Detachment. Right then the shooting began. Miguel
was bringing an M-1 and a cartridge-belt from one of the
wounded and the news that there were 21 men on the way to
Abapo and 150 in Moroco. We caused them more casualties
but were unable to determine these because of the confusion
that ensued. It took long to load the horses and Negro was lost
with the hatchet and a mortar that had been captured from the
enemy. It was almost 6 o'clock and more time was lost because
some bundles fell. The result was that in the last crossings we
were under fire by the soldiers who had become very bold.
Paulino's sister was in the clearing. Quite calmly she told us
that all the men in Moroco had been arrested and were in La Paz.

I hurried the men and went with Pombo, again under fire, to
the river canyon where the road ends and where the resistance
could be organized. I sent Miguel to take the lead with Coco
and Julio while I led the men on horseback. Covering the retreat,
there remained 7 men of the vanguard, 4 of the rearguard and
Ricardo, who fell back to reinforce the defense. Benigno, with
Pablo and Camba were on the right edge; the rest were coming
along the left. I had just given the order for resting at the
first opportune moment when Camba arrived with the news
that Ricardo and Aniceto had been hit while crossing the river.
I sent Urbano, Nato, and Leon with two horses, and sent for
Miguel and Julio, leaving Coco as forward watch. They crossed
without receiving my instructions and shortly thereafter Camba
reported that the soldiers had overtaken his group together with
Miguel and Julio, that the soldiers had greatly advanced, and that

he had returned to get instructions. I sent Camba again plus Eustaquio and only Inti, Pombo, Chino and I remained. At 13 hours I sent for Miguel, leaving Julio as forward watch and I withdrew with the group of men and the horses. While approaching Coco's lookout, they came to us with the news that the survivors showed up, Raúl had been killed and Ricardo and Pacho were wounded. The developments were as follows: Ricardo and Aniceto foolishly crossed an open space, the former got hit, Antonio organized a line of fire and between Arturo, Raúl, Aniceto, and Pacho rescued them, but Pacho was wounded and Raúl was killed by a bullet through his mouth. The withdrawal was very difficult. The two wounded men had to be dragged and there was little collaboration from Willy and Chapero, especially the latter. Later they were joined by Urbano and his group with the horses and by Benigno with his men, leaving the other wing unprotected, for which reason Miguel was overtaken. After an arduous march through the woods they came out on the river and joined us. Pacho came on horseback but Ricardo was unable to ride and he had to be carried in a hammock. I sent Miguel with Pablito, Dario, Coco and Aniceto to follow the outlet of the first brook on the right side, while we treated the wounded. Pacho has a superficial wound through his buttocks and the skin of of his testicles, but Ricardo was gravely wounded and the last plasma has been lost in Willy's knapsack. At 22:00 Ricardo died and we buried him near the river in a hidden spot, so that the police will not find him.

July 31

At 4, we left by way of the river and after crossing a short-cut, we went downstream without leaving tracks, arriving in the morning at the brook where Miguel, who had not understood instructions, lay in ambush and had left tracks. We walked some 4 kilometers upstream and went into the forest, erasing our tracks and camping near a tributary of the brook. At night I explained the mistakes of the action: 1) poor location of the camp; 2) poor timing which permitted them to shoot at us; 3) overconfidence which resulted in the loss of Ricardo and later Raúl in rescuing him; 4) lack of determination to salvage all the impedimenta. We lost 11 knapsacks containing medicines, binoculars and equipment such as the tape recorder used for copying the messages from Manila, Debray's book with my notations, a book by Trotsky, not to mention the political significance that the capture of these items has for the government and the confidence that it gives the soldiers. We calculate their casualties were approximately 2 killed and 5 wounded, but there are two contradictory reports: one from the Army reporting 4 dead and 4 wounded on the 28th. Another report from Chile mentions 6 wounded and 3 killed on the 30th. The Army later put out another report saying they had picked up their dead and that a sub-lieutenant was out of danger. Of our dead, Raúl hardly needs to be counted. He was an introvert, not much of a fighter or worker; however, he was continually interested in the political problems though he did not ask questions. Ricardo was the most undisciplined one of the Cuban group and the one that had the least determination in facing daily sacrifices, but was an extraordinary fighter and an old comrade in adventure during Segundo's first failure in the Congo and now here. With this loss there are only 22 of us left including two wounded men, Pacho, Pombo, and I with my asthma going at full speed.

ANALYSIS OF THE MONTH

The negative aspects of last month prevail, including the failure to make contact with Joaquín and the outside, and the loss of men; we are now 22 men, three of whom are disabled, including myself. Thus our mobility has decreased. We have had three clashes including the capture of Samaipata inflicting Army casualties of 7 killed and 10 wounded, approximate figures in accordance with confirmed reports. Our losses were 2 men killed and one wounded. The most important features are:

1) We are still completely out of contact.

2) The peasantry still is not joining us, although there were some encouraging signs from some peasants we know.

3) The legend of the guerrillas is acquiring continental dimensions; Onganía closes the border [of Argentina]; Peru is taking precautions,

4) The attempt to make contact through Paulino failed.

5) The morale and fighting experience of the guerrilla increases after each clash; Camba and Chapaco are still lazy.

6) The Army is still ineffective but some units appear to be more combative.

7) The political crisis in the government is getting worse but U.S.A. is giving small loans which on the Bolivian level are a great help and temper discontent.

The most urgent tasks are: To establish contacts, increase the capabilities of the combatants, obtain medicines.

[Ongañía is General Juan Carlos Ongañía, President-dictator of Argentina.]

August 1

A quiet day. Miguel and Camba began the footpath but did not go more than one kilometer because of the difficult terrain and vegetation. We killed a wild pony which should provide us with meat for 5 or 6 days. Small trenches were dug to prepare an ambush for the Army should it come through here. The idea is, if they should come tomorrow or the day after and do not discover the camp, we will let them through, then shoot them down.

Altitude 650 meters

August 2

The trail seems to have gone well, thanks to Benigno and Pacho who followed it through. It took them nearly 2 hours to return to camp from the end of the road. No further news about us since the radio reported the transfer of the body of an "antisocial." My asthma has been very good and I already used up the last antiasthmatic injection. I only have tablets for about 10 days.

August 3

The footpath was a failure; Miguel and Urbano took 57 minutes to return; we are going at a very slow pace. There is no news. Pacho is recuperating—whereas I am not well; I have had a difficult day and night, and there is no immediate relief in sight. I tried the intravenous novocaine injection, but to no avail.

August 4

The men arrived at a canyon which runs southwest and may empty into the arroyos that lead to the Rio Grande. Two pairs of men will go out tomorrow to check this and Miguel will explore what appear to be abandoned fields. My asthma subsided a little.

August 5

Benigno, Camba, Urbano, and Leon left in pairs to make more

progress, but they ended up at an arroyo which empties into the Rosita, and they continued crosscountry. Miguel went to explore the field but could not find it. The horse meat has been used up. Tomorrow we shall try fishing and day after tomorrow we shall kill another animal. Tomorrow we shall go up to the new water site. My asthma was implacable. Despite my strong feeling against a split-up, I will have to send a group ahead. Benigno and Julio volunteered to go. I still have to determine Nato's attitude.

August 6

We moved the camp; unfortunately it was a 3-hour journey instead of one hour, which means that we are still far away. Benigno, Urbano, Camba, and Leon continued to chop, while Miguel and Aniceto went to scout the new arroyo up to where it joins the Rosita. By night they had not returned, for which reason we took precautions, especially since I had heard something like the distant sound of a mortar. Inti, Chapaco, and I said a few words regarding today, the date of Bolivian independence.

Altitude 720 meters

August 7

At 11 in the morning I had given Miguel and Aniceto up for lost, having instructed Benigno to go up cautiously to the outlet of the Rosita to explore the direction which they took, if they had gone that far. However, at 13 hours the lost ones appeared. They simply had encountered difficulties along the way and it had gotten dark before they reached the Rosita. Miguel certainly had me worried. We remained in the same place, but the explorers found another arroyo and we shall move towards it tomorrow. Anselmo, the old horse, died today and we have only one left; my asthma continues and the medicines are running low. Tomorrow I shall determine whether a group should be sent to the Nacahuasu. On this date it is exactly 9 months since the guerrilla was formed and we arrived. Of the first six men, two are dead, one has disappeared, two are wounded, and I with a case of asthma which I am unable to control.

August 8

We walked for about one hour, which to me seemed like 2 hours because my mare was tired. At one point I stabbed it in the side, making a big gash. The new camp must be the last one in which there is water before arriving at the Rosita or the Río

Grande. The *macheteros* are some 40 minutes from here (2 or 3 kilometers). I assigned a group of eight men to carry out the following mission: They will leave from here tomorrow and walk all day. The following day Camba will return to report on their findings. The day after that Pablito and Dario will return to report. The other five will go on to Vargas' house, and from there Coco and Aniceto will return to report on the house. Benigno, Julio and Nato will go to the Nacahuasú to get my medicines. They are to take every precaution to avoid an ambush. We will follow them, and the meeting points will be: Vargas' house or further up according to how fast we can travel; the arroyo which is in front of the cave in the Rio Grande; the Masicurí, or the Nacahuasú. There is a report from the Army that they have discovered an arms cache in one of our camps. At night I got the men together and made the following admonition: We are in a difficult situation; Pacho is recovering but I am a mess and the incident of the mare indicates that there are moments in which I lose control of myself; that will change, but we must all share alike the burden of the situation and whoever feels he cannot stand it should say so. This is one of those moments in which great decisions must be made, because a struggle of this type gives us the opportunity to become revolutionaries, the highest step in the human ladder and also allows us to test ourselves as men. Those who cannot measure up to these two requirements should say so and abandon the struggle.

All the Cubans and some Bolivians said they would continue to the end. Eustaquio did likewise, but he made some criticism of Mugamga for having the mule carry his pack instead of carrying firewood. This brought about an angry rejoinder from the latter. Julio castigated Loro and Pacho for the same thing, and there was another angry retort, this time by Pacho. I ended the discussion by saying that two things of very different categories were being debated, one of which was whether or not we were willing to continue; the other one deals with small quarrels or internal problems in the guerrilla group, which detracts from the significance of the larger decision. I did not like the statements of Eustaquio and Julio, nor the responses of Moro and Pacho. In short, we had to be more revolutionary and more men of exemplary conduct.

August 9

The eight scouts left in the morning. Miguel, Urbano, and

Leon, the *macheteros,* proceeded another 50 meters away from the camp. I had a carbuncle in my heel lanced and now I can put my foot down, but it is very painful and I have a fever. Pacho is doing very well.

Altitude 783 meters

August 10

Antonio and Chapaco went hunting and caught a *visna* and a turkey. They explored the first camp, found nothing unusual, and brought back a load of oranges. I ate two and immediately I suffered an asthma attack but it was mild. Camba, one of the eight, arrived at 10 hours with the following report: yesterday they went to sleep without having had water and today they still have not found any. Benigno has explored the place and will set out toward the Rosita to look for water. Pablo and Dario will come back only if water is found.

Fidel made a long speech attacking the traditionalist parties, especially the Venezuelan. It seems that the behind-the-scenes fight was a big one. My foot was treated again; I am improving but I am not well. Nevertheless, tomorrow we should leave to get our base closer to the macheteros who progressed only 35 minutes in the entire day.

August 11

The *macheteros* are going very slowly. At 16 hours Pablo and Dario arrived with a note from Benigno reporting that he was near the Rosita and estimated it would take 3 more days to reach Vargas' house. At 8:15 Pablito left the waterhole where they spent the night, and at approximately 75 hours he met Miguel, so that there is still a long way to go. Turkey seems to disagree with my asthma (I got a slight attack), so I gave it to Pacho, We moved our camp to another arroyo which disappears at noon and reappears at midnight. It rained, but it is not cold. There are many mosquitoes.

Altitude 740 meters

August 12

A gray day. The macheteros made little progress. Nothing unusual happened and the food supply was low. Tomorrow we shall kill another horse which should provide meat for 6 days. My asthma is in a bearable state. Barrientos has announced the decline of the guerrillas and again threatened with intervention in Cuba. He was as stupid as usual. The radio announced a clash near Monteagudo resulting in the death of one of our men: Antonio Fernández of Tarata. It sounds very much like Pedro's real name. Pedro is from Tarata.

August 13

Miguel, Urbano, Leon, and Camba set out to camp at the waterhole discovered by Benigno, and will continue from there. They are taking enough food to last them 3 days, pieces of Pacho's horse which we killed today. We have four animals left and it looks like another one will have to be killed before the food arrives. If all goes well, Coco and Aniceto should get here tomorrow. Arturo caught two turkeys which were put aside for me because there is practically no corn left. Chapaco appears increasingly unbalanced, Pacho is making good progress, and my asthma has gotten worse since yesterday; I am now taking three tablets a day. My foot is almost cured.

August 14

A black day. It was gray as to the activities and there was nothing new, but at night the radio announcer gave reports about the taking of the cave which our messengers were to go to, with details so precise that it is not possible to doubt it. Now I am doomed to suffer asthma for an indefinite time. They also took all types of documents and photographs of every type. It is the hardest blow they have ever given us; somebody talked. Who? That is what we don't know.

August 15

Early in the morning, I sent Pablito with a message to Miguel that he should take two men to fetch Benigno, provided Coco and Aniceto had not arrived, but he met them on the road and so the three came back. Miguel sent word that he would stay where the night overtook him and asked for some water. Dario was sent with the warning that early tomorrow we should by all means leave, but he came across Leon coming to tell us that the road was completed.

A radio broadcasting station in Santa Cruz mentioned that two men from the Muyupampa group were taken prisoners by the army, Now no doubt remains that this is Joaquín's group. They must be very harassed and, on top of that, those two prisoners talked. It was cold but I did not have a bad night; another abscess in the same foot must be cut open. Pacho already has been declared cured.

Another clash in Chuyuyako was announced, without any losses on the army's side.

August 16

We walked for 3:40 hours and rested one hour along a relatively good road; the mule threw me clear off the saddle when it got pricked by a stick, but I did not get hurt; my foot is getting better. Miguel, Urbano, and Camba continued hacking away and reached the Rosita. Today was the day when Benigno and his companions should have arrived at the cave, and the planes flew over the area several times. It may be that they left some tracks near Vargas or that troops are going down the Rosita or pushing forward along the Río Grande. At night I cautioned the men regarding the danger of the expedition and precautions were planned for the next day.

Altitude 600 meters

August 17

We left early, arriving at the Rosita at 9. There someone thought he heard two shots and we thought it was an ambush, but nothing happened, The rest of the journey was slow. Continually losing our way and guessing wrong, we arrived at the Río Grande by 1630 and camped there. I had thought of continuing the journey by moonlight but the men were very tired. We have horse meat for two days, and *mote* for myself for one day. It looks like we will have to kill another animal. The radio announced that documents and proofs found in the four caves in the Nacahuasú will be presented, which indicates that the "cave of the monkeys" was taken. Under the circumstances, my asthma is not bothering me too much.

Altitude 640 meters. (This seems illogical, since yesterday it was 600.)

August 18

We left earlier than usual but we had to cross four fords, one of them rather deep and cut paths in some places. In spite of all this we arrived at the arroyo at 16:30 and we camped there, the men collapsed to rest, dead tired. There was no more activity: There are thousands of mosquitoes in the area and it continues to be cold at night. Inti told me Camba wants to leave because according to him, his physical condition does not permit him to continue, in addition to which he sees no future in the struggle. Naturally, it is a typical case of cowardice and it would be an improvement to let him go, but now he knows our future route to try to meet with Joaquín and I cannot let him go. Tomorrow I will speak to him and Chapaco.

August 19

Miguel, Coco, Inti, and Aniceto went scouting to try to find the best road to Vargas' house. A military post seems to be there but there is nothing in it and it looks like we should follow the old trail. Arturo and Chapaco went hunting and they were able to get a *urina* and while Arturo was standing guard with Urbano he killed an anteater after making us all nervous, since it took 7 shots. It will provide meat for 4 days, the *urina* will provide for one and there is a reserve supply of beans and sardines; total: 6 days. It seems that the white horse, the next in line, has a chance to be spared. I talked to Camba, and told him he could not leave until after our next step, which is the meeting with Joaquín. Chapaco said he would not leave, for that was cowardly, but that he wants the hope of leaving within 6 months to a year. I gave it to him. He spoke incoherently. He is not well.

The news reports are full of Debray. There is no mention of the other accused. No news from Benigno. He should have been here by now.

August 20

The *macheteros,* Miguel and Urbano, and my "public works department" Willy and Dario made little headway, so we decided to stay here at least another day. Coco and Inti didn't kill anything but Chapaco killed a monkey and a *urina.* I ate some of the *urina* and at midnight I got a bad attack of asthma. The doctor is still sick with what seems to be lumbago which is draining his general state of health and making him an invalid. There is no news from Benigno. It has become a cause for concern. The radio reports the presence of guerrillas 85 kilometers from Sucre.

August 21

Another day in the same place and another day without news from Benigno and his comrades. Five monkeys were killed, 4 by Eustaquio and 1 by Moro at close range; the latter continues to suffer from lumbago, I injected him with meperidina. My asthma resented the *urina*.

August 22

At last we moved, but before we did the alarm was raised because a man was seen running on the riverbank. It turned out to be Urbano, lost. I gave the doctor an injection in the spine and he was able to continue his trip on the mare, although he arrived sore. He looks better. Pacho made the trip on foot. We camped on the right bank and there is little cutting to be done to have the road ready to Vargas' house. We still have anteater meat for tomorrow and the day after. As of tomorrow, we will not be able to hunt. There is no news from Benigno. They were separated from Coco 10 days ago.

August 23

It was a difficult day because we had to walk on the edge of a very steep cliff. The white horse refused to go on and they left him buried in the mud without even taking the bones. We reached a hunters' hut which seemed to have been occupied recently. We laid an ambush and captured 2. Their story is that they have 10 traps set and they went out to check them; according to them, the Army is at Vargas' house in Tatarenda, Carguatarenda, Ipita, Yamon and two days ago there was an encounter in Carguatarenda wtih one soldier wounded. It could have been Benigno, driven by hunger or the encirclement. The men announced that the Army would come tomorrow to fish, they are coming in groups of 15 to 20 men. We passed around some anteater meat and some fish which was caught with in baskets, I ate rice which settled very well; the doctor is a little better. It was announced that Debray's trial has been postponed until September.

August 24

Reveille was sounded at 5:30 and we headed for the stream we planned to follow. The vanguard began the march and it had gone a few meters when 3 peasants appeared on the other bank. Miguel and his group were called back and we all laid in ambush. Eight soldiers appeared. The instructions were to let them cross the river ford in front of us and to shoot as they approached: but the soldiers didn't cross. They confined themselves to walking around a few times and they passed within rifle range without us shooting at them. The captured civilians said they are only hunters. Miguel, Urbano, with Camba, Dario and Hugo Guzman, the hunter, were sent to follow a trail which heads west but whose end is unknown. We remained in ambush all day. At dusk the macheteros returned with the traps, they caught a condor and a rotten cat. Everything was eaten together with the last piece of anteater meat. The only things remaining are the beans and whatever is hunted.

Camba is reaching the last stages of his moral deterioration. He trembles at the mere mention of soldiers. El Médico is still in pain and giving himself talamonal. I am quite well but ravenous.

The Army issued a partial report to the effect that it had found another cave and that there were two wounded "caused by guerrillas." Radio Havana reported an unconfirmed battle in Taperillas resulting in one wounded soldier.

August 25

Very little new. Reveille was sounded at 5 and the macheteros left early. The Army got as close as a few steps from our position but did not try to cross. They seem to be calling the hunters with their shots. Tomorrow we will attack them if the opportunity arises. The trail did not advance sufficiently because Miguel wanted advice and sent a message with Urbano. He transmitted it wrong and at a time when nothing could be done.

The radio announced a battle at Monte Dorado, which seems to be Joaquín's area, and the presence of guerrillas 3 kilometers from Camiri.

August 26

Everything went wrong. Seven men came but 5 went down river and 2 crossed the ford. Antonio, who was in charge of the ambush, fired too soon and missed, allowing the two men to beat it back to get more reinforcements. The other five fled and Inti and Coco pursued them but the soldiers barricaded themselves and forced them back. While watching the chase, I noticed the bullets were hitting close, in fact, they were being fired from our side. I broke into a run and discovered Eustaquio had been shooting at them because Antonio hadn't told him what was going on. I was so raving mad that I lost my control and mistreated Antonio.

We left with little speed since the doctor could not keep up the pace well, while the Army was advancing from an island in front of us in numbers of 20 to 30. It wasn't worth it trying to face them. They may have 2 wounded, at most. Inti and Coco distinguished themselves by their decisiveness. Everything went well until the doctor became exhausted and began to hold back the march. At 1830 we stopped without having reached Miguel, who was nevertheless a few meters away and he made contact with us. Moro stayed in a ravine without being able to climb the last stretch and we slept apart in 3 groups. There are no signs that we have been followed.

Altitude 900 meters

August 27

The day was spent in a desperate search for an exit, the results of which are not yet certain. We are near the Río Grande and we have already passed Yaman, and according to reports, there are other river fords; in other words we could go there to continue by way of Miguel's cliff but it cannot be done with the mules. There is a possibility we could cross a small chain of mountains and then continuing on the Río Grande—Masicurí, but we will only know tomorrow if this can be done. We have crossed heights of 1,500 meters, about the highest peaks in the area, and we slept at 1,240 meters in very cold weather. I am very well but El Médico is quite ill and we have run out of water, with only a little left for the doctor.

The good news, rather, the happy event has been the return of Benigno, Nato and Julio. Their odyssey was long because there are soldiers in Vargas and Yumon and they almost clashed with them; then they followed some troops who went down the Saladillo and up the Nacahuasú and they discovered that the creek has three paths made by the soldiers. The Bear Cave, where they arrived on the 18th, is an anti-guerrilla camp with 150 soldiers. They were almost discovered there but they managed to retreat without being seen. They were in Chaco del Abuelo, where they were able to get *jocos,* the only thing available since everything is abandoned. They passed near the soldiers again and heard our shots. They slept nearby and later followed our tracks until they caught up with us. According to Benigno, Nato performed very well but Julio got lost twice and was a little afraid of the soldiers. Benigno believes that some of Joaquín's men were in the area several days ago.

August 28

A gray and rather miserable day. We quenched our thirst

with *panes de caracare,* which is actually a way to fool our throats. Miguel sent Pablito along with one of the hunters to look for water and other things. He only had a revolver. At 1630 he had not returned and I sent Coco and Aniceto to look for him. They did not return all night. The rearguard stayed at the point of descent and we could not listen to the radio. There seems to be a new message. The little mare was finally slaughtered after accompanying us for 2 distressing months. I made every effort to save her but our hunger was getting worse and at least now we are only thirsty. It looks like we will not reach water tomorrow either.

The radio reported a soldier wounded in the Tatarenda area. The mystery to me is this: Why, if they are so scrupulous in reporting their setbacks, are they going to lie about the rest of their reports? And if they do not lie, who is causing them casualties in places so far removed such as Caraguatarenda and Taperillas? Unless Joaquín is divided into two or unless there are new, independent areas of activity.

August 29

A difficult and frustrating day. The *macheteros* advanced very little and at one point they mistook the route thinking they were going toward Masicurí. We camped at an altitude of 1,600 m. in a relatively humid place which has a kind of cane whose pulp quenched our thirst. Some of the comrades, Chapaco, Eustaquio, and Chino are collapsing for lack of water. Tomorrow we shall have to map a route to wherever water seems to be nearest. The mules are bearing up very well.

There was no great news on the radio, only that Debray's trial is being prolonged from one week to the other.

August 30

The situation was becoming desperate. The macheteros suffered fainting spells, Miguel and Dario were constantly dizzy, so was Chino, with the unfortunate results of diarrhea and cramps. Urbano, Benigno, and Julio climbed down a canyon and found water. They told me the mules could not go down. I decided to stay with Nato but Inti came back up with water. The three of us sat there eating mule meat. The radio was left below so we did not hear the news.

August 31

In the morning Aniceto and Leon left to explore returning

at 16 hours with the news that there is enough room for the mules to pass from here on in. I saw it and the animals can pass so I instructed Miguel to cut a path for us down the last cliff tomorrow, then continue, making way for us further ahead and we will take the mules down.

There is a message from Manila but it could not be copied.

ANALYSIS OF THE MONTH

It was, without a doubt, the worst month we have had so far in this war. The loss of all the caves with the documents and the medicines was a hard blow, especially psychologically. The loss of two men in the latter part of the month and our subsequent march on a horse-meat diet demoralized the men, leading to the first case of desertion, Camba, which would constitute a net gain except under these circumstances. The lack of contact with the outside or with Joaquín plus the fact that the prisoners taken from Joaquín may have talked, also demoralized my force a little. My illness caused uncertainty in several others and all these factors were reflected in our only encounter in which we should have inflicted several casualties on the enemy but wounded only one. Finally, the difficult march through the hills without water brought out the worst in my men.

The most important factors:

1) We still have no contact of any kind and have no reasonable hope of establishing any in the near future.

2) We still have not incorporated the peasants, which is logical when one considers the little contact we have had with them in recent weeks.

3) There is a decrease, I hope temporary, in the fighting spirit.

4) The Army does not improve in effectiveness nor in combativeness.

We are in a period of low moral and revolutionary spirit. The most urgent tasks continue to be the same as last month, that is: Reestablish contacts. Enroll combatants. Supply ourselves with medicine and equipment.

I should mention that Inti and Coco are becoming ever more steadfast revolutionary and military cadres.

September 1

We took the mules down early, after a number of incidents

including a spectacular fall of the jack. The doctor is still not well but I am, and I walked perfectly, leading the mule. The way was longer than expected and only at 18:15 we realized that we were in the arroyo near the house of Honorato. Miguel continued at full speed but he was able only to reach the main road and it was already nightfall; Benigno and Urbano advanced with caution and noticed nothing abnormal, and so we took the house which was vacant. Several sheds had been added for the Army which happened now to be unoccupied. We found flour, lard, salt, and goats. We slaughtered two goats and had a feast with the flour, even though the cooking kept us on the alert all night. At dawn we went to bed, posting a man in the house and another at the road.

Altitude 740 meters

September 2

Early in the morning we withdrew to the *chacos,* leaving an ambush in the house with Miguel in charge with Coco, Pablo and Benigno. A lookout was left on the other side. At 8 Coco came to tell me that a drover had come looking for Honorato. They were four. He was told to have the other three come through. All this took time, since we were an hour away from the house. At 13:30 several shots were heard and then we learned that a peasant was coming, along with a soldier and a horse. Chino, who was on watch with Pombo and Eustaquio, shouted: "A soldier," and he cocked his rifle. The soldier fired at him and started running and Pombo fired, killing the horse. I threw a spectacular fit, because this is the utmost in ineptitude. Poor Chino is embarrassed to tears. We released the four men who had meanwhile come through, and two prisoners of ours, sending everybody up the Masicurí.

We bought a small bull from the drovers for 700 pesos and gave Hugo 100 for his work and 50 for some items we took from him. The dead horse turned out to be one they had left at Honorato's house because he was crippled. The drovers said that Honorato's wife had complained about the Army because they had beaten her husband and had eaten everything she had. When the drovers passed 8 days ago, Honorato was in Valle Grande recovering from a tiger's bite. Anyway, there was someone in the house, since we found a fire burning when we arrived. Because of Chino's error, I decided to depart that night, heading the same way as the drovers and trying to get to the first house, assuming that the soldiers would be few and that they would be in retreat,

but we departed too late and we only crossed the ford at 3:45
without finding the house and slept in a cowpath awaiting daylight.

The radio brought some ugly news about the annihilation of
a group of ten men led by a Cuban named Joaquín in the area
of Camiri. However, the news came over the Voice of America
and local radio stations have said nothing about it.

September 3

Today being Sunday, there was a clash. At dawn we went
down the Masicurí reaching its mouth, and then up the Río
Grande a little way. At 1300 hours, Inti, Coco, Benigno, Pablito,
Julio and Leon left to try to get to the house if the Army was
not there and to buy the merchandise which will make our life
more bearable. First the group captured two laborers who said
the owner was not in and there were no soldiers and that considerable foodstuff was available. Other reports: Yesterday five
soldiers galloped by without stopping at the house. Two days ago
Honorato went by on his way home escorted by his sons. Upon
arrival at the *latifundista's* house, they found that 40 soldiers had
just arrived. There was a confused encounter in which our men
killed at least one soldier, the one who had a dog with him. The
soldiers reacted, and surrounded them but then they withdrew
on account of the shouts; we were not able to get even a jug
of rice. The airplane flew over the area and fired some rockets,
apparently over the Nacahuasú. Other reports from the peasants:
They have seen no guerrillas in this area and they had their
first news from the drovers who passed through here yesterday.

Again the Voice of America gave more reports about clashes
with the Army and this time it named Jose Carrillo as the only
survivor of a group of ten men. Since this Carrillo is Paco, one
of the "dregs," and the annihilation took place in Masicurí, everything seems to indicate that it is a big mess.

Altitude 650 meters

September 4

A group of eight men under the command of Miguel set up
an ambush on the road from Masicurí to Honorato's until 13
hours without incident. In the meantime Nato and León were
bringing a cow with great difficulty, but then they were able to get
two magnificent oxen. Urban and Camba were walking about
10 kilometers upriver. Four fords have to be crossed. One is rather
deep. The young bull was killed and volunteers were requested

to go searching for food or information. Inti, Coco, Julio, Aniceto, Chapaco and Arturo went, under the command of Inti. Pacho, Pombo, Antonio and Eustaquio also offered their services. Inti's instructions are the following: Arrive at the house at dawn and observe the movement, get supplies if there are no soldiers; go around it and continue ahead if there are soldiers; and attempt to capture one; remember that the basic thing is not to lose any men. Extreme caution is recommended.

The radio reports one killed in a new clash at Vado del Yeso, near the place where the group of 10 men was annihilated, which makes the report about Joaquín appear like a fraud. On the other hand they gave the full physical description of Negro, the Peruvian doctor, killed in Palmarcito and transferred to Camiri. Pelado collaborated in the identification. This one seems to be an actual person killed. The others may be fictitious or some of the "dregs." Anyway, there is something strange about the trend of the reports, which have moved to Masicurí and Camiri.

September 5

There was nothing new today, just waiting for the results. At 4:30 the group returned, bringing a mule and some merchandise. In the house of the landowner Moron there were soldiers who almost discovered the group because of the dogs. They seem to move at night. They surrounded the house and then cut through the jungle toward Montaño's, where there was no one but there was some corn which was brought. At approximately 12 they crossed the river and they fell upon the houses on the other side, which turned out to be two. All the occupants escaped from one, and there they got the mule. There was very little collaboration in the other one and it was necessary to resort to threats. The information they got is that up until now they had seen no guerrillas. The only instance was a group that went to Perez' house before Carnival (ourselves). They returned during the day and waited for night to avoid Moron's house. Everything was going perfectly but Moro got lost and he went to sleep on the trail and we lost 2 hours looking for him. They have left some tracks which could permit tracking if the livestock does not erase them all. In addition, they dropped a few things on the road. The morale of the people changed immediately.

The radio reports that it was not possible to identify the dead guerrillas but there may be some news any moment. We deciphered all the message that reports that the OLAS conference was a triumph but that the Bolivian delegation was a mess. Aldo Flores of the PCB tried to make himself the representative of the ELN and they had to give him the lie. They have asked one of Kolle's men to go to talk about it. Lozano's house was broken into and he is now undercover. They think they can trade Debray. That is all. Evidently they did not receive our last message.

September 6

Benigno's birthday looked promising. At dawn we made some porridge with what we had and we drank a little *mate* with sugar. Then Miguel in charge of eight men went off to set up an ambush while Leon tried to catch another young bull to take with us. Since it was getting late, after 10, and they had not returned, I sent Urbano to tell them to lift the ambush at 12. A few minutes later shots were heard and then a short burst, and a shot was heard in our direction. When we were taking our positions Urbano arrived in a hurry. He had run into a patrol with dogs. With nine men on the other side, without knowing their precise location, I was in great desperation. The path was improved to get out without reaching the bank of the river and Moro, Pombo, and Camba with Coco were sent on it. I was thinking of gradually transferring the packs and making contact with the rearguard if I was able to until the group could rejoin us; they, on the hand, could walk into an ambush. However, Miguel rejoined with all his people, hacking their way through. Explanation of what happened: Miguel forgot to leave a lookout for our trail and they got busy looking for the livestock. Leon heard the barking of a dog, and Miguel, just in case, decided to retreat. At the same time they heard the shots and noticed that a patrol had passed between them and the jungle through a trail and that they were in front, then they began to chop their way through.

We departed leisurely with three mules and three head of cattle and after crossing four fords, two of them rough, we made camp 7 kilometers from the old one and slaughtered the cow and ate our fill. The rearguard reported it had heard prolonged gunfire in the direction of the camp with many machine guns.

Altitude 640 meters

September 7

Short march. Only one ford was crossed, and then there was trouble because of the cliff, so that Miguel decided to camp and wait for us. Tomorrow we will do some good scouting. The situation is as follows: The air force is not looking for us here in spite of having reached the camp and the radio reports that I am the chief of the group. The question is this: Are they afraid? Not very probable. Do they find the upward climb impossible? With the experience of what we have had and which they know of, I do not think so. Do they want to let us advance so that they can wait for us at a strategic spot? It is possible. Do they think that we shall persist in the area of Masicurí to get supplies? That is also possible. El Médico is much better but came down with it again and spent a sleepless night.

The radio gave the news of the valuable information supplied by José Carrillo (Paco). He should be made an example. Debray refers to Paco's accusations against him by saying that on occasion he would hunt, and that is the reason they may have seen him with a rifle. Radio "La Cruz del Sur" announced the discovery of the guerrilla Tania's body on the banks of the Río Grande; this report does not have the ring of truth more than about Negro. The body was taken to Santa Cruz, according to the report of the radio station, only hers, not to the Altiplano.

Altitude 720 meters

I talked to Julio; he is very well but regrets the lack of contact and of new recruits.

September 8

It was a quiet day. An ambush of eight men was maintained from morning till night, under command of Antonio and Pombo. The animals ate well in a *chuchial* and the mule is getting over her blows. Aniceto and Chapaco went scouting upriver and returned with the news that the road was relatively good for the animals. Coco and Camba crossed the chest-deep river and went up a hill in front but without getting much intelligence. I sent Miguel with Aniceto and the result of a more prolonged check is that, in Miguel's opinion, the way will be very difficult for the animals. Tomorrow we will stay on this bank, although the possibility always exists that the animals can pass through the river unloaded.

The radio reported that Barrientos had attended the burial of the remains of the guerrilla Tania who was given a "Christian burial," and then he was at Puerto Mauricio which is Honorato's house. He has made a proposition to the disappointed Bolivians, those who have not received the promised salaries, to come to the doors of the Army with their hands on their forehead, and no measures will be taken against them. A small airplane bombed Honorato's house in the lower section as if to make a demonstration for Barrientos.

A Budapest daily criticizes Ché Guevara, a pathetic and apparently irresponsible figure, and hails the Marxist attitude of the Chilean Party for adopting practical stands in practice. How I would like to take power just to unmask cowards and lackeys of every sort and rub their snouts in their own filth.

September 9

Miguel and Nato went scouting and returned with the news that it is possible to cross but that the animals will have to swim across. The people can wade across. There is a rather wide arroyo on the left bank where we will make camp. The ambush was kept with eight men under the command of Antonio and Pombo. There was nothing new. I talked to Aniceto, he seems to be very firm although he feels there are several who are cropping up; he complains about the lack of political work on the part of Inti. We finished the cow, of which only the bones remain, for soup in the morning.

The only news on the radio is the suspension of Debray's trial until September 17 at least.

September 10

Bad day. It began with good promise but then the animals had a hard time with the very bad road and finally the donkey would not walk. It stayed back and had to be left on the other side. Coco decided it because of a violent rise in the river, four weapons were left on the other side, among them Moro's, and three anti-tank shells for Benigno's weapon. I crossed the river, swimming with the mule, but I lost my shoes in the crossing and now I am wearing sandals, something that is not very funny to me. Nato made a bundle of his clothes and weapons wrapped up in a rubber sheet and jumped in when the current was violent, losing everything in the crossing. The other mule broke off and jumped in alone to cross but we had to turn it back because there was no way to cross, and in attempting the same crossing with Leon, both he and the mule nearly drowned, because the heavy rush had come by then. Finally we got to the arroyo which was our objective, but El Médico was in very poor shape, complaining of aches in arms and legs during the night. Up to now our plan was to make the animals swim to the other side, but because of the flood that plan is canceled. Also, planes and helicopters have flown over the area; I do not like the helicopters because they may be leaving men in ambush. Tomorrow scouting expeditions will go upriver and upstream to try to locate our position.

Altitude 780 meters, Road = 3.4 kilometers

I almost forgot to mention that I took a bath today, the first in six months. It is a record which many others are attaining.

September 11

A quiet day. Scouts went out upriver and along the arroyo. The river scouts returned in late afternoon with the report that it would very likely be possible to cross when the river went down, and there are sandy stretches where the animals can walk. Benigno and Julio went to scout the arroyo but very superficially, and they were back by 12. Nato and Coco, supported by the rearguard, went to get the things that had been left behind when crossing the mule and leaving only one bag with the belts for the machine-gun bullets.

There was an unpleasant incident: Chino came to tell me that Nato had roasted and eaten a whole piece of meat in front of him. I stormed at Chino since it was his duty to prevent it but after investigating, the situation got more complicated because it was impossible to determine whether Chino had authorized the action or not. He asked to be replaced and I put Pombo in charge again, but it was an especially bitter pill for Chino.

In the morning the radio reported that Barrientos declared that I had been dead for some time and all that propaganda, and at night that he was offering 50,000 pesos [4,200 U.S. dollars] for information leading to my capture dead or alive. It appears that the Armed Forces gave him a [illegible]. Leaflets were dropped over the area, probably with my personal description. Roque Terán says that the Barrientos offer can be considered psychological since everyone knows the tenacity of the guerrillas, and the fact is that they are getting ready for a long war.

I talked at length with Pablito. Like all the others, he is worried about the lack of contact and he thinks that our basic job is to restore contact with the city, but he showed himself to be a firm and resolute partisan of *Patria o Muerte,* wherever it may lead.

September 12

The day began with a tragi-comic episode: Precisely at 6, reveille time, Eustaquio comes to warn that people are coming along the arroyo; he gives the alarm and everybody takes battle stations. Antonio has seen them; when I ask how many they are he holds up five fingers. In the end it turned out to be a hallucination, dangerous to the morale of the troop for immediately they began to talk about psychosis. I spoke to Antonio and evidently he is not normal; his eyes teared but he denied that he was worried and said that the only thing wrong with him was the lack of sleep, but he is demoted for 6 days because he left his post and later denied it. Chapaco disobeyed an order and was sentenced to 3 days' demotion. Tonight he spoke to me about joining the vanguard because, according to him, he cannot get along with Antonio. I refused. Inti, Leon and Eustaquio set out for a thorough scouting of the arroyo to see if it leads across a large mountain range visible in the distance. Coco, Aniceto, and Julio went upriver to try to scout the fords and the way to lead the animals if we go that way.

It seems that Barrientos' offer has provoked a certain sensation; in any case a demented newsman said that 4,200 U.S. dollars is little money considering how dangerous I am. Radio Havana reported that OLAS had received a message of support from the ELN, a miracle of telepathy.

["OLAS"—Spanish initials of the organization of Latin American Solidarity, Castro sponsored offshot of the Tricontinental organization; it held its first conference in July-August 1967, in Havana].

September 13

The scouts returned. Inti and his group went up the arroyo all day; they slept at a considerable height and quite cold; the arroyo apparently starts from a mountain range opposite us, running west. It is not practicable by animals. Coco and his companions tried unsuccessfully to cross the river; they went over 11 cliffs before reaching the canyon of a river which may be La Pesca, with signs of life, burnt *chocos* and an ox; the animals should cross to the other side, unless we all can do so together on the raft, which is what we shall try to do.

I spoke with Dario, presenting the problem of his leaving, if he wants to. First he answered that to leave would be very dangerous but I told him that this is not a refuge and if he decides to stay it must be for good. He said he would and that he would correct his shortcomings. We shall see.

The only news on the radio is of the warning shot they fired at Debray senior and the fact that they seized from his son all the documentary support for his defense on the pretext that they do not want it to become a political pamphlet.

September 14

A tiring day. At 7 Miguel left with the whole vanguard and Nato. They had instructions to walk as much as possible on this side and to make a raft where it was difficult to pass. Antonio remained with the rearguard. A couple of M-1's were left in a small cave which Nato and Willy know. At 1330, not having heard anything, we began the march. It was impossible to ride muleback and I, with the beginning of an asthma attack, had to leave the animal to Leon and continue on foot. The rearguard received an order to begin the march at 15, if there were no counterorders. Approximately at that hour Pablito arrived with the news that the ox was at the crossing point of the animals and that the raft was being built one kilometer farther up. I waited until the animals arrived, which they did at 1815, after the people were sent to help them. At that time the two mules crossed (the ox had done it before) and we walked a short distance to where the raft was. I discovered that on this side there were still 12 men; only 10 had crossed. Thus divided we spent the night, eating the last of the ox, half spoiled.

Altitude 720 meters, March = 2-3 kilometers

September 15

The ground covered was a little longer, 5 or 6 kilometers, but we did not reach the La Pesca River since the animals had to cross twice and one of the mules was stubborn about the crossings. We still have one more crossing to make and to look around to see if the mules can pass.

The radio carries the news of the arrest of Loyola. The photos must be to blame. The one bull we had left died, at the hands of the executioner, naturally.

Altitude 780 meters

September 16

The day was spent in making the raft and crossing the river. We walked only 500 meters to the camp where there is a small spring. The crossing was effected without incident on a good raft pulled by ropes from either bank. Finally, when we left them alone, Antonio and Chapaco had another incident and Antonio imposed 6 days of punishment on Chapaco for having insulted him. I respected this decision, although I am not sure that it was justified. At night there was another incident when Eustaquio charged that Nato was eating too much. It turned out to be some bits of meat off the hide. Another painful situation created by food. The doctor tackled me with another little problem, concerning his illness and what the men think of it, due to some comments made by Julio; it all seems unimportant.

Altitude 820 meters

September 17

A day of dentistry: I did some tooth-pulling on Arturo and Chapaco. Miguel scouted to the river and Benigno on the road; the report is that the mules can climb up but first they must swim, crossing and recrossing the river. In honor of Pablito we cooked a little rice for him. He is just 22 years old, the youngest of the guerrillas.

The radio only reports news about the trial's postponement and a protest against Loyola Guzmán's arrest.

September 18

The march began at 7, but soon Miguel came with the news that three peasants had been sighted. We did not know if they had seen us. An order was given to detain them. Chapaco began the inevitable brawl accusing Arturo of having stolen 15 bullets from his cartridge clip. This is dreadful, and the only good thing is that, even though he picks his fights with the Cubans, none of the Bolivians pay attention to him. The mules made the trek without having to swim, but on crossing a ravine, we lost our grip on the black mule which got hurt after being swept about 50 meters. We captured 4 peasants who were going along with their donkeys to Piraypandi, a river located upstream about a league to the east, and they reported that Aladino Gutiérrez and his people were hunting and fishing on the banks of the Rio Grande. Benigno committed the greatest imprudence by letting them see him and letting him, his wife and another *campesino* go.

When I found out I was furious and I called this a treasonable act, which caused Benigno to burst into tears. All the *campesinos* were informed that tomorrow they would go with us to Zitano, the ranch where they live, 6 or 8 leagues from here. Aladino and his wife are a little slippery and it took a lot of talking to get them to sell us food.

Now the radio reports that Loyola has attempted suicide twice "for fear of guerrilla reprisals" and also reports the arrest of several teachers, who if not involved, at least sympathize with us. It seems that they confiscated many things at Loyola's house, but it would not be strange if everything stemmed from the photos in the cave.

At night the little plane and the other plane suspiciously flew over the area.

Altitude 800 meters

September 19

We did not leave very early because the peasants could not find their donkeys. Finally, after I blew up, we left, with the caravan of prisoners with Moro. We walked slowly and when we reached the stopover of the river we received the news that three more prisoners had been taken and the vanguard had just left and expected to arrive at a sugarcane plantation about 2 leagues away. They were long ones, as long as the first 2. About 9 at night they reached the .ields, which were only one canefield, and the rearguard arrived after 2100.

At supper time I had a conversation with Inti about some of his weaknesses and he told me, upset, that I was right and that he would hold a public self-criticism session when we were alone but he denied some accusations. We went over altitudes of 1,440 meters and are now at 1,000 meters; from here to Lucitano is a 3-hour walk, perhaps 4, the people say. We finally ate pork and the sugar-mill people could have their fill of *chankaka* [toasted maize ground with honey].

The radio keeps harping on the Loyola case and the teachers are on full strike; the students of the Secondary School where Higuera, one of those arrested, worked are on a hunger strike and the petroleum workers are about to go on strike over the creation of the petroleum enterprise.

Sign of the times: I ran out of ink.

September 20

I decided to leave at 1500 to reach the Lucitano ranch by

nightfall because they told us one could arrive there easily in 3 hours, but various difficulties delayed the trip until 1700 and a complete darkness overtook us on the hill; despite the fact that we lit a torch, we did not reach Aladino Gutierrez' house until 23. It was not much of a grocery store, although we bought some cigarettes and other trifles; no clothing. We napped a little and at 0300 hours set out for Alto Seco which they say is 4 leagues away. We took over the mayor's phone but it has not worked for years and, moreover, the line was down. The mayor's name is Vargas and he has had the job only a short time.

The radio reports nothing of importance. We crossed over altitudes of 1800 meters and Lusitano is 1400 meters away. We walked some two leagues to the ranch.

September 21

Ot 0300 hours we left in bright moonlight along the previously scouted road and walked until approximately 9 without meeting anyone and crossing altitudes of 2040 meters, the highest altitude yet. At that time we came upon a couple of drovers who pointed out the road to Alto Seco, only 2 leagues away. In that part of the night and morning we had walked scarcely 2 leagues. On reaching the first houses on the slope, we bought some provisions and went to cook food at the mayor's house. We passed a corn mill driven by water power in the vicinity of Piraymiri (1,400 meters altitude). The people are afraid and try to get out of our way. We have lost much time because of our lack of mobility. The 2 leagues to Alto Seco took from 1215 until 1700 hours,

September 22

When we, the center, reached Alto Seco we discovered that the *corregidor* [local justice] apparently left yesterday to report that we were near. In reprisal, we seized all his grocery stocks. Alto Seco is a little village of 50 houses at 1,900 meters altitude, which received us with a balanced mixture of fear and curiosity. The urgency of getting supplies began to take effect, and we soon had in our encampment, an abandoned house near the waterhole, a respectable quantity of edibles. The pickup truck that was supposed to arrive from Valle Grande did not appear, which would confirm the report that the *corregidor* went to give the alarm. Nevertheless, I had to put up with his wife's crying, who, in the name of God and her children, asked for payment, something to which I did not accede. In the evening Inti gave a talk in the schoolhouse (first and second grades) to a group of 15 down-trodden and silent peasants about the scope of our revolution. The teacher was the only one present who responded, asking if we fought in the towns. He is a mixture of fox and peasant, illiterate and guileless as a child; he asked a lot of questions about socialism. A boy offered to serve us as guide but warned us against the teacher whom they call a fox. We left at 0130 en route to Santa Elena, where we arrived at 1000.

Barrientos and Ovando gave a press conference in which they revealed all the information about the documents, and declared that Joaquín's group has been liquidated.

Altitude 1300 meters

September 23
The place was a beautiful orange grove that still had a good quantity of fruit. We spent the day resting and sleeping, but we had to post a lot of guards. At 13 hours we got up and started out at 1400 in the direction of Loma Larga, where we arrived at dawn. We crossed over altitudes of 1800 meters. The men are loaded down and the march is slow. I got indigestion from Benigno's cooking.

September 24
We arrived at the ranch called Loma Larga. I was having a liver attack and vomiting and the men were exhausted from the long marches that did not accomplish anything, I decided to spend the night at the start of the road to Pujio and we killed a pig sold to us by the only peasant who stayed home: Sostenes Vargas. The rest flee at the sight of us.

Altitude 1400 meters

September 25
We arrived at Pujio early, but there were people there who had seen us down the hill the day before. We are being announced by word of mouth. Pujio is a small ranch located on a hill and the people who fled when they first saw us, later approached us and treated us well. A carabinero who had come from Serrano to arrest a debtor left at dawn. We are now at a point where the three departments come together. The road is very dangerous with mules. But I try to make things easy for the doctor, who is very weak. The peasants deny knowing anything about the Army in this area. We walked little by little until we

arrived at Tranca Mayo where we slept at the edge of the road because Miguel did not take the precautions I had urged him to. The *corregidor* from Higuera is in the area and we gave orders to the guard to arrest him.

Altitude 1800 meters

Inti and I spoke with Camba who agreed to stay with us up until we are in sight of Higuera, which is located near Pucara and there try to get to Santa Cruz.

September 26

Defeat. We arrived at dawn at Picacho where everybody was celebrating. This was the highest point we had reached: 2,280 meters. The peasants treated us very well, and we continued without excessive fear, even though Ovando had promised my capture from one moment to the next. On arriving at Higuera everything changed. All the men had left and there were only a few women. Coco went to the telegraph operator's house, where there is a telephone, and brought back a message dated the 22nd in which the subprefect of Valle Grande tells the mayor that there are reports of guerrillas in the area and any further news should be communicated immediately to Valle Grande, which will pay expenses. The man had fled but his wife assured us that they had not sent a message today as there was a *fiesta* in the next town, Jaguey.

At 13 the vanguard left to try to reach Jaguey and there make a decision about the mules and the doctor. A little later I was talking with the only man in the town, a very scared one, when a coca dealer arrived. He said he had just come from Valle Grande and Pucara and had not seen anything. He also seemed very nervous, but I attributed it to our presence. We let them both go in spite of the lies they were telling us. When we started for the top of the hill at approximately 13:30, the sound of firing all over the ridge told us that our men had fallen into an ambush. I organized the defense in the small town to wait for the survivors, and designated as the retreat route a road which would lead to the Rio Grande. A few minutes later Benigno arrived, wounded, and soon after him Aniceto and Pablito with his foot in very bad condition. Miguel, Coco and Julio had fallen, and Camba disappeared, leaving his knapsack behind. The rearguard quickly ran for the road and I followed, still taking the two mules; the ones behind were fired on at close range and they took longer. Inti lost contact. We lay in ambush for ½ hour, waiting for him, but after being shot at from the hill. we decided to leave him. But in a little while he caught up with us. At that point we noticed Leon was missing. Inti said he had seen a knapsack by the canyon through which he had come; we saw a man walking very hurriedly through a canyon and concluded it was he. Trying to throw the soldiers off our track, we sent the mules below and we continued through a small canyon where we found bitter water. We stopped and went to sleep at 12 since it was impossible to advance any further.

September 27

At 21 hours we started the march again, trying to find a place we could ascend, which we accomplished around 7, but on the other side of where we wanted to go. In front, there was a rocky hill which did not look difficult. We ascended a bit more to escape from the overhead planes, reaching a very sparse little woods, and there we discovered that the hill had a road even though there was no activity on it all day. In the evening a peasant and a soldier climbed up the hill and played there for a while without seeing us. Aniceto just made another scouting trip and saw a large group of soldiers in a nearby house. That was the easiest road for us but it was cut off now. In the morning we saw a column climb a nearby hill, their equipment shining in the sun. By midday we could hear scattered shots and some concentrated gunfire, and then shouts "There they are," "Come on out," "Are you coming out or not?," along with more shooting. We do not know who the man was but we think it was Camba. We set out toward evening trying to get down to the water on the other side. We remained in some bushes a little thicker than the previous ones. We had to search for water in the canyon as a cliff prevented us from getting it here.

The radio broadcast the news that we had clashed with the Bolivian company, that three men had been killed, and that they were taking them to Valle Grande for identification. It seems that they have not caught Camba or Leon. Our casualties have been heavy this time. The worst of all is having lost Coco, but, Miguel and Julio were magnificent fighters and the human worth of the three is incalculable. Leon had good promise.

Altitude 1400 meters

September 28

A day of anguish. At times it seemed as if it would be our last. At dawn we brought up water and then Luis and Willy went out immediately to scout for another possible descent to the canyon They returned at once as the entire hill in front was traversed by a road and a peasant on horseback was riding on it. At 10 a group of 46 soldiers with their knapsacks passed by, taking ages to get out of sight. At 1200 another group, this time of 77 men, passed by. At this moment a shot was heard. The soldiers immediately took their positions. The officer ordered them to go down to the ravine which seemed to be ours. Anyway [illegible word]; they communicated by radio and seemed satisfied, and continued their march. Our refuge has no defense against an attack from the height, and the possibilities of escape are remote if they discover us. Later a soldier who had been delayed passed by with a tired dog he had to pull along. Later still, a peasant guiding another straggling soldier went by. In a short time the peasant returned and nothing finally happened. But the fear when the shot was heard was really serious.

The soldiers all passed with knapsacks, which gives the impression that they are retreating, and we saw no fires in the little house that night, nor did we hear the gunfire with which soldiers usually welcome the evening. Tomorrow we will scout the whole day, all over the ranch. A light fell on us, but I do not think it was sufficient to erase our tracks.

The radio reported that Coco has been identified and gave some confused news about Julio; Miguel was confused with Antonio, whose duties in Manila were mentioned. At first they reported my death, then later denied it.

September 29

Another tense day. The scouts, Inti and Aniceto, went out early to guard the house all day. From early in the morning, travel began on the road, and at midmorning soldiers without knapsacks passed in both directions, in addition to others who led unloaded donkeys from below and returned loaded. Inti arrived at 18:15 and told us that the soldiers who had descended were in a clearing and they had not seen them again, and the donkeys seem to have been loaded there. With this news it was difficult to make a decision to take this road, the easiest of all and also the one most likely to have soldiers waiting in ambush. In any case there are dogs in the house which would give away our presence. Tomorrow two scouting groups will go out: one to the same place and another that will try to find a road uphill to see if there is a way in that direction, probably across the road the soldiers take.

The radio had no news.

September 30

Another day of tension. This morning it was announced on Radio Balmaceda in Chile that top Army sources revealed that they had Ché Guevara cornered in a jungle canyon. The local radio stations are silent. It seems as if there has been some betrayal and they are certain we are in the area. In a short while soldiers began to travel in both directions. At 12 o'clock, 40 soldiers passed by in separate columns. They stopped at the little house where they camped and set up a jittery watch. Aniceto and Pacho informed us of this. Inti and Willy returned with the news that the Rio Grande is 2 kilometers straight ahead. There are three houses in the canyon higher up and we can proceed without being seen from any angle. We got water and at 22 we started a tiresome night march, delayed by Chino, who walks very poorly in the dark. Benigno is very well but the doctor is not recovering.

ANALYSIS OF THE MONTH

It should have been a month of recuperation and it was just about to be, but the ambush in which they got Miguel, Coco, and Julio ruined everything and we have been left in a dangerous position, losing also Leon; as far as Camba is concerned, that is a net gain.

We had small skirmishes in which we killed a horse, killed and wounded a soldier, and Urbano exchanged shots with a patrol, and the fateful ambush at Higuera. We already left the mules and I think it will be a long time before we will use this type of animal unless I start having bad asthma attacks again.

Further, there may be truth in some of the news about deaths in the other group which can be considered liquidated, although it is possible that there is a little group of survivors wandering about, avoiding contact with the Army, because the news of the simultaneous death of all seven may be false or at least exaggerated.

The situation is the same as last month except that now the Army appears to be more effective in its actions, and the peasants do not give us any help and are turning into informers.

The most important task now will be to sneak out and look for favorable areas, and then make the contacts, even though they have wrecked the entire apparatus in La Paz where they have given us some hard blows.

The morale of the rest of the men remains fairly high, and I am only doubtful about Willy, who may take advantage of a skirmish to try to escape alone unless we talk to him.

October 1

Nothing much happened on this first day of the month. At dawn we reached a sparse woods where we set up camp, posting guards at different approach points. The 40 men went away through a canyon that we had planned to take, firing a few shots. At 1400 hours we heard the last sounds of gunfire; there does not seem to be anyone in the little houses, although Urbano saw 5 soldiers come down who did not follow through on any road. I decided to stay here one more day, for it is a good place and provides a guaranteed escape route because all enemy troop movements can be spotted. Pacho, Nato, Dario and Eustaquio went to look for water, and returned at 2100 hours. Chapaco made some fritters, and dried beef, so we are no longer hungry.

There was no news.

Altitude 1600 meters

October 2

The day went by without the slightest sign of soldiers, but some goats being herded by dogs passed by our position and the dogs barked. We decided to try to proceed alongside one of the clearings nearest the canyon and we started on our way down at 18 hours with plenty of time to make ourselves comfortable and to cook something before continuing the expedition; but we noticed that Nato had got lost and persisted in going on. When we decided to turn back, we got lost so we slept in the mountains. We had failed to make the crossing and we were very thirsty.

The radio provided details on the movement of soldiers on the 30th. According to news announcements on the Cruz del Sur radio, the Army reported having had an encounter with a small group of ours in Abra del Quinol but without casualties on either side, although they say that they found traces of blood in our flight. The group consisted of six persons, according to the report.

October 3

A long and unnecessarily active day: after mobilizing ourselves to get to the main camp, Urbano arrived with the news that he had heard one of the peasants passing them on the road say "those were the ones they were talking about last night." In all probability the report was inaccurate but I decided to pretend that it was perfectly true, and without quenching our thirst we again climbed a ridge that overlooks the road the soldiers were on. For the rest of the day there was absolute quiet and towards nightfall we came down and prepared coffee which tasted wonderful despite the bitter water and the grease in the pot in which it was prepared. We then prepared porridge to eat there and rice with tapir meat to take with us. At 15, after exploring the way, we set out and traversed the chaco without incidents and reached the glen we wanted next to the canyon, which has no water and shows signs of having been explored by soldiers.

The radio reported news about two prisoners: Antonio Dominguez Flores (Leon) and Orlando Jimenez Bazan (Camba). The latter admits having fought against the Army; the former says he turned himself in because he trusts the President to keep his word. They have both given abundant information about Fernando, his sickness, and all the rest, and who knows what they have revealed that has not been published. So ends the tale of 2 heroic guerrillas.

Altitude 1360 meters

An interview with Debray was broadcast: Very courageous in facing up to a student provocateur.

October 4

After resting in the ravine, we followed it downhill for about half an hour until we came to another one that joins it. Climbing up the second ravine we rested until 15 hours to escape the heat of the sun. Then we continued the march for more than a half hour, whereupon we met the scouts who had reached the end of the little canyons without having found water. We left the ravine at 18 and followed a cattle trail until 19:30 hours. At this time we could see nothing and so we stopped until 3.

The radio broadcast news of the transfer of the Army's Fourth Division's forward headquarters from Lagunilla to Padilla, to cover better the Serrano area where it is believed the guerrillas will try to escape. The radio also commented that if I am captured by the 4th Division they will try me in Camiri, and if I am captured by the 8th Division, I will be tried in Santa Cruz.

Altitude 1650 meters

October 5

We renewed our march with great difficulty until 5:45 hours, at which time we left a cowpath and we entered a little woods, which was sparse but high enough to prevent detection. Benigno and Pacho made several scouting trips in search of water, and completely circled a nearby house without finding any. Perhaps it is a little off to the side. As they finished scouting they saw six soldiers arrive at the house apparently just passing by. We set out at nightfall with the men exhausted from lack of water and Eustaquio making a spectacle of himself by moaning for a mouthful of water. After a stretch of very poor road strewn with rocks, we arrived at dawn at a small woods where we could hear the barking of dogs nearby. We can see a tall, bald ridge quite nearby.

We treated Benigno whose wound is a little better and I gave the doctor a hypodermic. Because of his treatment, Benigno complained of pain during the night. The radio announced that our two *cambas* were transfered to Camiri to be witnesses at Debray's trial.

Altitude 2000 meters

October 6

The scouting proved that there was a house nearby and also that there was a canyon a little farther away where there was water. We went over there and spent all day cooking under a rock overhang which made a sort of roof for us, despite the fact that I was worried all day because we had passed fairly populated areas in broad daylight and were staying in a hole. The meal was delayed, so we decided to go out at dawn to a tributary of this little arroyo, and from there explore more thoroughly to decide our future direction.

Radio La Cruz del Sur reported an interview with the *cambas*. Orlando was a little less villanous. The Chilean radio carried a censored news item to the effect that there are 1,800 men in the area looking for us.

Altitude 1750 meters

October 7

We completed the 11th month of our guerrilla operation without complications, in a bucolic mood, until 12:30, when an old woman grazing her goats came into the canyon where we were camped, and we had to seize her. The woman has not given us any trustworthy information about the soldiers, saying that she knows nothing, that there is a long time since she has been in that area. She only gave us information about the roads; from what the woman told us, we figure we are about one league from Higuera, one from Jagüey and about 2 from Pucara. At 5:30, Inti, Aniceto, and Pablito went to the house of the old woman, who has one daughter ill in bed and another half-dwarf. They gave her 50 pesos and commanded her not to speak to anyone, but with little hope that she will keep her word despite her promises. The 17 of us set out under a very small moon. The march was very tiring, and we left many traces in the canyon where we were, near which there are no houses but only potato patches irrigated from the same arroyo. At 2 we rested, for it was useless to continue further. El Chino becomes a real burden when we have to march at night.

The Army issued an unusual report about the presence of 250 troops in Serrano to prevent the egress of those encircled, numbering 37, giving our location between the Acero and Oro rivers. The news seems diversionary.

Altitude 2000 meters

ROLANDO'S DIARY

Kept in a small spiral-bound notebook, Rolando's diary covers the period from August 11, 1966 to April 20, 1967, a few days before his death. Like Pombo and Braulio, Rolando did not make a daily entry. Rolando was the only one of the guerrillas careful to use code in his diary to minimize its usefulness in the event of capture, and it contains many small symbols which mask the location of various guerrilla objectives.

Ché had known Rolando since he was a sixteen year old messenger during the Cuban revolution. He had intended to put his young protégé in charge of a second front in Bolivia and was greatly upset at his death.

Rolando gives a literate, straightforward account of the campaign. He is particularly valuable for his description of life in camp, and his excellent ability to clarify military engagements which appear muddled in the other diaries. At 24 he was one of the youngest in Ché's force.

1966

August 11, 1966
Today our training began.

September 1966
We met with Ramon at the S. Farm. We were extraordinarily moved when we recognized him. We continued our training until October 22, 1966, at which time we went on leave after having been visited by C., [Castro] who spent 3 days with us.

October 29, 1966
I left for P. [Prague] together with Urbano and Braulio, and arrived on Nov. 1.
In P. [Prague] we lodged together with Marcos, Joaquin, and Miguel until Tuesday, Nov. 16, 1966. On that date Marcos and I left P. We went through F., G., R., and S., [Frankfurt, Geneva, Rio de Janeiro and Sao Paulo] and on Thursday, November 18 arrived at Ricardo [in La Paz].

November 19, 1966
We left Ricardo for Ramón together with Rodolfo, taking with us some merchandise, weapons, and ammunition. On the trip we were able to get a general impression of the country: the more important cities and a multitude of little villages on the Altiplano as well as the tropical zone.

November 21, 1966
We reach our objective, meeting Ramón, Tuma, Pombo, and Pacho. Also in the place are 3 Bolivian comrades: Apolinar, Antonio, and Pancho.

November 22, 1966
Ramon goes out scouting with Tuma and a B [Bolivian].

November 23, 1966
Pacho and I go out scouting and return on the 24th.

December 23, 1966

By now we are in a more secure and more habitable camp. The other comrades of our group arrived without major trouble on the following dates: Pombo, Tuma, Ramón, and Pacho on November 7; Marcos and I on November 21; Joaquin and Miguel together with Inti and the doctor on November 27. On that same date Urbano and Braulio together with Coco. On December 8, 1966 Apolinar was officially admitted. Alejandro, Benigno, Arturo, and Morogoro together with Nato, Orlando, and Carlos arrived on December 11.

December 23, 1966

Today a hunter (the vg [Vallegrandino, man from Vallegrande] who works for the g) made remarks to the effect that he had seen several men, armed and carrying knapsacks; after [we] tried to downgrade his remarks with the story that it might be a group of hunters, he admitted that they might be hunters.

December 24 1966

We celebrated Christmas Eve with roast pig and some drink, and then organized a sort of cultural event, having a good time.

December 31, 1966

Today Mario arrived; we had been awaiting him since the 25th. He arrived together with Papi, T., R., and S. [Tania, Ricardo and Suarez]. Also two new comrades joined us: the secretary of the J [youth organization] and Pedro.

1967

January 1, 1967

At 0800 Mario pulled out after having had the discussion with Ramón. Briefly, his statement was to this effect: a. He disagrees with the established strategy. He thinks that the most appropriate way would be to have a general uprising and, if this uprising is arrested, to retreat to the mountains; nevertheless, he would be willing to come along on the basis of three conditions: 1. He would be the leader. 2. The P. CH. [pro-Chinese Communist Party of Bolivia] would not participate. 3. He would make a tour of Latin America to get the support of brother P's [Parties] and the recognition of the C. D. He ended up [saying] that the P. Ch. could participate, but suggested the public adherence of the (xxx). There was no agreement on this point. Ramón said that although he did not see the usefulness of point 3 he had no objection to it. Point 1 was discussed time and again with no agreement. The net result was that help. But today, 1, he withdrew without setting a new date for a meeting, and ship in the Party]. I feel that this is his maneuver to see if he can strengthen his authority in the P. Although it is not easy to imagine what upheaval there may develop in the P., the most likely thing is that there will be a split and some people will come over to us.

January 10, 1967

We are still at the same camp on Arroyo 1 of the N [Nancahuazú River]. We have been accumulating merchandise, something we had been doing since we settled down here. In the last 10 days three scouting expeditions have been conducted by groups led by Marcos, Joaquin and Inti, who returned on the 5th and left again, to come back on the 12th at the latest.

The rest of us are continuing our routine jobs and attending the classes being given by Ramón, with considerable progress.

I must report that on the 7th we held the first staff meeting of all the personnel at which Ramón pointed out a number of cases in which we had been careless, in violation of discipline. He pointed to the lack of interest of some comrades in the lessons, explaining the experiences of Manila and the C. with regard to self-sacrificing but uninstructed comrades, and how in Manila this compelled placing not-quite-qualified persons in certain posts, etc. He pointed to the prospects of fighting and reiterated his statements with regard to the time it would take us to attain the objectives we seek, at the same time cautioning us against false illusions, etc. He indicated how we should introduce standards and methods that would make our guerrilla unit into an iron-strong group in which every new member would feel upon his arrival the positive influence of the group. Then he referred to the need to set up a political organ of leadership, analyzing the present difficulties and concluding that we could do without it for the time being.

Further on, Ramón explained why he had designated Joaquin as second-in-command instead of Marcos. He said a few things concerning one and the other. He concluded by assigning the various duties and reporting on his forthcoming interview with G., [Moisés Guevara Rodríguez] and its consequences.

January 10, 1967

Today I am on sentry duty in a beautiful place where [I am sorry] not to have a camera to take a few pictures of the area around me. I am on a mountain which is the equal of the most picturesque ones I ever saw at the movies. On my right the river runs swiftly over great rocks which produce thunderous falls. Beyond the river there begins a mountain range which is extremely steep and covered with heavy vegetation and which rises almost vertically from the arroyo, forming a number of peaks. The top portion of each of these is shrouded in heavy fog while below the warm morning sunshine brightens up the place and makes me interrupt my reading (I am reading *The Charter-house of Parma*), remembering my loved ones; my wife, Eliseito, Marisela, and Renecito. I think of my mother, of the surprise that she must have had when my father told her that I am fighting by the side of . . . with P. In front of me there is a deep ravine covered with trees and at a distance of not over 200 meters there is a mountain.

January 24, 1967

These days we have been going on scouting expeditions, *góndola* trips, doing some camouflaging, etc. Ramón has devoted even more attention to the teaching of the personnel: to Spanish, mathematics, and history, Quechua has been added (taught by Aniceto and Pedro), and there has been a beginning on political economy, attended by those who wish. Also, at the request of some comrades, a course in French has been started, with the attendance of eight or ten.

On the 19th the P. [guerrilla sentry] at the house came to report that the police had made a search of the house and con-fiscated a revolver, telling Bigote when they finished that he would have to go to Camiri to explain. This, and the fact that Coco was more than 10 days overdue from La Paz made us think that he might be in prison. The next day, the 20th, the sentry reported than Algaraña had been at the house together with an American who was carrying an M-2, which according to Algaraña he had bought from a police lieutenant. The sentry also reported that Algaraña was carrying a [V/]-brand [weapon] which at

another time he had said had been confiscated from him by
- - - - -, and at this time he said that he had lent it to - - - - -.
All this, together with the fact that several days earlier he had
told Bigote that he had observed strange movements in the area
and that he was ready to participate in the activity, whatever
it was, coca-making or whatever, makes him very suspicious. He
may even have been the one who alerted the police to suspicious
movements around the farm, since we know that he had instructed the man from Valle Grande in trying to uncover a presumed coca plant that in his opinion was on the farm. In view
of this situation, security measures were taken: a place was found
from which to watch the house of the G.; a messenger was sent
to Coco: camouflage arrangements were made; and a defense was
prepared to try to destroy the enemy in ambush and cut their
retreat, the relation of forces and the progress of the fighting
permits. On the 21st the situation changed with the arrival of
Coco, although the possibility could not be overlooked that the
enemy might have some indications as to movements in the area.
It was very probable, however, that they were going after a
cocaine plant, as it makes no sense that, if they had indications
that there were guerrillas in the place, they would be so stupid
as to send four policemen to make a search.

On the evening of the 21st Ramón reported on a letter sent
by the PC (MM), reading it and telling about the interview with
the sg [secretary-general?]. The letter is addressed to F [Fidel
Castro] and it contains the three points made by Mario to Ramón;
although it does not reproduce precisely the letter of his proposal,
nevertheless the intent is the same and does not define anything.
It is worth pointing out that M.'s attitude can be gauged by the
fact that he persuaded three B comrades coming back from
Manila not to take to the mountains.

January 31, 1967

From the 21st to today we have continued to study economics,
Quechua, French, Spanish, mathematics, and geometry, and kept
up the routine activities: *góndolas,* hunting, sentry duty, cooking,
and cave-making. Antonio, Inti, and I have continued recruiting
and screening candidates for the cl[andestine] org[anization] and
the guerrilla unit.

Ramón made a reorganization and divided the men into several
study groups, making me responsible for checking up on the
studies. Two groups were organized in each platoon, and Rubio,

Alejandro, and Benjamín were assigned to teach. Ramón continues to handle Group 1.

On the 23d or the 24th the man from Valle Grande was seen spying on the house of the N. On the 26 G. arrived, and today he agreed with Ramón's ideas and promised to rise up together with [us?].

Today, January 31, we are ready to leave for N. d R.G. [north of the Rio Grande?]. The second phase of the first stage of L. [liberation struggle?] begins now.

February 11, 1967

This is the 11th day of our trip, the purpose of which is to contact peasants and familiarize ourselves with the territory. Until today we have walked normally and have eaten fairly well (one meal upon setting up camp and soup and coffee at noon; in the morning we have taken coffee, tea or chocolate). The distance traveled can be covered in 5 or 6 days, but we have had to camp several times for unavoidable reasons. On the sixth day we arrived at the N d Rg, where we stayed 2 days. The first day was spent scouting and on the second we had to build two rafts to cross the . . . River, because the first one we built was carried off by the river after only three trips across. On the 8th day we resumed the march at 0800, when the last of us had come across the . . . River. Until sundown it was one of the worst days in our march because we had nothing to eat all day, and the water gave out at noon so that we had to continue without water all afternoon. On the 9th we made contact with . . . [#] I at 1000 hours and our situation changed. We decided to take a supply for 3 days (9th, 10th, and 11th) and so we would be able to save the last two we have for the 12th and 13th. Since we have a general idea of the area we have ahead of us, where several peasants live, it will not be hard for us to find food. Among the features of this area we find that a road is being built by 300 soldiers assigned by the government; there is a village named [name indicated by wavy line]; and . . . I reports that in this area there is a magistrate who whips the peasants and commits all sorts of abuses.

February 13, 1967

We spent the 12th walking on the m n [north bank] of the [symbol] We advanced slowly because it was necessary to hack our way through. At 1500 we stopped until 1900, when we found a path along which we walked until midnight. We passed

close to the house of . . . II (MO). We cooked some oat broth
and camped overnight, and today (the 13th) we set out to look
for another campsite in the area while something to eat is being
prepared at the house of . . . II. The plan was to leave at 0500,
but the rain that has been falling prevented it; the river is so
swollen that it is impassable; since the soldiers who are building
the road are on the other bank we are in no danger of surprise,
but nevertheless the greatest precautions were taken as to camouflage.

February 15, 1967

We spent yesterday camped at A [symbol] while a group of
six *macheteros* opened a way to enable us to get to the north
bank of the [symbol]. Today we started out at 0630 and walked
until 1000 and then stopped to enable six *macheteros* to open
up another stretch, since we have walked the entire previous
stretch. At 1200 we shall set off once more. We are bringing three
humitas each for the day's meal, and our breakfast was *lagua*—
green-corn porridge. Today we may meet a middle-class peasant,
and depending on his attitude we shall decide whether to continue
or come back.

February 16, 1967

Yesterday at 1900 we arrived before the house of . . . III.
Today we moved to an appropriate place near the house of . . .
III where we camped in order to prepare food for four days'
travel which we shall spend traversing a mountain range where
there is not supposed to be any water.

February 17, 1967

Today we were unable to continue because it rained from
1900 last night until noon today (17 hours).

February 18, 1967

Today we left at 0630 and walked until 1600, at which time
we camped in an arroyo we found at the base of Loma Pelada.
Marcos and Tuma went scouting up the mountain itself and
found that it was not possible to get to the other side that way,
so tomorrow we are going back one kilometer to find another
pass.

February 19, 1967

Today we walked 1½ hours to the first arroyo of the [symbol] where we shall camp while we do some scouting to find a pass to get to the [symbol]; we have already consumed two days' ration of food.

February 20, 1967

The scouting was fruitless, so today we advanced somewhat further to the right to the second arroyo, from which Pombo and I went scouting for a pass or to proceed to the point where there was no pass. We walked from 0740 until 1400 and went back then to avoid spending the night away from camp. When we got there we found that the column had moved to the fourth arroyo, so we set off in that direction but had to stop at the third arroyo because the night had become very dark.

February 21, 1967

Today at 0700 we caught up with the column in the fourth arroyo, from which we shall depart at 1030 to try to go over Loma Pelada. It seems that from this point, as well as up the third arroyo, it is passable.

February 22, 1967

Yesterday we walked up the fourth arroyo until 1900. We had to set up camp in the arroyo itself, hanging the hammocks from bushes on its edge, because up to that point and even there the arroyo was between nearly unbroken walls rising from 20 to 50 meters. Today we managed to leave the arroyo and climb along a ridge on the bald mountain, arriving at one of the main massifs at 1800, and camping there. There travel was very difficult because the terrain was extremely steep and we had to make our way through brambles and bushes.

February 23, 1967

Today we proceeded toward the main massif of Loma Pelada which faces east and then went down in that direction. Thus we walked until 1900 and set up camp without having found water, and so we will not be able to cook the *mote* we still have. Tomorrow we shall go without eating all day, because even if we were to find water the *mote* takes more than 6 hours to cook. I twisted my right foot and am limping a little.

February 24, 1967

Today we are to continue walking east. My foot hurts quite a bit although the medic bandaged it up for me. We are out of water and have no idea how long it will take us to get to [symbol] River.

February 25, 1967

Yesterday at 1800 we arrived at a small stream where we camped and cooked the *mote* we still had, together with two turkey hens we hunted. We ate the turkeys and some of the *mote;* the rest we have eaten today. At the campsite we found several *corojo* palms. We cut them down and ate the hearts of palm as a salad and also some of the fruit. We camped all day waiting while a group of *macheteros* opened a way to the [symbol] River. At 1900 we heard about an incident between Marcos and Pacho. At 2030 we heard that the comrades who were opening up the way had reached the river.

February 26, 1967

We resumed the march at 0630; at 0800 we made a stop and held a meeting of all personnel at which Ramón gave an account of the result of the trip thus far, pointing out its usefulness and emphasizing the way we have begun to experience the hard and difficult moments of the guerrilla activity, and stressing that what we have experienced is infinitesimal compared to what will come in the future. He explained that the Manila people, as he had pointed out earlier, had the advantage over the Bolivians of having undergone tests of this sort of combat. He related how in the time elapsed our shortcomings had become evident; how 7 years of revolution had influenced some comrades who, when they got the services of chauffeurs, secretaries, and others, had become accustomed to giving orders and asking to have everything done for them; how a relatively easy life had made us forget somewhat the sacrifices and rigors of the life we were now living again. Ramon went on to say that among the Manilans there were some who, although they had been in combat, had never gone through the hard experience we were having. He ended this portion of his remarks by saying that all those from Manila were known to him and that was precisely why we had come; but that he had to admit his ignorance concerning the character of comrade Marcos, and that Pacho had proved that he was still very far from being a true guerrilla. The merits of the Manilans had only given them the right to take part in this glorious and extremely important fighting. "I," he said, "did not have friends but comrades in Manila, and whenever I defended someone in trouble it was because I was right and not for the sake of friendship. Here, the man who by his attitude deserves it, can have responsibility and the opportunity to set the example. Comrade Pacho, next time he has a problem of this nature," he said, "will be dismissed dishonorably and returned to Manila, and comrade Marcos must change his way of addressing his comrades, because the manner he employs speaks against his authority because it is insulting." He declared the meeting finished and ordered the march resumed until 1800 hours.

I must point out that this meeting was due to the incident that took place between M. and P. [Marcos and Pacho] the day before, because when he got them together to clear up the situation, as Ramón told me later, he had decided that P. had failed to obey an order of M's and after the incident had given a false version of it.

We resumed the march and at 1030 we arrived at [symbol] and continued along its left bank. At 1600 there was a very regrettable and painful accident: Benjamín made a mistake, left the just-opened path, and when he tried to return to it slipped and fell into the river. I was then about 100 meters from the spot; other comrades, such as Ramón, A. [Alejandro] and R. [Rubio], were about 60 meters away. We ran to the spot and jumped into the water but it was impossible to find him. The current dragged me about 600 meters, while I was searching, in less than 10 minutes. This gives some idea of the current speed at this point, and the depth was enormous. I touched bottom only about 6 times. He did all he could; he did not scream, Ramón pointed out.

February 27, 1967

Yesterday we consumed half the beans we had left over, and today, after walking until 1700 hours along the river bank we reached our objective, the [symbol]. We camped and consumed our last ration. Now we have three cans per person: one of milk, one of sardines, and one of broth.

February 28, 1967

Today we built a raft and got hearts of palm and a fish. For lunch we made fish soup, and for supper we have the hearts of palm flavored with a hawk I killed. At 1600 the vanguard crossed [symbol] on the raft, but it reached the shore one kilometer downstream and had to be broken up. At sundown we, Chino,

Alejandro, Rubio and myself, came back to the camp. The stream took us about 500 meters away. At night we built another raft.

March 1, 1967

It is raining since dawn and the river is very swollen. Ramón orders Marcos to have the vanguard advance on the other bank toward [symbol]. We shall await to see if tomorrow the river will be passable.

March 2, 1967

We wait until 1200 hours, and since the river is still impassable, we march until 1700. Two men from the center and four from the rearguard chop down *corojo* palms and extract the hearts to make our meal together with three cans of meat. We have now consumed six cans.

March 3, 1967

We keep marching from 0600 to 1800 hours, at which time we arrive at the Arroyo de Las Panas. We eat another three cans of meat, for a total to date of nine.

March 4, 1967

Miguel and Urbano go out to cut a trail. The rest of us go out to look for hearts of palm or hunt. We, the collectors of hearts of palm, get enough for two rations for everybody; the hunters kill two little monkeys and eight small birds which we divide between the two platoons.

March 5, 1967

Braulio and Joaquín continue with the trail. Miguel leads the hunters for hearts of palm, and the rest go out to hunt meat. We get 10 small birds and enough hearts of palm for today and tomorrow and the day after.

March 6, 1967

We continue to march on the left bank of the [symbol], setting up camp at 1800 hours, and eat birds caught along the way, and hearts of palm.

March 7, 1967

We march all day and camp at 1800 hours. Today we ate

three cans of meat with the hearts of palm we had left, so that we have six cans left.

March 8, 1967

At 0530 hours, eight of us go out hunting until 0900, and return for the day's march. I bagged six little birds and two monkeys; Marganga and Chinculine killed nine parrots, and with that we made a broth. At 1200, Urbano and Miguel, who had gone out at 0600 hours to cut trail, arrived at a place from which they could see the opposite bank, a water turbine, and two or three people. Ramón decided to send Inti and Chinchuline to find out what there is, with orders to buy every possible merchandise, if any is available. When they cross the river with their clothes on, the river drags Inti, who is forced to shed his clothes, and with Chincho's help is able to reach the shore, but in his drawers. We posted a watch opposite the place, but the entire day goes by and the comrades are not seen. This worries us all, and Ramón decided that tomorrow Alejandro and I are to cross over on a small raft, carrying our weapons, to see what has happened, and if there are police in the place to attack them and rescue the comrades.

March 9, 1967

At 0830, when the small raft is being finished, Inti and Ricardo are observed on the other side, building a raft, and so our mission is cancelled. At 1400 the comrades are able to cross the river, bringing sugar, cigarettes, tobacco, and merchandise for 5 days, counting six remaining cans.

March 10, 1967

We kept on going until 1800 hours, when we camped.

March 11, 1967

We kept on going.

March 12, 1967

Today Miguel and Tuma go out to scout the area of some cliffs by the river which seem to be impassable. They stayed out until 1900 and then only Tuma returned, since it had apparently gotten too late for Miguel.

March 13, 1967

We marched until 1800 hours. By 1100 we arrived where Miguel was.

March 14, 1967

We march until 1200 hours, at which time we reach [symbol], but the troop cannot cross because the river is swollen and it is extremely dangerous to do so. We only have *mote* and [illegible word] for today, and since the troop is unable to cross, Urbano is prevented from going to the camp to ask them to send food. I ask Ramón to let me go; I can walk less than Urbano but I can swim and cross the river. Ramón agrees. I leave by myself with the rifle, my clothes, and a coat. I start out at 1430 and walk until 1730; I stop, build a fire, and eat the *mote* they gave me for the trip, and then hash.

March 15, 1967

I continue toward the camp, sometimes in the river and sometimes along the bank until 1900, when I arrive at the cave on Arroyo #1 for my overnight stay. With two small birds I killed and plenty of guavas I found I have enough food till I get to the camp.

March 16, 1967

I resume marching at 0700 hours, after having picked up 80 guavas. At about 1030, I meet Benigno and three other comrades who are going to the mouth of Arroyo #1 to wait for Ramón with food for four meals. I tell him that he is to go on till he meets Ramón, which is the order I have, and he agrees. From this I deduce that if on the 15th Ramón was able to cross the river, by the 17th or 18th he will receive the goods and they will be without food only 2 or 3 days. I go on; it is no longer necessary, however, for me to get to the camp today, so I decide to stay at Bear Camp. Among the things Benigno told me was that the Army had been at the farm again on the 13th, so that they are expected to advance toward the camp.

March 17, 1967

(Today I got a letter from my wife, dated December 29, 1966.) I leave Bear Camp together with four visitors and Julio, a Bolivian doctor who has joined the guerrillas. At 0930 I detach myself from them because they are going slowly, and arrive at the camp at 12:30. There they give me plenty of bread, sweets, and an oversize lunch. I tell Marcos and Antonio my mission. They tell me that two recruits brought by Guevara have deserted and apparently have been captured and betrayed the position. The deserters know about the presence of Ramón and Debre, Tania, Carlos, and Chino, who are visitors and who will leave when they have talked to Ramón. At 1900, we are told that the Army has gone to the farm during the morning, ten men in a pick-up truck presumably including personnel of the DIB. Antonio and Aniceto also report that while they were coming toward the camp they found that about 60 police were going downstream, taking with them a mule and prisoner. We figure that the man may be Salustiano, a comrade being sent by Loro with information from the farm to the camp. We examine the situation and conclude that tomorrow the Army will advance again; so tonight we shall set up a watch with four men under my command and tomorrow we shall lay an ambush.

[By "DIB," Rolando meant the DIC—Departamento de Investigacion Criminal, Bolivia's FBI. For some unknown reason, Pombo uses the same erroneous initials, "DIB."]

March 18, 1967

We discuss the best place for the ambush. Marcos thinks it should be the maneuvering ground, whereas I think it should be the defense position. Marcos's argument is that in the maneuvering field we can guarantee that the Army will not pass, regardless of their numerical superiority. I argue that with seven or eight men in the defense position we can also guarantee that they shall not pass. Marcos gets upset at this suggestion, and says to me: "There you have the men; guarantee it." I say: "You are the chief; give your orders and I shall comply." Antonio cuts in and points out that it is true that in the maneuvering position we only cover the entrance in the event that the Army advances up river; if it comes downriver it will slip right into the camp while we are in ambush 45 minutes from the entrance. Marcos says that eight men should not be split up into two groups, because that way neither place would be guaranteed. We tell him that is not the intent, but to have a single group at the entrance where both directions come together. He points out that we have told him he is the chief, and yet we are not accepting his decision. Antonio replies that that is not the intention; that he is suggesting our setting up the ambush where he proposes and posting two men at the entrance to the camp. He agrees to the proposal and I keep quiet, because the decision is not what I had in mind. We set out for the ambush and half an hour after we arrive Loro comes up and tells us that yesterday afternoon, when one of the guards who had gone into the house was coming toward his watch post, he was forced to shoot him dead, after which the Army left the place. Under these changed circumstances, Marcos proposes moving the ambush to the lower corner of the right wing of the defense position, and we do so.

For a complete idea of the positions involved in the discussion, see the sketch on the following page.

In the last position we stayed the 18th until 1600 hours, when Aniceto and I stayed on guard and the others withdrew. At 2100 we were relieved by four men who stayed until 0600.

March 19, 1967

We decide that I take charge of Bear Camp to accelerate the transfer of the supplies and look for a safe place for the visitors, the sick, and some of the new men who do not look combat-worthy. At this camp Nato will be put in charge and I will rejoin the ambush. While I am leaving for Bear Camp, Marcos and Antonio will attend to the ambush and start forwarding together with half of the personnel a certain proportion of the supplies which we have considered strategic. They are also to transfer the individual reserves for the people who are coming with Ramon. We decide that the ambush be moved to one kilometer from the camp in the direction of Bear Camp. I leave at 1030 and reach Bear Camp at 1500.

March 20, 1967

At 0700 hours Nato leaves with the *gondoleros* to look for supplies, I hide the stuff brought in the night before, and leave for the scouting expedition to look for a place with water to which to take the personnel I referred to yesterday. At 1830, I return without success. I meet Ramón, who is arriving at the camp, and I explain to him in broad outline the steps taken until now. He criticizes us for having wasted experienced personnel such as Pacho and myself on tasks other than defense, and tells me about the latest incidents on the way: the center group crossed the river on the 15th and the rearguard on the 16th, but when it crossed because Tania was here. He refers to Iván, one uninteresting the raft overturned, with the loss of six weapons and six packs, and Carlos drowned when he became exhausted.

When we got to the camp we met a messenger from Marcos and Antonio with a note summoning me for 1600 hours to place midway between the ambush and Bear Camp. They were asking for cooking kettles and supplies. When asked what the kettles were for, the messenger replied that all the personnel had returned from the ambush and were to camp at the place to which I had been summoned, and tomorrow they would proceed to the camp. This did not seem logical to me, but when the messenger affirmed it I told Ramón, who ordered the messenger to tell Marcos and Antonio that he was forbidding them to come to him and that they were immediately to occupy the defense position. It was unbelievable to retreat without a fight, and it was a serious error, he said.

March 21, 1967

I join the center group and go out with Alejandro, who is bringing specific instructions for Marcos, and four other men. Alejandro, in bad shape because of his swollen feet, decides that I should walk ahead with the instructions and the personnel and that he will follow more slowly, as his legs permit. I arrive at the camp at 1600 hours and I tell Marcos that Ramón's instructions are as follows:

1. Set up an ambush downriver where he thinks best.
2. Organize the defense at the entrance to the camp.
3. Send a group of experienced comrades to scout downriver.

When Alejandro arrives, Marcos meets with us and we decide that I am to go to the ambush. With another four men, it will be set up in the maneuvering area. Antonio is to go with Miguel and Loro on the scouting expedition. I am to escort them to the Loma del Avispero, a distance of 1½ hours on foot, and come back to the ambush. Marcos and Alejandro are to attend to the defense with the rest of the personnel. This will be done on the 22nd, at daybreak.

March 22, 1967

We depart at 0600 hours on our respective missions. When we get to the cave of the Avispero, Antonio tells me he understood I was to wait for him in ambush in the [word missing] and that this has . . . [an entire page is missing.] . . . forming an angled strip ending in a small stone mountain about 80 meters from where I place the machine gun.

In sending the message explaining the position, I ask for two more men. I have two men keep watch all night, and at 0100 hours of the 23rd the two men arrive and one more. I get the order to leave Benigno in charge of the ambush and withdraw to the camp.

March 23, 1967

At 0700, as I was explaining the ambush to Benigno, the enemy force arrives. I decide not to withdraw. I open fire as planned. The gunfire lasts about 6 minutes, the enemy force agrees to surrender. A tally of enemy casualties shows 7 dead, 6 wounded, and 11 prisoners out of a total of 32, and 8 have escaped. The materiel taken includes three 60-mm mortars and 8 cases of grenades for them; one 30-cal machine gun with 500 rounds; two BZ submachine guns; two UZZIs machine pistols; 16 Mausers and 2,000 rounds for them; two radio sets, etc. The prisoners included two captains.

[NOTE: A few pages follow which Rolando apparently did not keep in chronological or sequential order. The editor has consequently been forced to take the liberty of selecting an arbitrary order which would seem to conform to the diarist's intent.]

At 1600 hours I get to the camp and I report to Ramón the action in the ambush and the attitude of the personnel, only one of whom (Walter) got cold feet. The B comrades Coco, Pedro, Guevara, Paco, and Chino behaved very well. At 6, I join the defense ambush.

March 24, 1967

Still entrenched in the defense point; part of the day I am in charge. At 2200 hours, I am relieved and I retire to sleep.

March 25, 1967

We go back to the defense point. I take charge because Alejandro is ill and needs his rest. At 1000 hours aircraft bomb and strafe the area of the camp and environs. Yesterday the wounded and other prisoners were set free and were given permission to remove their dead within 3 days. At 1800 I get orders to lift the ambush and leave a reinforced watch.

At 1830, Ramón holds a meeting with all personnel and reviews the marches that have been made. He notes the deeply felt loss of Benjamin and Carlos, and stresses the qualities of the latter who, though not physically strong, had a high degree of spirit and morale. He discusses the comrades who have been exemplary on the training march: Miguel, Inti, Pombo and Rolando. He notes that there are few Bolivians among the examples and adds that this is natural, since among the Manilans there are comrades who are not going through this experience for the first time. But he hopes that on future trips the number of Bolivians will be much greater.

Then he refers to the case of Marcos, listing his errors and incorrect attitudes, although he is a very meritorious comrade. Among the defects, he indicates his tendency to have others serve him; his tendency toward lack of discipline; his despotic attitude toward his comrades; self-sufficiency and lack of authority. He accuses him of not complying with the order which Ramón had given to return by way of the Nancahuasú; having come to the farm in full daylight against orders, at which time a shot had been fired at him by a presumed collaborator of the Army and he had failed to report it: also of having camped at the home of a peasant who accompanied him for 3 leagues and then led the Army in his pursuit, who was unable to catch up with him but it was verified that he died in the ambush of 23 March 1967 while guiding the Army.

In conclusion, he announces the removal of Marcos as chief of the vanguard and third in command of the guerrilla band, and gives him the choice of returning to Manila or staying on as an ordinary combatant. He points that Marcos has ruined a large part of his good record. In place of Marcos, Miguel is to be chief of the vanguard. Marcos agrees to stay on as a fighter, and is assigned to the rearguard.

Ramón goes on to explain that among the personnel brought by Guevara there are comrades who are not guerrilla material because they are dregs: Chingolo, Pepe, and Paco. They want to do no work; they want no weapons; they want to carry no loads; they feign illness, etc. These, in addition to two deserters from the group. What shall we do with these people? We do not want to [illegible word] as soon as possible. Meanwhile, a warning: if they do not work, they will not eat. As soon as we have hidden our possessions, Ramón said, without their knowing where, we will give them a few pesos—this money belongs to the people—and let them manage as they best can.

He again emphasized the toughness and difficulty of the struggle and the long time it will take, so that the new recruits may decide whether they want to leave or not. He referred to the case of Eusebio: thief, liar, hyprocrite, who also says he wants to leave because he is tired. He will be treated the same as the other three brought in by Guevara.

He reported on the statements made in Manila by the Party, to the effect that it would not demand the leadership of the war but collaborate with us, and that it intended to send a commission to talk with Ramón. We are ready to discuss, Ramón declared, and to accept that collaboration, but in deed, not in words; let them give us cadres to work in the city; let them get us arms and give us economic help: that is, a form of help. But while there is talk of helping, comrades Aniceto, Pedro, and Loyola have been separated from the Youth, and the deeds are once more at variance with the words. We shall again discuss and we shall hide nothing from them, comrades; we shall keep them informed on all political and [illegible word] matters. We have to trust this group, and the important thing is, the comrades who have firmly decided to fight and make the [true] . . . [words missing] Ramón concluded [from top of p. *8*].

March 26, 1967

6 a.m. In ambush all day til 1800 hours and the Army does not advance. I take charge of the ambush because Joaquin and Alejandro are ill.

March 27, 1967

At 0600 hours we take our positions in the ambush. I take charge, as Joaquín and Alejandro are still sick. There is news brought by Antonio and Inti that the Army is at the mouth of the Yaqui River (about 9 hours' walking distance from here). At 1200 I send out scouting teams in both directions to look for points from which the enemy advance can be observed; since today's observation post did not yield that information (because the comrades assigned to it did not find the place), I send Urbano to locate it exactly. At 1215, I receive the order to send three comrades along the maneuvering area to pick up a parachute that the flyers have dropped on the little hunting plain about 45 minutes from here along the river. Antonio, Marcos and Pablo set out to execute the mission, with instructions that if they meet soldiers and these are few they are to capture them and if not they are to leave them alone. At 1730 they return with the information that it was not the place mentioned earlier but further on, toward the area of the Yaqui River, because they had searched the little plains well and had found nothing. At 1800 hours, I get orders to withdraw with the men comprising the ambush to attend a meeting with Ramón. At 1830 the ambush is lifted.

Ramón points out that there are three things to take care of, besides maintaining the ambush:

1. To hide all the confiscated materials and the supplies we own, for such a time as we are ready to take out the four dismissed men.

2. The visitors will have to remain with the guerrilla band until we can get them out by some road which is closer to the city.

3. The need to send 10 men to get corn from the farm, going very carefully so that the Army will not take them by surprise; in any event, if they see the Army advancing upstream they are to set up an ambush and wait for them. Braulio is to head this mission; I am to remain with the main ambush with another 12 men.

March 28, 1967

At 0600 hours, we take our position in the ambush and stay there until 1830, at which time I go on to the reduced watch group and the other personnel withdraw. At 2145, Braulio returns from his mission and reports that they got to the farm and he set up several watch points. One of them saw eight members of the Red Cross approaching, together with four soldiers in mufti. The watch stopped them and talked to them. Just then a truckload of soldiers arrived. Braulio told them that soldiers were not to come there if they were to carry off the bodies, and the truck left with the soldiers. After that, the men Braulio sent to gather corn returned with only three packs full and two horses, one of which is to be slaughtered tomorrow. At 2200 hours they relieve me.

March 29, 1967

At 0540 hours, we leave for the ambush again, and take positions at 0600. At 1200, two planes machine-gun the area, but at a safe distance from our position. At 1830, I pull out of the ambush. I feel a little ill.

March 30, 1967

I stay in camp, resting, and I use the time to get my things in order in preparation for leaving at any time. Antonio takes over the ambush.

March 31, 1967

At 0540 hours I return to the ambush, where we stay until 1830.

April 1, 1967

At 0540 hours, we set up the ambush with only part of the center force and the rearguard, because the vanguard has gone off to scout our farm and, if the Army is not there, to set up an ambush between Pincal and the farm. After that they will gather corn. At 1400, Tuma reports that they have seen three soldiers proceeding downriver. The ambush is strengthened and Ramón takes over himself. He orders me to try to capture the three soldiers who have been seen 300 meters from the watch point. At 1800, I get orders to return to my position. In the note Ramon tells me that the little soldiers have disappeared. He also orders me to pull out the ambush at 1830. At that time the rearguard takes over the night watch. He also orders me to take over the rearguard in place of Joaquin, who is still ill, and to make everything ready to leave this same night. At 2230 we are ready to start, but it is postponed until 0400.

April 2, 1967

I start out leading the rearguard and with instructions from Ramón, either to:

1. Join the vanguard, reinforce the ambush they are maintaining, and with the rest of the personnel open a path to the arroyo in the Piraboy Ravine, transferring there all the corn possible and one or two head of cattle; or

2. Set up an ambush between Pincal and Lagunillas in order to surprise them on their rear (if the vanguard has not been able to get to the farm because the Army is there.

Once either mission has been completed, to establish contact with the center at the entrance to the Arroyo de los Monos after having placed an ambush on the Nancahuasú River between the ravine and our farm.

At 0730, I arrive at the farm and Miguel and I put the first alternative into practice. By nightfall we have finished at the farm and move to the P. Ravine.

April 3, 1967

I place the ambush at the point indicated (the Nancahuasú River), at 0630 hours. At 1000, we make contact with Ramon. At 1830, I pull out the personnel from the ambush and at 1930 I attend a meeting of leaders with Ramón, at which he explains the plan to follow after tomorrow.

April 4, 1967

The column leaves for Piraboy. I put Pedro in charge of six men of the rearguard to continue with the column, while I stay behind with another four to cover the entrance to the ravine to make sure that while the column carries out the operation in Pirirenda the Army will not cut off our retreat.

April 5, 1967

At 0800 hours, two comrades arrive from Ramón to report the impending arrival of the column, which was able to get only to Pirirenda and not Gutiérrez, because there is an Army force of 150 men camped in Pirirenda which is moving toward the Nacahuasu, and their path runs more or less by the ravine (the place for our retreat) or close to it. At 1000, the column arrives; the rearguard regroups and continues its normal march. At 1900, the comrades who stayed at the ambush site report that the Army continues to occupy our house, the old camp on the trail which goes from the house to the river, the clump of trees on the bend of the arroyo as it enters into the Nacahuasu. In addition, shots are heard on the Algarañaz farm and on the path on the left bank coming from the camp just abandoned by us. Miguel also reports that, at the mouth of the arroyo of the ravine at about 300 meters on the right bank, about ten little soldiers were seen bathing. Ramón decides that we pass by the mouth of the ravine at 0300 hours and go into the jungle in the direction of the Arroyo de los Monos.

April 6, 1967

Reveille at 0200 hours. At 0300 we start for the arroyo, and finish crossing it at 0430 or thereabouts, but we only advance a few meters so as not to make any noise. At 0700, while we are still on the left bank of the Nancahuasú, 80 or 100 soldiers go up the right and into ambush opposite us, about 25 meters away. We stay hidden where we are while the center group withdraws and then we of the rearguard withdraw at 1000, with the soldiers unaware of our presence. After we go off about 100 meters distance, we go on toward the northwest until it gets dark, when the vanguard sees four drovers coming upstream. We hold them until 2000 hours. They report that they are taking the cattle to the Army camped at Pincal. We take two cows from them and explain what ELN [National Liberation Army] stands for. They promise not to tell the Army about us but to say that they located only part of the cattle, which are scattered along the banks of the river. They furnish a few data of interest. After releasing the drovers we proceed along the river to the Arroyo de los Monos, where we go in about 300 meters and make camp.

April 7, 1967

The camp is moved about an hour's march away while the vanguard does some scouting and opens up a path to Gutiérrez. I go into ambush with the rearguard on the Nancahuasú River until dark.

April 8, 1967

The vanguard continues to open trail and scout; the center transports merchandise for the sick; the rearguard stays in ambush in the same spot as yesterday.

April 9, 1967

The rearguard continues in ambush; it is reinforced with three men for the vanguard, so that we are ten in ambush. At 1815 hours we retire to the camp.

April 10, 1967

We maintain the ambush with ten men. At 0950 hours, I am told by the watch that the Army is coming down the river; he puts their strength at about 20 men. At 1020 the fighting begins. At the end of 3 minutes one enemy is dead and three wounded, two of them dying afterward, and 7 are captured (11 casualties in all). Four soldiers flee. We take six Garands, ten M-1s, one [illegible], and four Mausers. We lose our comrade Rubio, shot in the head. Ramon sends the entire vanguard as reinforcements and then orders me to retire to the second position. I explain to him that I have advanced about 250 or 300 meters to prevent the four soldiers from escaping, and that the terrain enables us to prevent the enemy from entering to our depth, and he orders me to continue in my ambush. At 1700, the watch reports that the Army is advancing downstream. At 1710, a battle begins that lasts about 15 minutes. We inflict 26 casualties on the enemy: 7 dead, 6 wounded, 13 prisoners, including the major commanding the column, comprised of 120 men. We take one Browning, one Billallol [sic], one mortar, 15 Garands, 4 M-3, 2 M-1, and 5 Mausers.

April 11, 1967

At 0600 hours we release the prisoners and permit them to remove the dead and wounded from both battles. They are granted a 24-hour truce as of noon to pick up their dead, on condition that this truce applies only along the river bed; if they go into the jungle the truce will be broken. The major agrees as we escort him one kilometer upstream. On our way back we check the places from which the Army fled and pick up the things they left. Then we withdraw to the second position and the vanguard and rearguard go into ambush until 1700 hours and then withdraw; meanwhile the center transports the captured supplies and equipment.

April 12, 1967

I turn over command of the rearguard to Joaquín, who has recovered from his illness and has come back to duty. At 1200 hours the center group leaves for camp; the vanguard had left at 0700; the rearguard will take a 2-day rest in the third position and then join us in the camp on the Nancahuasu. We set up camp at 1800.

April 13, 1967

We continue marching toward the camp. Our first group arrives at 1500 and the rest at 1830. We learn that the Army failed to find the main cave when it took the camp a few days ago.

April 14, 1967

At 0600 hours, I take over the defense with six men from the center and seven from the vanguard. At 1820 I lift the ambush.

April 15, 1967

At 0600 hours, we take up defense positions until 1500, at which time the rearguard takes our place. At 2000 we have a meeting with Ramón, at which time he tells us that we are going to move toward another area (to the south, on the Sucre-Monte-agudo road). He points out that in this area are peasants among whom we have to establish our base. He explains that this time we shall be in contact with many more peasants; that we must bear in mind that their first reaction will be one of fear, and it is possible that their reaction may at first be unfavorable to the guerrilla band and some may even tell the Army of our presence. He advises that we treat them carefully and earn their trust. Another purpose of the trip is to get food, to get Danton and Carlos out, and become familiar with the area.

Ramón also reports that 20 cans of milk are missing from the cave and explains that this is not the case of a comrade picking up a can and drinking it, which is blameworthy but not as bad as this, which is a premeditated action; that the man who is capable of doing this does not deserve to be one of us and should be shot; that if milk continues to be lost and the thief is not found he will stop buying milk for 6 months. Finally, he reads Communiqués #1 and #2, which we are trying to get to the press.

April 16, 1967

At 0600 hours we go south on the Nancahuasu River, arriving at the village of Ticucha at 1930 and camping in the jungle while a meal is being prepared.

April 17, 1967

We stay in the area of the village while the Bolivian comrades make contact with the local peasants. At 2200 hours, we continue south in the direction of Muyupampa, stopping at 0430 on the 18th at a small mountain on the edge of the road.

April 18, 1967

At 1300 hours we start again and walk until 1530, at which time we make a stop while a meal is ordered, prepared at the home of a peasant in the place known as [blank space]. The peasant is surnamed [Cala?].

April 19, 1967

We stay in the place until 1800, when we continue toward Muyupampa, arriving at the highway at midnight. We hide the pack and advance [several words missing] of the little town. The vanguard meets a patrol of four residents and arrests them, confiscating two M-3 and two revolvers. Among the arrested is an agent of the DIB. Under interrogation he reveals that in the afternoon three truckloads of guards arrived. This seems to be the result of the report made by the brother of peasant [space blank], this being confirmed by the statement of the independent British newsman, [name omitted], who contacted our guerrilla band at 1500. We detained him and brought him to Muyupampa, where we released him after he promised to help Carlos and Danton to get out. At 0300 hours we withdrew from Muyupampa, leaving Carlos, Danton and the British newsman hidden in the area of the village, and releasing the residents who made up the DIB patrol.

April 20, 1967

At 0900 hours we arrive at Don Nemesio's house.

POMBO'S DIARY

Pombo's diary covers from July 14, 1966 to May 29, 1967. Despite his uneducated style, Pombo had a keen political insight and is the most valuable diarist in describing the political infighting between Ché and his various Communist allies and opponents. He also reports on his observations of the guerrilla group itself and the many personality conflicts within it.

While loyal to Ché, Pombo occasionally will indicate his objection to Ché's handling of a situation. He was primarily responsible for the establishment of the base at Nancahuazú and his coldly realistic counsel, when Ché followed it, was an extremely valuable counterbalance to Ché's theoretical enthusiasms.

A 27 year old Negro, Pombo led the three Cuban survivors through the heart of a hostile Bolivia and finally to safety in Chile, in February of 1968.

1966

July 14

We left Prague by train, via Frankfurt, at 1000 hours. The only inconvenience we had to face was with the Czechs at departure time, who claimed that our visas were for air travel so we could not leave by surface transportation. In this city, we stayed at the Hotel Royal.

July 16

We left for South America via a Lufthansa flight, our itinerary being Zuri[ch], Dakar, Río and Sao Paulo, which is our destination.

July 17

We had a great fright at the airport because they took away my baggage as if they were going to make a special inspection of it at Customs. I was told it was overweight. We stayed at the Hotel Broadway.

July 19

After taking all the necessary steps to get visas for Bolivia, we sent a cable to Papi in which we told him that we would arrive on the 22nd.

July 21

We took a Cruzeiro do Sul flight to Santa Cruz de la Sierra in Bolivia. We were informed at the airport that we would be making a stopover at Corumba and that we would continue on the next day. But at the airport at Campo Grande, we were told that the plane would go on and that we passengers for Corumba would continue our trip on the 22nd at 0004 hours. We met a Bolivian girl called Sara Polo (She is very nice).

July 22

We continue our trip to Corumba. We are told there is no flight to Santa Cruz until Monday the 25th. We try to get the airline to pay our room and board, but they refuse to do so. We are seven passengers all told (2 Brazilians, 2 Bolivians, 1 German, and we 2 Ecuadorians). We stayed at the Gran Hotel.

Bolivians: the girl we spoke of earlier, Sara Polo Ariñez—very interesting. The other one is Sr. Mario Urquídez Cordana, representative of a German firm; he behaved well, but tried to find out if we were smugglers. The Brazilians were the wife and daughter of Mario. I liked the little girl, Claudia, very much. Because of the restlessness in her, she reminded me a lot of Harry Andrés.

That evening, while we were eating, another Ecuadorian arrived who said his name was Diego—I don't remember his family name—son of a former Minister of his country. He worried us a bit.

[Pombo speaks of himself and his travelling companion, Tuma, as "we Ecuadorians" because both travelled on false Ecuadorian passports. With this in mind, the reader can appreciate the humor in Pombo's subsequent reference to "another Ecuadorian."]

July 23

This group of the "Latin American Confraternity," as Mario christened it, decided to split up so that Sara could get home as quickly as possible [because] they had been expecting her now for four days.

July 24

We were invited to attend Mass, but decided instead to go to a movie.

July 25

We got up early because I had promised to take Sara so that she could leave in the morning. After this, we went to get our inoculations against yellow fever. We left at 1400 hours. On our arrival at Santa Cruz, we were very happy to see the familiar face of Comrade Mbili, who awaited us. The Bolivian comrades took care of arranging our documents, etc.

We conversed with Mbili, gave him all the necessary papers and explained to him what Ramón had told us, verbally, for his orientation (the Tania matter, the need to acquire a farm farther north in the zone of possible operations because of Emiliano's people. Ramon's trip to the Island possible duration of their stay there). We were very surprised when he asked me where the house was to be, for he had received no specific guidance in this regard. We told him that it was our understanding, because they had told us separately, that they had sent word to him about the location of the farm, that [our] principal efforts in Bolivia would be concentrated thereabouts; although we knew very little about this because we were so compartmented that we were only suppliers of merchandise. He said that if they had given him more time, he would have had everything ready; but that now we would have to begin to look for a place for us because the house of Tejada Zoyano had been given up and he didn't want the one belonging to República Dominicana "blown." If necessary, he would send Mongo to the farm. He could not go himself because it was located practically inside a military encampment (3 kms. away). We left for La Paz with the idea of helping out to whatever extent possible. Because, as he had told us, we would have to get started because nothing had been done.

We discussed the new alignment with the representatives of the Party, beginning with the conditions in the country for the struggle. We tried to get a commitment from them to join in the struggle even though Estanislao opposed this. We suggested that, from their standpoint, the best thing was to put it to Estanislao that they were certain that their position would be to join in the armed struggle; and that if he did not agree they were prepared to go along with us. We tried to learn of the plan for an uprising that would have the characteristics of a *coup de main,* and which, if it failed, would serve to awaken the consciousness of the people. El Negro had got us four men to prepare things in Argentina or Peru, and promised to get us six more.

["República Dominicana" is the name of a street in La Paz where Ché's urban group had one of many rented houses used in connection with preparations for the guerrilla campaign and the urban insurrection which was scheduled to follow.]

July 26

We left Santa Cruz for La Paz early in the morning. The road is very hilly because here the ascent begins to the high plateau of the Cordillera Oriental of the Andes. (It has very good tactical possibilities for operating, although it does not appear to have an abundance of water.)

July 27

We reach La Paz. It is a provincial city, situated in a concave depression, completely surrounded by mountains. We went to the home of a man called Tellería, a member of the CC PCB [Central Committee of the Partido Comunista Boliviano, Bolivian Communist Party], who is in charge of the supplies that we will need (arms, medicines, food, clothing, etc.). About a month ago, Papi had told us that this comrade was looking for a house, and he had still not found one for God-knows-what reasons. The only solution remaining was to go and see Estanislao to see if the organization has an available house where we can leave Camba, a Bolivian comrade who is still working with Papi. The rest of us will stay in the República Dominicana house.

July 28

Papi discusses with Estanislao the new situation created by the guidelines from The Island. It was agreed to begin the armed struggle immediately, keeping the plan for a general uprising alive but first organizing the guerrillas. The bad parts of the plan were explained to him [Estanislao], because it requires the cooperation of the [Cuban] Armed Forces. Without that, a great number of men would face the possibility of confronting the enemy at a disadvantage. But we had to let the matter drop, to be discussed later by Mongo when he arrives. The guerrillas can count on 20 men provided by the Party.

July 29

We informed Sánchez, the Peruvian comrade who serves as liaison between us and El Chino, of our Government's decision to begin the struggle, first in Bolivia and later in Peru, We explained the fact that, for the moment, conditions were better in Bolivia, beginning with the way in which things had developed in his country which would spell disaster for the armed struggle (the death of De La Puente, the imprisonment of Calixto, the disappearance of Lobatón, etc.). He understood the matter perfectly. We asked that he continue to collaborate with us, that his organization send men to be trained here, as had been planned. But instead of being trained alone, they would participate with the Bolivians in some of the actions, and later they would form the nucleus of the guerrillas in his country, along with some of our compatriots.

[Luis de la Puente and Guillermo Lobarón were the two top leaders of the Peruvian Movement of the Revolutionary Left (MIR), a guerrilla group with some peasant elements which was wiped out in 1965; Lobarón is believed dead too. Calixto and Gadea were also leaders of the MIR.]

July 30

We talked with Comrade Guevara. This comrade has an organization that is of the pro-Chinese faction. He says he favors the armed struggle. We proposed that he join the guerrilla group we are organizing, with the idea of building a united front in the struggle against Imperialism in Bolivia. We discussed the points that he had raised with Francisco (Emiliano), in which he had not been entirely sincere and open as to what he required, since at that time he had only asked for money.

He was asked to submit a new report outlining his real activities. We explained to him that the money for arms and equipment would not be given to him because the central command would be in charge of equipping the men on a centralized basis; but that he should make a detailed report so that a Manilan who was passing through here could take it back with him. These negotiations were carried on through Comrade Sánchez. The report will be delivered within two days.

We sent three comrades under Coco's orders to look for a farm where we can train, one that is in the possible zone of operations.

A report was received from Ramón asking for a detailed account of the situation. We proceeded to discuss with Mbili the most correct way of informing him.

ANALYSIS OF THE MONTH

(REPORT)

CZO #1 s/c. ARIEL. It appears that El Flaco has not informed correctly, for which reason I have talked with Pombo. I have asked a number of questions and have not received any guidance regarding them: the Guevara matter, the Sánchez matter.

As for the situation, I will tell you that we have experienced some difficulties. Estanislao vacillated a great deal at first. With the arrival of the four, we have managed to put pressure on him through Coco. Everything is going well. The man seems committed and has promised to go along with the Plan, although he proposes doing so by means of an uprising in the capital that would serve as an awakener simultaneous with the struggle in the mountains. For the latter he has promised 20 of his best men with whom we will start work.

I went on a reconnaisance to the poultry farm. It will not do because it is within a [illegible] of those here. I am looking for one in the zone indicated. I hope to have one within 20 days.

I have been obliged to inform Sánchez of our intention of concentrating our principal effort here, instead of Peru, for the time being. In general, he seemed to take it well. I see a good chance of success. I believe this is the time to tell Estanislao that Mongo is participating in this. We have sounded him out and he has indicated to us his decision that, if that happens, he will fight at his side wherever it may be. As for myself, I am not in any danger at the moment. The boys feel it is necessary to get a man to take charge of the work in the city so that I can go to the farm. I think you should send some more money as a reserve. An *abrazo*. TACO. 30/7/66.

August 5

A message was received from Manila which acknowledged receipt of the notice of our arrival; at the same time it mentions bilateral [illegible word] after the 13th. (They are crazy, because nothing is ready here.) In addition, they ask for military maps of the country. They say nothing about my report. Apparently it has not arrived.

It is suggested that Mbili not establish direct contact with Moisés, that it should be done through Sánchez—that Moisés be told we are awaiting a reply from our Government, which is studying his budget.

August 6

Two Peruvian comrades arrive with messages from El Chino, in which he states that he does not understand the reason for giving priority to Bolivia. He feels that they, although they are working slowly, have taken the decision to begin the struggle, and that whatever conditions for the struggle may be lacking, will be created. (The truth is that, in our judgment, Ramón cannot go there. There are still many things to be cleared up, such as how the capture of Calixto, the death of De La Puente, the disappearance of Lobarón, and the capture of Gadea took place. It looks, from the way things were going, as if Calixto gave himself up, through the doctor, perhaps on condition that they guarantee his life.)

Tumaini has left with Sánchez to watch the civic and military school parade—(Yankee-style majestic waste of [time? money?] of the schools).

August 7

Today there was a military parade that culminated with the unfurling of the flag by the conscripts and military schools (Army, Red Battalion, Navy, Pre-military Cadets, Rangers, etc.). Throughout the parade there was much anti-Chilean propaganda, based on the [Bolivians'] need to get a seaport. The people from the Party told us that this is a way of distracting the attention of the masses from their internal and international problems.

We are somewhat concerned about how long we have already spent in this house (12 days) without having managed to find one with better security conditions.

General Barrientos' speech was a fabric of lies, calling for unity on the basis of love of country in order to achieve a new, industrialized Bolivia with its own blast furnaces. He called on his collaborators to fulfill their responsibility to the people, for which reason it was their obligation to work night and day to make Bolivia a great nation, with its own outlet to the sea and respected by everyone.

August 8

In the evening, we visited Estanislao at his home. There, Mbili stated his need for some men in addition to the 20 that he [Estanislao] had promised. He [Estanislao] asked, what 20? He did not remember any such promise and said, furthermore, he did not have anybody who could be put in charge of an intelligence and counter-espionage apparatus, to be used as a last recourse. He explained that he had some high officials in the Government who had promised to supply him with information. He gave us the names, but it is much better that I not repeat them here. When Mbili called his attention to the 20 promised men, he replied that he was having trouble with the rest of the Central Committee, which was putting pressure on him not to enter the armed struggle, feeling that the recent elections had been a success for them because they had gotten 32,000 votes, about double what they had previously obtained. From the little progress we were making, one could see that there was something in the air; more precisely, a great deal of uncertainty about the decision to join in the struggle. In fact, it is a dead issue; and we face the problem that there is little enthusiasm for the affair. In fact, Mbili has to keep breathing down people's necks just to get anything done at all; tremendous apathy. We are the ones who are doing all the organizing, and they aren't helping us at all.

August 10

For the second time, I am having sharp stomach pains and diarrhea. We went to see Dr. Herrera to get some pills, and he told us that it is [dysentery?] but that it is nothing to worry about.

August 12

We received a report from Manila in which they say that Pacho departed for here on the 20th with a list of instructions from Mongo. He will arrive on about the 24th. Unfortunately, they did not say they were sending anyone to make contact with the front as we had hoped.

August 15

Bigote arrives with the data on the farms they had visited, indicating the one most suitable for our purposes. It was agreed that we would send Camba and Tumaini to buy the most suitable one because Mongo will probably come with Pacho.

August 19

Mbili had a meeting with Estanislao at which they discussed currently outstanding problems, Estanislao threatening to withdraw the four, [saying] that he could tell them not to join in the revolt. We said that we knew this, but that if he was not prepared to fulfill his promise, given in Manila and repeated here just a few days ago, we would have to report this to Manila. He replied that he was a man of his word and that he would keep all his promises, but he would like it understood that he had to talk it over with the men; that he would let us know before we were ready to leave for the mountains, because many of these people that had been assigned to us by him still did not know that they had been designated for this job. This was the explanation for the boy that had refused to accept because he didn't think conditions were suitable.

August 20

Bigote left with arms for Santa Cruz.

August 21

We had an argument with Comrade Sánchez, who was offended because he felt he had been left out of things. We explained to him that, to the contrary, we were fully intending to use him and that he had no reason to feel left out.

August 23

We test-fired Mbili's pistol on the outskirts of the city.

We discussed what should be done in the event that using Guevara should be approved. Sánchez suggested not entrusting Guevara with knowledge of the designated place for the zone of operations and concentration, etc. The best thing, he suggested, although it might cost a little money, would be to put his organization to a practical test. For this purpose, he could be asked to assemble his people in Cochabamba, ready to revolt. He would be given 15 days to do this, and asked to find out how much it would cost for fares, house rentals, etc. In this way, we could ascertain if he really has any people who are ready to revolt. Prior to this, we could ask him to clarify some points in his report, which would give us some additional idea of how he plans to carry it out, what his real objectives are.

August 24

Today, finally, we obtained the house that we have been looking for to rent for more than two months. The comrade [blank, no name] who had been suggested was not willing to "go into the mountains" because he had no confidence in our success, he did not feel that conditions in the country were ripe for the struggle. Later, he said that he had confidence in the people, that the masses are aware of Barrientos' political farce but that conditions are not ripe in the Party for the struggle, for what he had been told by a leader on the Central Committee differed from what had been told to him by the Secretary General. Therefore, as he sees it, there is no unanimity of opinion. Our opinion is that this comrade should talk with Mario and stay in the city to work, because he could stir up discontent among the men in the mountains. Which might oblige us to take drastic measures (shooting), which would not be a good start for the struggle.

August 26

Mario talked with the aforementioned comrade and demanded that he stick to his promise. It was agreed that he would go to the mountains.

August 27

Now Mbili has talked with the comrade. He explained the conditions under which the struggle would be carried on, that it might take 7 to 10 years to achieve final success. Mbili also told him about our attitude of not permitting unfavorable comments about the cause. We made it clear that he was mistrusted and that, therefore, he would be in a very difficult position in the mountains because he is a Party [PCB] man, and would not be able to adapt himself to our discipline, so that, although it had been agreed with Estanislao that he would go into the mountains, it would be preferable for him to stay in the city.

August 29

We invited Dr. Herrera to eat some chicken fricassee à la Manila with us. We discussed the political situation in Bolivia, the methods and means of struggle that, in his opinion, must be used to bring the left to power. He said he felt that the first thing we must do is to divest ourselves of historically traditional notions, that power is seized by means of a general uprising, a *coup de main,* without accepting the possibility of a much longer and harder struggle, a struggle that could go on for many years. The second thing for us to do would be to make emerge from the masses a leader capable of carrying on this struggle. Mario is very good as a theoretician, but is not of the caliber for this. Dr. Herrera didn't want this to be taken as criticism of our people, ·but it was the truth; he [Mario] is not the man capable of guiding the country after the victory and would be better as Minister of Education and Propaganda.

The third thing is to analyze carefully the failure in Peru, Argentina, and the current situation in Venezuela. He believed that the errors have been basically tactical military ones. To avoid them in this country, we should take full advantage of the many experiences that might help us; we should avoid repeating the mistakes previously pointed out. Fourthly, an objective analysis of the possible zone of operations should not ignore the search for a means of mobilizing the peasant masses. When beginning the struggle, we must not lose sight of the characteristics of our peasantry; we must not forget how little the fight for land means because we have thousands of hectares of idle lands. For example, in the Beni area (not in our zone of operations), a situation is about to be created which could be taken advantage of: The United Nations is querying Barrientos about control over the *coca* plantations as a means of checking cocaine smuggling. When such steps are taken, discontent will increase because for the Indian, *coca* is something more than a stimulant. It is fetish related to everything in his life. It has to do with future harvests, with hunger, with his and his children's future, with the passing of his forebears, etc.; in short, with his whole religious outlook.

There is talk behind closed doors of sending a contingent to Vietnam. In case it is decided to send troops, this can be exploited on the national level.

Sánchez, the Peruvian comrade who is working with us here, arrived a bit late at a meeting we had with somebody called Roberto, one of Guevara's people. This didn't bother us because there is always a lot of drinking at these meetings and we never talk about anything very important with these people. Mbili thinks Sánchez is not too happy, and, with the matter of his country suspended, he is considering a return to Peru. If that suits him, we agree. We will talk frankly with him about the matter, and, if that's the way things are, we'll send someone to look up El Chino to learn what Sánchez knows about Ramon, and then act accordingly.

August 30

I talked with Sánchez. He stated that it had been proposed to him that he should stay and collaborate with us until the proper conditions could be created for his return to Peru voluntarily, and that he had accepted, that when he had taken this decision he had been fully aware of what he was doing and he was determined to stand by this commitment. But he wanted to let us know that it had greatly pained him that at times we had not trusted him. We tried to explain the thing to him, telling him that we had never, in any way, mistrusted him; that, on the contrary, we had had the greatest confidence and faith in his fulfillment of the tasks that had been assigned to him.

September 3

Pacho arrives from Chile by train. He presents the matter of the zone selected by Mongo (Upper Beni), seeking our opinion; that Guevara is to get $500; the visit of Danton, whose mission is to make a geopolitical study of the chosen zone and discuss Guevara's reports with him. Mongo's idea is to come without advance notice. He will concentrate on Guevara's group.

All these things conflict with the work that had been done, that was started by some people in the zone around Camiri with, primarily, the group from the Party, these people having been told that Mongo would arrive ahead of time to make the reconnaissance and checks, etc. We have practically everything we need (the farm, 45 rifles, clothing, etc.); part of this equipment's in the Santa Cruz area. So, on account of Mongo's plan, we are forced to move the supplies again to La Paz en route to the Beni. We have to get someone from the Party to take charge of the farm and [illegible] without arousing too much suspicion.

September 5

I went to the movies with Pacho. We discussed several things. He knows that Mbili's attitude toward the new plans that have come is one of hostility. I explained that, basically it is because he is displeased to learn that it has been decided to pay attention to Guevara. All Mbili's relations are with the Party, which, although not committed to join the struggle, has supplied the people who have been helping most to buy arms and equipment. Although the Party plan is for a general uprising, they have promised to give us 20 men for the guerrillas. If the thing should fail (that is, the general uprising), all of them will flee to the mountains. I also told him how Estanislao had been giving us the runaround about these [20] comrades; that he has even gone so far as to threaten to withdraw the four men that, in accordance with his agreement with Manila, were to be at our unconditional disposal regardless of where the fighting should take place. Then I told him how Estanislao had said he did not recall his promise of 20 men. But Mbili, who is fundamentally under the influence of the Party, is prejudiced against Guevara, regarding him as a trouble-making prick incapable of really revolting. This, Telleria had told me. I also expressed Sánchez' opinion of the man, believing that his opinion has some value because he is the one who deals with Guevara. None of us has had any contact with him. Sánchez thinks that Guevara is of some value, that he has proven capable of organizing his group which has decided to join the struggle, and that he has no alternative but to accept our aid or fight on his own, since he is a dissident from the official Party and the Zamora group, the pro-Chinese Party.

Mbili is used to working alone and it is now very difficult for him to accept the fact that he does not have contact with the people that are going to revolt. I understand this sort of jealousy because when I arrived here, although Mongo had told him in the letter to consult with me, he told me that was a lot of nonsense on Mongo's part, that he was sure that El Flaco was the one to blame for this by having certainly spoken hogwash. This forced us to adopt the attitude assuring him that we had no interest in running things and that the right to mutual consultation would be worth while, thereby giving him confidence in us as comrades and friends. This attitude caused me problems with Tumaini who wanted to talk with him, citing what Mongo had said. Because when we arrived here we ran smack up against the fact that no preparations had been made. (To start off, there wasn't even a house for us to stay in, there being only the one in which Mbili and Sánchez were living.) The farm was right next door to an Army Division. There were only about 7 guns and we had counted on 20. We didn't know if we had 20 men from Guevara, or only the four from the Party, who didn't know that the fighting was going to take place here, but rather were collaborating under the misapprehension that it would take place in Peru or Argentina. Later on, they became aware of the fact that the fight was to take place in Bolivia because it was considered that conditions were better here. It was agreed to discuss the new situation with Estanislao because he complained that El Flaco had told him nothing about where the fighting was to take place. (We proceeded to explain the conversations with Mongo when El Flaco left for here [Bolivia]. Then it was necessary to begin to organize things.)

September 6

With Sánchez and Mbili participating, we proceeded to analyze the situation that the new guidelines created for us, and the best way to solve the problem. The most complex problem is that of our relationship with the Party, now that we have decided to organize things with Guevara, and got orders to practically cut off our relations with the Party, at least temporarily. The other problem is that of the farm that has been bought near Santa Cruz, which we now find ourselves forced to get rid of.

It was agreed to send someone to take charge of the farm so

as not to arouse suspicion by leaving it vacant. And go urgently to the Beni zone to acquire a farm with the minimum requirements. We are hoping to hear something from Manila about the matter of breaking off with Estanislao, or at least to hear that they authorize us to go ahead with the 10 men that we have. To keep things at their present level, it is necessary that Ramon and Paile get together with Estanislao. As soon as we acquire the farm, we will go there and transfer the stuff we have at Santa Cruz (arms and ammunition).

September 8

We are continuing our discussions with Pacho about the most convenient way for Mongo to travel, and about the date of his return to Manila. And about the best way to solve the new problems brought on by the new instructions. We had to agree on making a report in which we would cover, more or less, the points discussed and which would amplify those on which we had reached agreement.

September 9

We showed him samples of the equipment we have acquired: uniforms, boots, water bottles, radios, shelter-halfs, hammocks, machetes, some arms. We will also carry the items that we have to use as means of contact, our foodstuffs, etc.

September 10

We proceeded to draw up the report of our activities to date.

1

In accordance with our instructions, we have proceeded to take appropriate steps; primarily, acquiring the farm in the indicated zone. We also wish to inform you of our opinion regarding some of the steps taken and the difficulties arising out of them.

1. We want to let you know that all our relationships for the organization of the dance have been established with the Party and with Estanislao. You should be made aware of the fact that we have agreed with Estanislao that he will join in the armed struggle. As we informed you earlier, this attempt will be in the nature of a general uprising that will, in a few hours, be capable of bringing them to power. Clearly, this is not our conception of the armed struggle. For this reason, we have discussed the need of having the guerrilla struggle organized in the mountains. There-

fore, we have obtained from Estanislao a commitment to give us 20 of his best men, of whom we have 10 with us. We are fully convinced that if Mongo talks with Estanislao, he can convince him to concentrate all his efforts on the guerrilla activities. He has told us of his intention to go ahead.

By giving priority to the negotiations with the Guevara group, we have been placed in a difficult position. In addition, because of what preceded this, we do not feel that this was the right thing to do because we could organize a unified, central command which would include both the Party's and Guevara's people. For this reason, we cannot break off contact with the Party, at least not with the 10 men that we already have (of whom five have been trained there already) until you arrive and decide about the rest.

Perhaps we are somewhat influenced by our relation with Estanislao's people, but have only worked with them (good and bad). We are aware that this overt type of organization (Party) runs the risk of penetration of its ranks, but you may be sure that we are being very careful in our selection.

Despite the fact that we have had no contact with Guevara, we have formed an opinion of him on the basis of his reports, the things we found out through Sánchez, and others. Certainly this opinion is not a profound judgment, a matter which we hope the Frenchman will resolve.

Personally, we feel that he is not to be trusted in the way that you trust us. He has displayed some vacillation: in small things, but noticeably so. For example: Through Sánchez, he has sold us a [illegible word]. If he is planning to engage in the struggle, why would he part with his arms, He has said one thing to Francisco and another to Sánchez. When this was pointed out to him, he tried to alibi his way out of it, only proving his inconsistencies. We have explained all this to Pacho in detail.

We cannot fail to recognize that he has stated his decision to fight openly for our line, guerrilla warfare. That his is a group of working class extraction (miners); peasants, people who are dedicated to fight. Almost all of the militants are ready to join in the struggle, 20 men.

The reconnaissances of the possible zones of operation;

His closed organization;

His willingness to integrate commands. For the moment, we have a problem of leadership.

2. The question of the selection of the chosen zone. The Alto

Beni zone is, in our opinion, very good. We want to fill you in on what we have done in this regard. After discussing with Estanislao what would be the best of the three following zones (Karanabi [sic; Caranavi], Las Yungas, Santa Cruz—the first two in Beni), we had to decide on Santa Cruz for the following reasons:

a. Because it is a tropical zone;

b. It is an inhabited zone, as are the other two;

c. It has great formations for houses [sic; caves.] and is right at the foot of the eastern range (Cordillera Oriental) of the Andes;

d. It is an economically important zone for the country because it has petroleum and cattle. We felt that in this way we could make an impact on the economy, not only nationally but internationally because the petroleum company has a pipe line to Chile, where the petroleum is shipped out to the U.S.

From some of these standpoints, the Yungas zone of Alto Beni, that had been selected, is acceptable if we consider only the economic aspect. This is the zone that supplies La Paz with vegetables, grains, etc., and through it passes a great part of the cattle that is consumed, coming from the great plain areas of the Beni.

In the Santa Cruz zone, we found that some of the required conditions already exist. We have acquired a farm, located at Pincal, near Lagunillas and Gutierrez. This is a Chiroguana Indian region. As can be seen from the sketch that is being sent with this report, it is located among low hills. In addition, we have one house in Santa Cruz in which we stored about half our arms. We have started organizing in coordination with Party, a supply and intelligence network.

This farm has been left in the care of a family. They raise pigs on it, which avoids the arousal of suspicion. We are taking appropriate steps in regard to the remaining matters. As for the arms. We have started organizing in coordination with the Party, a there.

3. I do not understand how our substitute can work under orders to keep himself isolated from the Party and from Guevara. Actually, everything we requested we obtained today, and on prior occasions, with their assistance (acquisition of arms and other equipment, and our knowledge of the country.)

We have not been able to acquire the documents because in regard to this instruction, we have never, for reasons of security, made contact with the people who could supply them. Therefore, there is no other solution but to fall back on our last resort; that is, to use the Party's channels.

4. In our previous report, we asked for guidance in the matter of how to resolve the question of Peru. And, at the same time, we told Sánchez that he should inform El Chino about the Bola affair and we reiterated our decision to continue to aid him, on a secondary level, in regard to the Bolivian matter.

El Chino replied, graciously, that Sánchez would collaborate with us in the Bolivian Plan. But, at the same time, he let us know his opinion, in which he stated that although the work had gone a bit slowly, it had been done so competently that his organization is standing by its decision to join in the armed struggle.

We request that you give us some guidance as to whether or not he has been told that there will be a temporary suspension of aid; and if not, if it is to be kept up, what form it will take and where it will come from.

5. If it is possible, send us comrades Fredy Maimura and Lorgio Vaca, and speed up Inti's and Coronada's training.

6. It is necessary that you send us some addresses in Prague to establish contact so that those who travel will be met at the airport and avoid having an entry stamp affixed.

7. At the recent Congress of the Uruguayan Party, comrade Kolle had to support the members of the Brizola group that expressed to him their determination to initiate the armed conflict, and they asked for the Party's assistance in buying arms and equipment. At the same time, they asked for personnel who would serve as guides for the purpose of entering Brazilian territory. They also asked for the good offices of the Party to see if comrades Comodore Arau and Capt. Alfredo Riveiro Damut, an F-86 pilot, could be sent there for the purpose of reporting and holding discussions for aid. Authorization is requested, in the event this is approved, for providing travel costs to and contacts in Prague.

8. If it is possible, send us an FAL grenade launcher adapted to the Mauser.

9. [Sic; this point deleted by author]

The last point we wish to bring up is your decision to travel without alerting us of the possible date of arrival and the route. We would forestall any possible danger. We could wait at any point in the country and afford proper protection; we can even go and do likewise in Chile, where we have the appropriate cover. We have told Pacho how inadvisable it is to do the traveling by road alone, because aside from dangerous road conditions many control measures are imposed. In addition, it is impossible to obtain the documents required for moving from one country to another in the time available.

Our plan for your trip is through Brazil: Frankfurt to Sao Paulo and then Santa Cruz, where we would meet you and leave directly for the farm, which is twelve hours away. There are no controls at this airport. Brazil would be the only place where controls would be encountered, and I have told Pacho what they are, concluding that they are not half of those in Chile. Also there will be a landing at only one country in America, whereas another route would involve several. We say this for your consideration and decision.

["Brizzola" is Leonel Brizzola, former Governor of the State of Rio Grande do Sul, Brazil, and brother-in-law of deposed President João Goulart. Since fleeing Brazil after Goulart's ouster, Brizzola has been periodically reported as leading guerrilla forces in southern Brazil. "Comodore Arau" and "Capt. Alfredo Riveiro Damut" appear to be dissident Brazilian Armed Forces officers who belong to Brizzola's group.]

September 11

The report is completed with several points we had forgotten (not numbered), the report on the location of the Nancahuazú farm and listing of arms and equipment.

The Nancahuazú property is located in the southwest region of Santa Cruz province, in a mountainous area of exuberant vegetation but scant water in the general area. The property itself has plenty of water. Nancahuazú is in a canyon between the Serranías de las Pirirendas to the east and the Serranías Incahuasi to the west; their highest peaks are its eastern and western borders. These ranges join up farther south and continue into the Salta range in Argentina. The farm is bounded on the north by the Iripiti property, unoccupied, owned by the same man who sold us the farm, Remberto Villa, who lives on a farm called Terrazas near Lagunillas, about 20 kilometers from Nancahuazú; on the south by the farm of Ciro Algaranaz, who raises pigs. The property is 255 kilometers from Santa Cruz on the Santa Cruz–Camiri road, and is relatively isolated. It can be reached without going into Lagunillas, which is 25 kilometers from Nancahuazú taking a side road about 6 kilometers south of Gutierrez.

By this route you only go by the Aguada Grande property of Eudol Leon, a young peasant. Ten people, all of whom speak Guarani, the prevailing language in this area, live in this house. Leon's house is on a hill about 200 meters from the road so that one can go by without being detected. About 3 kilometers short of the farm is Algaranaz' house, which is on the road. This man is the only risk in the work because he is the closest neighbor and is extremely curious. During Paz Estenssoro's administration he was mayor of Camiri. After we bought the farm we heard that he said we were going to take advantage of the isolated location of the farm and set up a cocaine plant. He is interested in our buying some cattle and pigs from him, and so he has good relations with us. He lives in Camiri, where he has a butcher shop. On weekends he goes to Camiri, returning Monday evening. Sometimes he stays longer.

Aside from this drawback, the farm has the specifications for this sort of work, but not on a large scale as yet, although we shall establish the proper conditions by building a house farther in so that it cannot be seen, as the present one is right where the road ends. The problem, however, lies in the transfer of the people, because we have to fool Algaranaz.

The trip from Santa Cruz takes twelve hours in the dry season, in spring. The stretch from Mora to Rio Seco becomes almost impassable, and the delay may amount to two or three days.

The farm is 1,227 hectares, and has a considerable amount of timber. On this basis the legal cover plan is to raise pigs and later on build a sawmill.

An important point is that toward the north it is possible to travel to Vallegrande through a mountainous and heavily wooded area; from there on the woods become sparser. Toward the south it is possible to go through terrain of similar nature to Argentina.

The following matter, not in the report, have been discussed with the bearer:

1. The matter of General [Expiellor?].
2. The matter of the scholarship holder.
3. The matter concerning Uruguay.
4. The matter of the grenade launchers.
5. Opinion on the forthcoming trip.

September 12

We sent Pacho off on his return trip to Manila. We agreed to buy at least four pair of boots in Paris and send them to the commercial addresses we gave him, because the local ones are not worth a damn. We waited for Tania's book and nothing was delivered.

September 13

Mbili leaves with Rodolfo to look for the farm in the area of Alto Beni.

September 16

Mbili returns from his tour; he did not stay all the time necessary because the Frenchman is in that area and it is inadvisable that he sees them too often.

This is a homesteading area. Sixteen thousand families (10 hectares per family) occupy the entire area. In the woods we come across hunters or people searching for *cinchona*. One man will sell us his parcel (10 hectares) and another one is undecided. The trouble is the excessive number of homesteaders. It is possible to get a lumbering concession from the Forest Reserve Area, but this requires a number of steps and some time. We are trying to get authorization to settle 400 hectares.

September 19

We go with [Ricardo crossed out by author] Mbili to give protection to one of our buyers of arms. While we waited about two blocks from where he was going to make the delivery, we talked about the new turn of events (Mongo's decision to work things out with Guevara). Our discussions were mainly directed to trying to find the way that would guarantee the success of our endeavor. In this connection we were thinking of the need to invest wisely in this region, to avoid waste of energies, to plan well, calmly and big, to try to tie all ends together in order to avoid failures to organize things well with the neighbors or with neighboring territory, in case it becomes necessary for Mongo to cross over to any of those countries.

We must now forget the notion that the struggle [in Cuba] started with twelve men. The struggle under the present conditions must begin with the largest force possible. Also, we should keep in mind that the impact of guerrillas on the continent is not the same as on a narrow island.

Mbili's replacement must be someone whose facial characteristics are similar to the others here and he should have a good cover.

September 23

Mbili has been summoned by Estanislao to discuss some problems. Everything indicates that this meeting is brought about by the activities of the Frenchman.

Also, Facundo tells us that we have received a message from Manila. He gave us the name and room number of the hotel in which the messenger was staying; that is, he was following us.

September 24

Message No. 5   ARIEL

In the previous message we raised some questions about the Party; these questions must now be modified because of the Party's change in attitude.

Several days ago, we were located and summoned to a meeting with Estanislao in the presence of the four. We were told that, apparently, our government was establishing some contact with the splinter groups through the Frenchman, Debray, because he has offered a trip there [to Cuba] to some people. (I might add in this connection that they do not trust me nor do they agree with me.) Also he has been seen with Zamora (they have no news from Guevara). For this reason they would like to have the situation explained to them. They are not willing to be taken advantage of nor to join a single command group with these people, because they are their enemies in all things.

We stated that we were unaware of the Frenchman's mission in this matter, and that our government had not told us anything about him either, but that we would like to take this opportunity to point out a few things: 1. They have shown no confidence in guerrilla warfare; 2. They have made no efforts to organize themselves, rather, they view it all as not solving anything. They added that they had been concentrating all their efforts toward a general uprising and considered guerrilla warfare as secondary. We asked them what they had done to date; they replied, "Nothing." We told them we could not sit around 20 years waiting for them.

They suggested sending an emissary to Cuba to discuss the problem.

In a conversation with Coco he mentioned that Mario had asked him to go to Cuba, to discuss the matter of his resignation from the Party leadership so that he could become part of the guerrilla struggle. In our previous message, we had raised the problem of our relationship with the Party, but it is not easy to break commitments. We are waiting for instructions.

During a trip in search of the farm we met the Frenchman who tried to photograph us. I didn't let him photograph me, but he did photograph the jeep driver. I don't think he recognized me because he was photographing everything that looked official.

The area surrounding the farm as far as I can detect is populated and therefore one runs across peasants, hunting, fishing, or looking for *cinchona* bark. Thus, a regular group runs the risk of being discovered in a short time. The area is divided into grants of 10 hectares per family (16,000 families). There is an Army work team building a highway (Caranavi to Santa Ana). The main camp is at Palos (the labor troops are not part of the regular army but they are armed just the same).

All these problems have made us keep our distance and for this reason we have requested we be granted 400 hectares in an unpopulated area under the pretext of settling the land and devoting ourselves to farming and pig raising. The property on which a house will be built will be located between Santa Ana and Palos. In addition, we will buy two plots (20 hectares), 3 km. away from Belen near the road. This would serve as an outpost to get to the other farm because the latter is on the opposite bank of the Beni River and the only way to reach it is by river. A map is attached.

We will leave the jeep under guard, and store provisions at this farm.

In case we are delayed by some unexpected event, it will be easy for us to go there to orient and inform ourselves better about the situation.

September 28

Accompanied by Ricardo we met with Estanislao; we were to be informed of the questions to be sent to Manila.

Estanislao began by stating that his commitment to Leche was to help organize the matter of the south; that is, make four men available to him and turn them over to Mbili; and, in addition, to coordinate with Brizola the matter of Brazil. He said that the strategic plan gave secondary importance to the matter of Bolivia, and that the organization and direction of the Bolivian plan was his responsibility and that, at the proper time, he would ask for aid. He added these were all the commitments made in Manila. He also stated that he had discussed things with the Soviets, who promised him they would consider giving their full support. Now, considering the arrival of the Frenchman, who for the second time has dedicated himself to criticizing the Party, Estanislao said the Frenchman is closely tied to Zamora's Party; that in the name of our government he is proposing trips there [to Cuba]; that he has visited the Caranavi zone; that from there he ordered a change of location of the farm to the upper Beni region, an area from whence a guerrilla cannot move out to other countries. He [the Frenchman] has been able to establish that the central point of the plan is Bolivia and that he is on the edge of everything.

For this reason Estanislao believes that it is the duty to inform the Party of what is going on. He [Estanislao] added that, although he supports the armed struggle, he has nothing to do with the matter because he is outside the whole issue, and that, therefore, he accepts the proposal made by the secretariat that he would dissociate himself from the leadership. This would benefit the organization. He believed he was fulfilling his part of the agreement and that there had been meddling in the affair on our part.

We told him we could not accept his argument because it is contrary to everything. All developments have been reported to our country. Above all, two months back we informed Comrade Estanislao that the plans for the south today are secondary and that the headquarters was here because it was thought that this country, at the moment, was the one that had the best conditions. (He agreed with this.)

We decided to leave the area because the farm is almost within limits of a military post. We thought it best to begin looking for a better location. Four zones were discussed: Alto Beni, Yungas, Cochabamba and Santa Cruz, we agreed to send men to explore these areas. Because the men recruited were from Santa Cruz, they were sent to this area. They were given the jeep, etc. Simultaneously, we had transmitted the names of the four zones to Manila. Within a matter of days, we selected one.

Estanislao, I cannot understand why you say that you know nothing of the matter, and I don't see where, at any time, we have interfered. Because if you were not in agreement, you would have mentioned it two months ago.

He continued maintaining that he knew nothing of the change in plans until now; that we had told him about the conditions as though they pertained to the south. But when Facundo spoke to him about the change in zones, he understood that we were talking about Bolivia. We appealed to the four. They also knew about it because Mbili had told them what his agreement was with him.

He admitted that the matter of Bolivia was his idea and that Bolivia was the ideal place, but said he could not tolerate goings on behind his back; that he was going to participate in the struggle, but he was going to direct things politically. He cannot accept being a puppet in our hands, he went on; in his opinion, things should be better organized; he is participating in the fight with the complete support of the Party. There was a need for him to take part in the matter in order to assign tasks to the Party organizations, by means of which better organization would be assured.

He declared that he is ready to join any group with any organization, but that he is sure the Zamora will not join in the struggle.

He explained that he feels it necessary to mislead the Secretariat because its members talk too much. Because, in Uruguay, Arismendi was told about our presence here and about the possibility of reinforcements for the affair in the south. Arismendi demanded that all party secretary generals be informed, and if not, he would see to it personally.

It was agreed to report the matter immediately to Manila. We were told that if we decided not to take part in the struggle here, we could not count on receiving the promised personnel or the support of the four unless they should decide to go personally, that is take the risk. As we were leaving, the other members of the Secretariat, Kolle and Reyes, arrived; they told us that Debray had returned from Cochabamba and was leaving on Tuesday.

In discussing the situation, we concluded that the matter of Uruguay should be decided before Mongo leaves because it is necessary to send someone to Manila. We thought of Sánchez, but Mbili badly wanted to go, as he had told me a few days before.

Therefore, it was agreed to prepare an agenda and send Mbili. Meanwhile, with Rodolfo, we would take up the problem of the farm.

September 30

We agreed to make a clean breast of things and tell Rodolfo about the state of our relations with the Party and to ascertain his attitude in the event that the decision is made to go ahead with the struggle using other people. We agreed that nothing has been accomplished with the Party with reference to its position. The same thing was done with Coco and they both replied that they have decided to fight. Mbili thinks that it is [illegible] to raise it and keep it on the farm without knowing what questions were discussed with Mario; and when the matter is resolved in Manila as to whether or not he will continue with us. I oppose this because I feel that the man who comes to arrange things should be knowledgeable about conditions and should not have anything to hamper his work or justify his desertion when he is forced to deal with the hardships of this life. These are the sacrifices that success demands of us.

October 2

Rodolfo leaves to buy the farm.

October 4

Mbili left for his land to explain the foregoing matter. The plane suffered slight damage and he had to reroute himself. We discussed again with Sánchez the contents of the message received last night which, when deciphered, read as follows:

Taco:

Beginning October 10 you alone should make the following daily trip on foot, at 21 hours: start at the Plaza del Estudiante (where Prado begins) go up Calle Mexico to Calle Almirante Grau. Renan will intercept you on this walk. He has orders to contact you just once.

As for the message Pacho brought: 1. We are not sure at all of Guevara. We are only collaborating without commitment. Don't worry about the political relations between us, Estanislao and Guevara. The important thing is to ensure the necessary conditions.

Continue relations with Estanislao, avoiding arguments. Aid requested will be considered later.

2. The present farm is good. Get another but don't transfer the arms to it until I notify you.

3. The proposed supply network should be put into operation. As for Renan's method of operation, don't worry about it. Follow instructions to a T. Documents are not necessary.

Aid to Chino will be controlled from here; ties with Sánchez will be maintained in this matter. Acquisition of equipment must be done with great prudence at this stage. Lorgio Vaca left here 24/9. Send proposals to invitees by January 1.

Brazilian matter will be dealt with by other means.

Send cable signed "Gloria" to postoffice box. Request return receipt.

Abrazos to all. Ramon. End.
9/26/66

October 5

Mbili is leaving for his country. Rodolfo arrived and reported that he had acquired the farm, but he believes we should not leave for the farm because it has not yet been surveyed and our presence there might attract the attention of the Engineers, etc. Also, in his opinion it is much better to go there on Tuesday, the 12th. He also said that, after being in the zone for three days, he decided that our stay there would be shortlived because soldiers are combing the area. Nevertheless, we decided to survey the area and decide for ourselves whether we would move there or to Nancahuazú and let Rodolfo decide whether we should continue living along the river bank.

October 6

A message was received which when decoded was taken to Mbili at the airport.

October 8

We talked with Facundo about the land which had been requested and about when we would receive the memorandum authorizing us to take possession of the land. He told me that [our request] had been denied and that our only alternative was to accept 15 km. farther in; or, if not that, accept as [illegible] 16 hectares in the originally requested zone. We feel that, in order to accept [land] farther in, we would have to have legal permission to do business. This would probably mean that we would have to take our products to market because, being this far from the river, there would be no means of communication. Therefore, in order not to attract attention, we would have to insist that [the land] border the river because building a road would be much more expensive than the overall investment, which does not need to be justified because, first, of the amount of land to be exploited and, second, because of its income possibilities.

We checked the list of equipment bought, to standardize it. Therefore, we tried to outfit 30 men, although this cannot be done systematically because Mbili only ordered equipment for 25 men. We are waiting until Ricardo arrives to order 30 more knapsacks.

The original list included equipment for 50 men but, I don't know why, Ricardo changed it without having any idea of the cost involved.

We are buying foodstuffs to stock secret dumps which will be of great use to us during the first period.

October 10

We have been told that Mario wants to talk to us about the results of meeting with the CC. He said: "I was informed that the CC had taken a positive step by unanimously accepting the line of armed struggle as the correct way to seize power. Nevertheless, I believe that many support armed struggle only verbally and that they are incapable of physically participating in it."

Discussion centered on seizing political power in Bolivia. The meeting opened with a report on armed struggle as a vehicle for the seizure of power. We explained that conditions are becoming more acute; everything points to a possible coup d'état or cabinet crisis and that the regime is preparing to liquidate the leftist organizations. We conceive of armed struggle as a civil war, and civil war as guerrilla warfare. I explained the favorable conditions for guerrilla warfare, and that it is possible (or rather, they are convinced) that this is the country with the best specifications. We should not delude ourselves. We face an implacable enemy, and one which has great resources of gringo imperialism at its disposal, a fact which makes it impossible for us to achieve power easily. Therefore, we must believe that our country will create the necessary conditions or will accelerate them with determination, so that the other Latin American countries may begin the struggle, and possibly might distinguish themselves before we do; this is our mission in accordance with the development of events.

When Mario finished his statement, we were addressed by some of our comrades who stated that they would speak openly because Comrade Mario had merely outlined what took place at the meeting and was keeping back the rest, not mentioning what Cuba's role was; Comrade Mario was not telling everything he knew. Mario answered these questions by asking if anyone had more to add because this was all he had to say.

As for the Cuban position on this mattter, Comrade Major Fifo told me that we could count unconditionally on their support (men, equipment, etc.).

After the matter was settled, a question on the Party leadership's place was raised, especially Estanislao's. They suggested that [Estanislao and the others] should be in the mountains with the rest of the combatants. It was agreed that this would be discussed later. It was proposed that Reyes be sent to Manila to discuss the problem there, but, on Ramirez' suggestion, it was decided to send Estanislao too, because he is more familiar with the problems. Also, they will attend the congress in Bulgaria.

I told him that I agreed with his reasoning but that I did not think it necessary for them to travel to Manila to carry out the mission which (according to the foregoing decision) Coco had been assigned. He explained that Coco was not qualified to discuss or report anything; not being familiar with the CC's attitude he was in no position to negotiate. Also, what had been previously discussed was a problem raised by Estanislao on his own and not on behalf of the organization he represented.

I felt like impressing on him our feelings about this flaw in his personality, but we had to follow instructions and not get involved in arguments, so we put this aside and continued [with other matters]. One should remember the decision that Estanislao stay in the mountains, and I believe that this is right, but one must not lose sight of the Julio affair, etc. To which he answered and a thousand others, but I do not think that this is vital. In any case, I added that the most important thing was that the political leadership be located in a secure zone where the enemy could not easily wipe them out; and the most secure zone is the front because of its mobility. Moreover, security measures allowing the Party to go underground whenever necessary should be taken.

We must not for a moment forget what happened in Santo Domingo. Although you have already explained to me that your concept of armed struggle is civil war in its guerrilla warfare

form, in any case consideration should also be given to a decision
for a general uprising. Santo Domingo is the precedent for Yankee
intervention in the affairs of any country which, in their opinion,
is menaced by international Communism. The decision to intervene in Santo Domingo was made on their own because many of
the countries previously participating in intervention do not have
facilities for maritime landing. But here, any one of them can
cross the Bolivian borders by land and this would constitute a
joint intervention. Therefore, considering this possibility, we must
be prepared for guerrilla warfare.

[The Dominican Republic is often referred to by the name of its
capital, Santo Domingo, because the island was originally called Saint
Dominique. Pombo is referring, of course, to the American armed
intervention there in 1965.]

October 12
     A message was received from Mongo in which he reported
on Mbili's return trip.

October 15
     We talked again with Facundo about purchasing equipment
and foodstuffs and asked that we be shown a budget for them,
because I am unsatisfied not knowing how the money is being
spent, as is the case of the $7,000 which was given him. We told
him we were interested in having a physical inventory of what
we presently have because, to date, we do not know what equipment we have available to us.

     CZO #16: Pombo, Mbili arrived ok. Will leave for there
Saturday, October 15. You and Tumaini should [stay in La Paz]
until new orders.
October 13, 1966

October 21
     Ricardo arrives and tells me about the plans he has and the
questions Mongo posed.
     He told me that there had been no reason for him to travel;
Mongo had told him that the trip was a waste of time since he
was thinking of going to La Paz that Saturday, that he had made
a lot of mistakes and that his greatest mistake had been in send-

ing him because he was a good-for-nothing. This hurt [Ricardo] very deeply because his presence there is not because of any especial interest in Bolivian affairs, but rather because of personal loyalty to Mongo.

He told me about the Tania matter: she accused him of violating the security rules and of getting fresh with her. Mongo is to leave for here this Saturday, the 22nd, to meet with Renan at the place specified in the message. Afterwards [Renan] has to take Tumaine to Santa Cruz with six weapons to pick up Mongo who would go there by "gondola." From there they will go to the farm and then return to La Paz. Another man and I will go to the farm.

October 22

We spoke with Facundo, who told us that Estanislao said to him that he was traveling to Manila to discuss the decisions of the Central Committee on the question of the armed struggle; that they want their people to receive military training in Manila to prepare them for leadership positions in case of any spontaneous uprising, and that we should go south because we have tried to interfere in the internal affairs of the country. Also, if Mbili has anything to discuss with Estanislao, he should say so, so that a meeting can be arranged. Mbili said he had nothing new to discuss since instructions from Manila were to be sent with Coco, according to previous instructions, when he returns. But, offhand, he wants to tell him [Estanislao] that he learned from Coco that things are not the same as what we had previously discussed.

October 24

Mbili meets with Estanislao, who tells him that he is going to Manila to discuss the Bolivian matter, or better yet to demand fulfillment of all agreements and commitments made to him, such as that we should go South and then he would be in charge of matters in Bolivia. At the same time, he blamed Mbili for many of the things that have occurred here and reminded him that one day history will judge him. Mbili let Estanislao's statement ride because of instructions received from Manila to the effect that Mongo had the mission to contact all organizations, including Lechín's, in which Mario has a primary role. History will judge the attitudes of both and decide who is mistaken.

Mbili has been too lenient with Mario; he should have made him more responsible by impressing on him what could happen in our area. Due to an error on our part, they are the only ones who know the tactical plans in detail.

Estanislao had to request $2,000 from Mbili to pay the Party's salaries. Mbili refused to give him any, claiming that he had only $500 and that he would not be left without money when he was responsible for several comrades. Estanislao stated then that he would not ask for a loan, but instead would ask for an amount to cover the boys' fare to Bulgaria, thus disregarding the previous agreement whereby the Bulgarians would pay the fare from Chile to Bulgaria and we from Bolivia to Chile. [Mbili] told him we would not tolerate deception from anyone and that his request was just that. Seeing his error, he changed his attitude. Then he tried further pressure by mentioning the people he had given us. He then made an analysis of the $25,000 given to him in Manila and the $20,000 given him in a lump sum for the FLIN, and which they had not delivered, claiming that they are not going to let themselves be manipulated and that the families of the men with us cannot be permitted to go hungry. We agreed to give him $1000. He stated that he did not believe that Fifo had received the results of our reports, while reiterating that this was a result of our meddling. Our reports show the contrary, but our big mistake was to have taken him into our confidence and kept him informed about almost everything.

October 27

I reminded [Rodolfo] that Mbili had promised him that if his family wants to, they can go to Manila without any problem. But he answered that Estanislao already accused him of being mercenary and he doesn't want to give him cause to justify his accusation.

October 28

Mbili told us Renan has arrived and to pack Mongo's things in a little bag.

November 4

Mbili told us Mongo has arrived and asked us not to say he had told us because Renan says Mongo doesn't want us to know. This surprised us because it seems inconceivable that Mongo doesn't trust us. Worried about this, I couldn't sleep and neither could Tumaini.

Mbili arrived at about 2 a.m. and told us that there was a misunderstanding on Renan's part, because what Mongo had asked was that we all not go together to see him, that we should be ready to leave by nightfall and that he can drive himself, because he has Bigote's drivers license. I will ride with him in the second jeep.

November 5

Mbili and Tumaine set out at 6:30. I said goodbye to Cuqui and Maria on the pretext of taking refuge in Canada. I could not do that with Augusta nor Mirtha, the pathetic one. It was about 10 hours.

November 6

We reached Cochabamba at 9:30 a.m., having learned at the control shack [illegible] that the other vehicle had passed at 0800 hours.

We continued walking and about 9 p.m. we had reached the Santa Cruz road crossing, there we took a short cut through the Camiri road and were on the banks of the Río Grande about 4 a.m. Although we still did not know where to cross the river on the raft.

November 7

After 6 a.m. we found the crossing point and joined the other jeep waiting there. We agreed to cross separately and then look for a place to spend the night. After looking for the entrance of the road leading to the farm, we stopped at a remote place where Mongo, while we were eating, introduced himself to Bigote, who in turn told him of his decision to come to fight in Bolivia because it is the country with the best conditions for guerrilla warfare on the continent. He is aware that the plans together with his presence would delay the possibilities of quick victory but we cannot afford to dream about a revolution in Bolivia alone, without at least having a revolution in a coastal country, even if not in all of Latin America. If that doesn't happen, this revolution will be smothered. He said he came to stay and the only way he is leaving is dead or shooting his way across the border. I want to talk with Mario because I think he can help the revolution a great deal. He asked two favors: 1. That [Mongo?] help him bring in the men; 2. That he not tell the Party of his presence here because he knows what that would mean for a militant.

November 8

We cleaned the weapons and went into the bush; we are close to the game.

November 9

Mongo and Tumaine leave on a scouting mission and to test the little radios.

November 10

I went out walking with Pacho. After about four hours we found a spot where we can set up camp in its third phase. There is an arroyo up the hill, as well as tall grass. On our way back, when we came close to the house, we were seen by the chauffeur of Algaranaz, a gentleman who owns a nearby farm. Because of this Mongo decided we should go to live in the bush. We will build a house like the ones we used to build when I was a child. And so we will go to live with the bugs, mosquitoes, chiggers, etc.

November 14

We have begun construction of a place in which we can leave some supplies hidden. We talked with Mongo about the possibility of proving ourselves by attacking an Army barracks. He said we couldn't do it unless it was a small one because we can't take the risk of starting out with a defeat, but must give the men a chance to build up their confidence.

November 15

Mongo told us about the points he is going to outline to Estanislao. 1) That he has no political power in Bolivia. He does, however, feel he has enough experience to direct military operations and control finances. Because this is where the money is needed. We could ask help from China and the USSR, explaining to the Chinese that without any political commitment on China's part, we could send Guevara [to China] with a letter from us to Chou En Lai and we could also send Mario with a companion to the USSR so they will at least tell us how much they will contribute.

Mario has to understand that the struggle in Bolivia will be long because the enemy will concentrate all its forces against it.

Bolivia will sacrifice itself so that conditions [for revolution] can be created in neighboring countries.

We have to make another Viet Nam out of America, with its center in Bolivia.

November 18

Pacho and I went out scouting around the camp to find a place near the arroyo to set up camp in its third phase (when everyone arrives; but we have to await Mario's arrival before beginning). The place is well hidden. The only trouble with it is visibility; you can only see about 10 meters away, which means the enemy will be sighted when he is on top of us. There is a possibility we could post guards at the entrance to the arroyo, or on one of the distant hills, and report over the radio or telephone, thus saving much time.

November 20

San Luis and Pinare (Marco and Rolando) arrived. [Identities have been reversed: San Luis refers to Rolando.] Ricardo stayed behind due to the fact that the rest of the comrades in the first group still had not arrived in La Paz. Rodolfo came. Mongo asked him if he knew who he was and he answered, yes, because Mbili had already told him.

November 21

We moved to the new camp located on the little hill in front of the house.

November 24

Marco and I went scouting around the hills. He asked me some things about the struggle. He seemed optimistic, which pleased me very much. I used a kind of revolutionary frankness. He asked if Ramón was happy with the group and I told him Ramón thinks not even Manila can produce another group like this one. He said that pleased him very much but that there are two things bothering him: Machin and Suarez Gallol [sic: misspelling of Gayol] but that time and events would tell in the end. I like the comrades to be people who are easy to get along with; there are two who are very aggressive, Braulio and [name omitted]. He then referred to Tamayo and told me about a cer-

tain problem he had with Tamayo about the fact that he claims
to be Ramón's assistant, when in fact he is only his bodyguard.

November 27

The rest of the comrades in the first group arrived: Joaquín,
Urbano, Braulio, Miguel and the Bolivian comrades Inti and
Ernesto (the doctor).

In welcoming them, we toasted the success of the armed
struggle with a glass of Singani (a hard liquor made of grapes).
The comrades from Manila are actually called Vilo, my brother
Tamayo, Manuel and so on (Israel).

November 30

We went out exploring in the direction of the first arroyo on
the left and following the compass we proceeded in the direction
of *Las Misiones*. So far we have explored the bed of the Río *B*
and its arroyo and possible convergence with the Yaqui River.
We came back from this expedition after walking for two days
without food, arriving at the camp on the night of December 1,
1966.

December 4

We had a meeting with Ramón in which he gave a lecture on
discipline and our duty to be an example to the Bolivians since
we have the guerrilla experience.

He then said in substance:

"Some of the comrades have taken courses on how to handle
weapons and are better prepared than many of us (referring to
the Bolivians) who have been involved in political action and
have overlooked these things.

"We have the privilege of being proven soldiers, we have felt
bullets, we have passed all the tests of guerrilla life which are
harder than [illegible] and we have overcome them. We are the
authors of a successful revolution, so that our moral obligation is
much greater because we must be true Communists, full of an
immense spirit of sacrifice.

"All the security measures are not enough. We have examples
of guerrillas who have been wiped out in America. We had the
luck to receive blows to dislocate us, surprises like the Algeria
del Pino, Alto de Espinoza. We had no experience, we lacked
the most elementary knowledge, and yet we survived these surprises. Fidel's spirit, his ability to organize the men, saved us

from failure, a lucky break which our comrades in Peru and Argentina did not have. In Venezuela things are still in the balance. The question is not victory or failure, after the first blow they did not have to go through the formative stage.

"Problems of the guerrilla band: leisure time must be spent in fighting leisure time. We should not fall into brooding or do only what is absolutely necessary. For example, yesterday I conducted a little test: there was a lantern which had fallen on the ground and I watched to see who would pick it up but no one did. If you were home you would have picked it up, but no one did. In my struggle against laziness I try to overcome feelings of indifference about things not our own because this can destroy the internal rapport essential to guerrilla unity. The Manilans will temporarily occupy positions of leadership to start forming the Bolivians, the future cadres that will lead the struggle for continental liberation in this country. The [illegible] will be formed from the liberation armies of brother countries."

December 20

We had a meeting at which Ramón explained what this struggle entails and repeatedly pointed out that it will not be done quickly because we will need 10 years or more before the insurrectional stage is finished. [We must] seize power in Bolivia but unless some other neighboring country does the same, we will be inevitably annihilated because [illegible] and a block like the one against Cuba would be enough [to destroy us].

[Note: Following were not in chronological order in original].

December 31

Arrival of Estanislao after several days of waiting.

December 24

We celebrated Christmas Eve with much merrymaking and happiness. We had roast pork, beef, drinks, etc. We got drunk, we sang, we danced, we recited, etc. Ramón recited a poem of his own invention well put, with eulogies of the Chilean, Urbano and Braulio.

December 31

Mario arrived with Mbili, whom we have been awaiting since the 25th. He was accompanied by Tania and Sánchez as well as two other Bolivians who have joined us, Pedro and Walter. We waited for New Year's Day to celebrate the anniversary of the Cuban revolution, guide and shining beacon of all who, like ourselves, struggle in America to free their countries from imperialist exploitation. Mario talked to us, pointing out what an enormous endeavor we have undertaken, what faith all the peoples of America have placed in it. He intimated his decision to fight; this statement disconcerts us because we already know that he and Ramón have not been able to agree about who should lead the struggle. He maintains that as Secretary he cannot submit himself to Ramon's orders in political or military matters, even though as Estanislao the individual he would be proud to do so. Mario also asked that the pro-Chinese line be rejected and all parties be united, proposing that he would take a trip all over the continent getting Party support, demanding that the Venezuelan comrades recognize Douglas Bravo. There was mutual agreement on both these points: Ramón accepted the proposal about approaching the parties and the thing about Douglas even though he pointed out that this was a waste of time because from the parties' point of view that would be negating their own policies.

Estanislao agreed to go along with the pro-Chinese. In regard to the first point, Ramón told Estanislao that he could be titular chief, so as to save face, but Ramón would be the real chief. He added that this would not, however, be in line with Marxist method. He said that Estanislao only aspired to be leader of the struggle in Bolivia during this first stage, but that his [Ramón's] strategic plan was to direct the continental struggle, and he could not at the moment allow the guerrilla movement to be turned into a political instrument to obtain political position, as had been the case in Venezuela and Colombia, etc. It is only a means to the end, which is the seizure of power. The kid from Peru arrived.

1967

January 6

A meeting of a select group of those designated to various responsibilities was held. Ramón analyzed some of the weaknesses of the work accomplished thus far. He criticized Comrade Marcos for his treatment of the men and explained why, even though Marcos was leader of the group in the beginning, he was not named second in command, a position which is occupied by Joaquín.

January 10
Joaquín, Inti, Marcos, Miguel, Benigno, Braulio go out on a scouting mission to find the Fria River and the Pampa del Tigre and to see if they can be used to get to the Río Grande, the area in which we hope to establish contact with the peasants.

January 11
A monotonous day.

January 13
Joaquín, Marco and Co. return. They think they have found the Fria River. After their report, a discussion ensues. Ramon says that if the river they found empties into the Nacahuasu instead of the Río Grande, it can't be the Fria River.

January 15
We had a meeting at which Ramón announced his intention to set out after the arrival of Comrade Guevara, who should join us on the 25th.

January 16
Góndola day (named by Tuma), that is what we called the activity of moving our supplies and equipment.

January 18
Today is my third wedding anniversary (leather anniversary). I remember my wife and son with great affections on this date. A thousand kisses for Harry and Custi (a million kisses.)

January 29
Guevara arrived accompanied by La Loyo. He is ready to join us, but needs two weeks to recruit some men, in other words, until after carnival. Loyo has been made responsible for finances on a national level.

January 31
Explanatory meeting to outline the objectives pursued: 1)

The need to adapt to the vicissitudes of guerrilla life such as hunger, thirst, sleepiness, exhausting hikes, factors which are equally if not more important than combat itself from the standpoint of molding the future revolutionary soldier. 2) Formation of the peasant support base or better, exploration of possible areas where the peasant base of the (ELNB) can be started. 3) To explore and broaden territory scouted by our forces.

February 1

We set out on a scouting mission for 25 days after I suffered intense pains from drinking too much water. We reached an arroyo where we camped.

February 2

We got past Marcos' little house, but did not reach the arroyo.

February 3

Although a torrential rain was falling when we woke up, we climbed over very rugged terrain until we reached an arroyo which we at first thought to be the Frias River. Marcos waited for us with a fire and coffee made, we cooked and set up camp.

February 4 .

We set out early along the banks of the Nacahuasu. After walking along it for 6 hours, we camped.

February 5

Very early, at about 11 a.m., we received a radio message in which the vanguard advised they had gotten 2 horses. They also ordered us to take precautions and said they have reached a river which, from its dimensions, must be the Río Grande.

During a Sunday meeting, Ramón discussed the organization plans which were set up a few days ago at a meeting at which we, comrades Marcos, Rolando, Pombo, Miguel, Pacho, were not present, although the main item on the agenda was the function of the political instructors. The duties assigned the comrades are the following:

Second-in-Command: Joaquín; Chief of Operations: Alejandro; Political Commissars (the only duty assigned to 2 comrades), Rolando and Inti; information, collection of data, organization of troops etc.: Antonio; Chief of Supplies: Nato (Camba);

Chief of all services; Pombo (supplies, medicines, transportation etc.). He discussed each man's responsibility in his job, and the absolute duty of all the men to comply with the orders of each leader in a specific area. He also pointed out that the political instructors were subordinate to the Military Chief; that the political leader is the receptacle, the catalyzing agent for political situations of the troops (he is responsible for the morale of the men and their problems); he must keep the military chief informed of them at all times. We do not ask him at any time to be too strict; on the contrary, all the men should look to him for guidance and help in difficult times. We of Manila who have already experienced these things should analyze our experiences so that we do not repeat our mistakes here. Take the case where the center party of the guerrillas exists as a political organ. The political bureau cannot operate; that is, it cannot make decisions on guerrilla matters. The political as well as military command should be one. Within a few days, Comrade Estanislao will visit us and I hope we can decide on the future organization of this budding revolutionary struggle. I also hope we can count on the complete support of the vanguard organization of the working class and of the Bolivian Party. It is not necessary that we select a name for our movement now but we should choose one some time in the future. On our future marches, the Bolivians, who are still few in number, will have to carry the heaviest burden of the work since we of Manila cannot also remain in the front. Because of this, the Bolivians will have to sacrifice a great many things and have a great capacity for work. The main things we have discussed, that is, the designation of areas of responsibility, need no further explanation because this was done previously and the specific duties of each job are simple; those who have been assigned are familiar with them. All leadership posts which we currently occupy are transitory because ultimately the leadership cadre for this struggle will arise from these Bolivians: its officers, its future economists, administrators, etc.

February 6

We organized the scouting expeditions and celebrated their return with 2 dinners. The scouting mission led by Joaquín revealed that we cannot cross to the other side even though the path indicates there must be a *baado,* he says he walked 8 kms. Marcos' scouting expedition revealed that 1) the path leads nowhere 2) he found a place where we can cross.

February 7

We began to cross the river at 1 p.m. in order of columns: Vanguard, Center, Rearguard. After Marcos and his men crossed, the raft was swept away by the current so that the Center was divided, half with the Vanguard and half with the Rearguard. We will continue the crossing tomorrow.

February 8

At dawn, we the remainder of the Center who could not cross yesterday (Muganga, Rolando, Chinchu and I) began to cross as well as all the rearguard. By 8 a.m. all the men had crossed. We passed through a short period of thirst when we had to go around a loop of the river that blocked the way and we had to climb up a hill, without any water. On descending to a valley we found a pool of water as well as some pigs who were bathing in it. We camped in the valley.

February 9

Ramón, Inti, Alejandro, Chinchu, Tuma and I set out in the direction of the river, reaching a corn field that had tender young corn. Inti and Chinchu went on a scouting expedition and found a road and some peasants. They sent for the men. The house belongs to a peasant called Honorato. We bought corn and pigs and we stayed.

February 10

We stayed to take advantage of the peasant's offer.

February 11

We spent the night in Honorato's house, being careful to take necessary precautions so that the peasants across the road don't see us. The water from the arroyo is very cold, so we baptized it "arroyo frio."

February 12

We reached Montanes' house who was not at home. According to his son, he has been away for over a month, The son is about 20 years old and had never seen a hammock which filled him with admiration. His great discovery, though, was the *guayo* for shelling corn which we made out of a tin can. He asked us to give it to him.

February 13

Some set out on a scouting mission to find or continue cutting paths (Miguel and Marcos).

February 14

We continued cutting a path to the next house which must belong to a rich cattle rancher because it has 50 head of cattle.

February 15

We reached the house we were looking for, but instead of finding the cattle-rancher we found his brother lives there. Of course we were a little afraid he would inform on us. It turns out he is exploited by his brother who owns the land. He seemed very well disposed toward us.

February 16

The river provides plenty of water. We know the Army is in Masicurí but they are engineering troops assigned to fixing roads and they have few weapons etc.

February 17

It started to rain and lasted 16 hours so we camped in the same place again.

February 18

We had a meeting with Ramón in which he announced that due to the Army's presence in Masicurí, and the fact that it is not advantageous to attack them, we will head for the Rosita River. To get there we will have to cross the entire Masicurí mountain range, and after reaching the mouth of the Rosita we .will return to the Nacahuasu via the Río Grande.

February 19

We set out to cross the mountains. We camped in a dale about 100 meters from the summit.

Marco and Tuma were sent out to scout and they discovered that the hills end in cliffs, making it impossible to go down the other side.

February 20

We were forced to go back to a cow path which descends a

ravine to a stream where we camped. We had to cross this stream near its mouth days before.

February 21

We set out early, crossing a little hill and reaching a stream at 10:39. Two scouts explore the area: Marcos goes upstream looking for a way out, and Joaquín goes downstream. The latter found a clearing with tender corn.

February 22

We continued the march. Upon reaching the long stream, Rolando and I go on a scouting mission to look for a place where we can cross.

The stream is extremely long and after a day's walking we still hadn't reached its source. Along the way, we killed a *visna*. When we returned to our starting point, Rubio and Pedro were waiting for us. The rest of the men continued the march to the Arroyo del Muchacho.

February 23

We reached the Arroyo del Muchacho early in the morning. We had spontaneously baptized the stream by that name near which we camped while we were in the mountains. We decided to continue upstream after Marcos gave us a quick run-down in which he guaranteed we could cross in that area. We had some difficulty in the arroyo, because we found 4 *jocos* that were blocking the way. We managed to cross by making bridges out of sticks. I slipped on one of them and almost fell into the water which is quite deep.

February 24

After passing over some very dangerous places, we managed to leave the arroyo and climb up a ridge. We found a water hole in a valley.

February 25

Marcos, Braulio and Tuma are sent out to find a spot where we can descend. At 11 a.m., we reached the spot where Marcos was waiting for us and he points out the Río Grande to us, where he thinks it meets with the Rosita and the Masicurí. We started to go down an almost vertical cliff where the man who had the least falls, fell 10 times. We walked along a creek until

6 p.m. We couldn't find water so we didn't cook and we were advised to reduce our use of water.

February 26

After walking for 6 hours, we reached an arroyo in which there were lots of *tatais* [correct spelling is singular, *totoi*] plants from which we prepared hearts of palm salads.

February 27

Marcos, Miguel, Braulio and Tuma go scouting. Pacho was also sent to maintain communication with the walkie-talkie. Pacho returned in the afternoon with the news that Marcos had ordered him to come back. Later on he confided to Ramón that Marcos had threatened him with death and had struck him with the handle of a machete.

Ramón called Inti and Rolando and told them what had happened, saying this was the last straw and that in a revolutionary army no abuse of any kind can be tolerated.

February 28

Ramón, Marcos, and Pacho meet together. All the comrades are advised that a general assembly will be held so that everyone can see that the *Manilenses* who have come to help are nothing more than a bunch of softies.

The meeting:

"Everyone knows," Ramón began, "what the point of this reunion is, but it has been a great surprise to us to witness the fact that comrades who have already been proven are the first to be a problem. We are on this march to enable the Bolivian comrades to adapt themselves to the vicissitudes of guerrilla life, which in our opinion are the most difficult part of the struggle. We wanted them to become accustomed to hunger, to thirst, to constant walking, to the loneliness of the bush, etc. and we have discovered that it has not been the Bolivians who encounter difficulties, but comrades who could be classed as veterans because of the many times they have been in these situations. But this should be a lesson to us for the future: men who once gave their all for a cause have become accustomed to office life, have become bureaucratic, have become used to orders, to having everything solved in the office, to having everything reach them already solved. This is the case of comrades Marcos and Pacho, who cannot adapt themselves to this life; I would not like to think that they have constant problems with the other comrades because they do not have the brains to say they want to get out.

"Comrade Marcos has been the head of large units and this case is typical of him. Comrade Pacho is a comrade who has fought but needs to go through guerrilla training school because he is not a complete revolutionary and is an incomplete guerrilla fighter. If we have any more problems with Pacho, he will be thoroughly chastised and sent back to Manila, because he lied about how things developed. At 2 p.m. Comrade Benjamín fell into the river and drowned. This struggle has begun with a sad resemblance to the one in the Congo during which Comrade Mituride, the chief of staff, drowned."

March 1

We reached the Rosita river. Our food is all gone. Only the center group has some beans and 2 boxes of oatmeal, which are distributed among the vanguard and the rearguard. We had some soup (very bad). We built a raft and one segment of the vanguard, excluding Miguel, crossed. The current swept the raft away. It started to rain heavily.

March 3

The rain continues. We tried to make radio contact with the vanguard but were unable to do so. We posted a guard in case anyone appeared on the river bank but this did not happen either.

March 11

The rain stopped at 10 a.m. We went out to follow the path at the point in which it crosses the trail leading directly to the hills. We covered 8 or 9 kms of this path until we lost it. We camped with the intention of returning to the path we made that goes up into the hills.

March 5

In the afternoon we reached the arroyo from which we had set out towards the Rosita River a few days ago.

March 6

Miguel and Urbano went out to start cutting the path and the rest of us spent the day looking for *palmito*. For the past few days we have been eating nothing except a few small birds we hunted and the *palmito*.

March 7

Joaquín and Braulio go out to help with the cutting of the path: Braulio fainted and is hardly able to walk.

March 8

We camped about 4 or 5 kilometers away from where we were, still on the banks of the Río Grande.

March 9

After passing through dangerous areas because they were so rugged, we reached a water tank that pumps water into the village of Tatarenda. Ricardo and Inti cross the river, pretending to be members of a hunting expedition, and they are left without food. They take longer than planned, making Fernando very impatient.

March 10

Since we heard no news about what had happened we began making a raft so that an expedition could cross over to see what was going on. After all the men crossed, we planned to capture a house. While we were preparing to cross, we posted Miguel and 2 other comrades as undercover guards with orders to open fire at first sight of any suspicious movement on the other bank.

At 9 a.m. Miguel reported a raft was crossing from the other side; to our joy it turned out to be our men returning with food (rice, coffee, sugar, pigs, etc.). We learned that Marcos had pretended to be a Mexican engineer. Inti almost drowned when he got a cramp.

March 11

We continued the march in search of the mouth of the Nacahuasu.

March 12

The same.

March 13

We camped after crossing the most difficult and dangerous

terrain encountered on the trip thus far. Miguel has demonstrated great fortitude in cutting the path and has done it in only one day.

The rain started falling. I waited to hear Poni's speech. I talked with Mbili about several things Ramón had asked me to approach him about a few days ago, concerning his attitude. We tried to find out what he was thinking without letting him know that Ramón had said anything to me.

He said he feels he has been deceived, that he has been given a raw deal, and that he is not given enough responsibility. We explained that Ramón has no choice but to give the positions of leadership to members of the Central Committee. He said he understands this but that things are going very badly in the city, and he thinks the only one capable of solving organizational problems in the city is someone who feels it *personally* when something is done badly. Mbili said he does not think Ivan will stay because he's getting jittery about the situation adding that if these people are not supervised or disciplined they do not work.

"Ramón treats me very badly, Pombo," Mbili said, "and he is making a big mistake because I am here only out of commitment to him. I would give my life a thousand times over for him because you know that he is our teacher and guide."

But we cannot tell all this to Ramón. I told Mbili that Ramón told me he is going to talk with him shortly.

March 15

We reached the banks of the Río Grande. We wanted to send Urbano to the main camp with a message to send us some food but the river swelled up and prevented our crossing. Since Urbano does not know how to swim, we sent Rolando in his place.

March 16

The men in the center group crossed over on the raft we had made a month and a half ago, but the strong current carried the raft away and the men in the rearguard were unable to cross.

March 17

We received the news that Joaquín and his men have showed up and that, to our sorrow, Comrade Carlos drowned when their raft turned over. Comrade Carlos, who was one of our most

valuable men, was from Santa Cruz. On top of this irreparable
loss, we also lost 3 weapons and 7 knapsacks.

March 18

Headed towards the camp after having regrouped our forces
somewhat because we had to kill the *patianca* yesterday that was
running around loose with its mother along the river bank.

We killed a *visna* and after having to wait about three hours
for the men who stayed behind, we had to make a great effort
to get to the spot where we camped the last time. I had a heated
discussion with Urbano during which Fernando had to intervene.
Urbano had refused to do the cooking and I was insisting because
I am responsible for organizing things like this. I am constantly
having arguments with Urbano and Ricardo because they are
always refusing to work.

March 19

We set out with the aim of reaching the little stream we had
used to get to the Nacahuasu camp, and later continue on to the
spot where we made the first camp when we started out. Ramón
voiced his suspicion that something must have happened because
a plane flew over the river, apparently on a reconnaissance mission. Besides, we should have met some of the men sent from
the main camp. Those behind killed another *visna*. Ramón suggested that I carry some of the things Alejandro was carrying
as he was loaded down. This made it difficult for me and I had
to make a great effort to keep up with those ahead. The truth
is I only managed to make it in the first place because of the
example of Ramón, sick but still among the first, greatly impressed me; second, because men I consider weaker than myself
were doing it; and third, because I don't think any man should
let himself be overcome by fear. When we reached the arroyo
we found one of the comrades who called us and said he had
come with Benigno. This comrade is the Peruvian Negro doctor.
Benigno reports about what is going on at the main camp: Two
of the men Guevara brought in have deserted; the Army has
seized the house; Loro had a clash with the Army, killing one
soldier. We cooked some *cangui* and we ate it with meat, coffee
etc.

March 20

We met Pacho halfway along the road to Marcos' little house

and he gave us this message: he repeated what Benigno had told us adding that the visitors are at the first campsite which is now called Bear Camp. He also reported the path they followed for their return. We expect to reach the little house before 4 p.m. and if we do, we will continue on to the camp. We reached the camp at 6:30 p.m, When we arrived, Rolando gave us a message from Antonio and Marcos advising that they are withdrawing their ambush from the place in front of the campsite to a spot behind it known as the "elevator." This angered Ramón who said this was not very appropriate, for who ever heard of retreating before ever making contact with the enemy.

March 21

In the morning, Alejandro and the men of the center continued on, under orders to set up an ambush further ahead along the river. The men in the rearguard set out in the afternoon. They did not reach the camp so stayed in the [space left blank].

We are having a problem with the things we were keeping in reserve. Nato does not know where the things in the caves have been put and accuses Antoio and Marcos of having taken them out. They in turn accuse him.

March 22

We set out early with the visitors. (Visitors: Dantón, Carlos, Chino and Tania.) They were waiting for us at the main camp with bread and coffee.

Ramón sent Antonio and Miguel . . . to reconnoiter the house without being seen.

I criticized Antonio for his decision to withdraw, and he claimed it was taken by Marcos. Upon calling the latter's attention to this behind his back, he commented on the experience he had acquired at Pani's side in the field of correct tactics, etc., alleging that this was an error.

Antonio and Miguel's reconnaissance was poorly done because they crossed the roads without taking any precautions: and later, when this was pointed out to them, they claimed that if the Army had been about it would have fired at them, so they had crossed the road with confidence. The matter developed into a heated debate with Antonio which got to the point where Ramón had to intervene. ("Shut up right now; I am the chief and you will listen and obey.")

March 23

An Army patrol was ambushed and 18 Mausers, a .30-calibre machinegun, three 60mm mortars, and various other pieces of equipment were captured.

[Blank] were killed and [blank] were wounded. Two horses belonging to Alganaraz, which the Army had seized, were recovered.

March 24

The prisoners were set free. We shared what little we had with them.

They were given three days to recover their dead, and it was explained to them that thereafter we would resume hostilities.

March 25

Some planes flew over the ambushed area. A man was seen.

March 26

Peaceful.

March 27

Same.

A meeting was held at which Ramón reported on Marcos' performance as chief of the vanguard, and on the assignment of Miguel to that post. This was done after considerable discussion between Ramón and Marcos, Marcos being inclined to speak ill of Ramón, alleging that Ramón's tactic was in error.

April 1

All possible steps were taken to guarantee success in case the Army should advance with superior forces.

From the observation post, Tuma gave the alarm because he had seen three soldiers who, it would appear, had also seen him because they ran. It was decided to send the vanguard to the camp at the little house to see how the house was. They seized some cows and checked on the Piraboy Falls.

The horse was killed because it was necessary to leave the meat for Joaquín and Alejandro who were ill and had to remain in a camp that had been quickly put up for them. The doctor stayed with them for company, as did Muganga and Eustaquio and [sentence unfinished].

April 2

We began early to transfer everything that, of necessity, had to be left for the sick men.

The departure plan to have the center group meet the rest of the troop on the trail to the mountain was changed, because it was considered better to leave by way of the river.

April 3

We left at 3 in the morning, arriving at the farm at 9 a.m. with no complications.

We set out to make contact with the people. In the afternoon, we got to where they were camped. They had one of our cows.

April 4

We set out for Pirirenda and continued on to Gutiérrez in the hope of supplying ourselves with goods for the sick men and ourselves. Before we got to Piraboy we found traces of an Army ambush that had been vacated about two days ago. During the night, we entered the settlement. The first house we came to was empty; its owner had left. Some Army equipment was found, things that we took. A meal was prepared from what we took from the other houses and we tried to ascertain if there were Army troops in Gutiérrez. Due to our carelessness, one of the peons from the house escaped, which made it necessary for us to suspend operations. We began to fall back to the foot of the falls.

April 5

On arriving at the head of the falls, where we had left the rearguard in ambush under the command of Rolando, we learned that there was an Army unit encamped about a kilometer, more or less, away. They had come to the falls to bathe, etc. It was decided that we should cross the Nacahuasu River without waiting for dawn, leaving at 3:00 a.m.

April 6

At the planned hour, we proceeded to cross the river. We rested there until the dawn light permitted us to continue with what we planned. We heard the Army arrive and camp at the foot of the falls.

We continued on and got lost, so we decided to try to get back to the Nacahuasu River during the night. We stumbled on some cattlemen who were bringing cattle for the Army. We took the cattle away from them and paid them.

We camped in the "Los Monos" arroyo.

April 7

We set up an ambuscade and began to search for a place that would serve as an observation post.

April 8

We sent Urbano and the Doctor to the vanguard; and Julio to look after the sick men or, rather, to ask if they could walk so as to send them into hiding,

April 9

We began cutting two trails to Pirirenda and from there to the highway to set up an ambush for the Army.

April 10

An Army patrol fell into the ambuscade while advancing. It appeared that they expected to find us in the zone. We suffered our first loss in action, losing Rubio who was a very good man, both for his organizational abilities and as a future soldier. This was his first combat. In the afternoon, the Army returned to recover their dead and, inexplicably for us, they seemed completely confident and again fell into the ambush that had been established. There were 120 men under the command of a Major Sanchez, who was taken prisoner. This officer conducted himself with dignity because he refused to surrender the rest of his troops to us.

We captured arms [blank], ammunition [blank], [blank] other equipment.

April 12

On the road to Tres Cabezas, we met the sick comrades who had been sent into hiding and were to stay in that arroyo in case we should not have had an encounter with the Army: Muganga had told them I was well.

We left them as a rearguard, to continue on their way two days after we have left. Alejandro stayed with them.

April 13

We arrived at the camp in the afternoon, where the vanguard

was waiting for us and had set up an ambush. To our surprise, but they had done it nevertheless, they had found the caves.

April 14

We proceeded to inventory all the provisions. Everything was there except for 22 cans of milk which were missing from cache No. 1.

We came to the conclusion that it had been some passerby who had committed this theft.

April 15

Ramón talked to us about what our future activities would be like: Wiping out the enemy on the roads and trails by means of ambuscades; the necessity of winning over the peasantry so as to be able to organize our rural base.

An appeal was issued pointing out the great truth of the incompatibility of theft with socialism, which also makes it incompatible with the principles followed by this guerrilla band. Therefore, anyone caught committing this crime would be punished, up to and including the death penalty.

April 16

We arrived in the afternoon at the settlement called Buena Vista (or Bella Vista) which is all the way upstream on the Nacahuasu River. Our objective is to get to the Sucre-Santa Cruz highway in the area around Muyupampa or Monteagudo, with the idea of taking out Carlos and Danton and stocking up on supplies.

April 17

Another peasant has escaped from us. We spent the day waiting.

April 18

We are waiting for the arrival of Alejandro and Tania who had been left with the doctor (El Negro) at the Iquiri River to take care of comrades who are ill.

The rearguard stayed behind with the sick men in the zone awaiting our return, which should be within three days at most. We walked all night. At dawn, we stopped in a canefield until full light, and our people rested and slept.

April 19

We took a peasant prisoner and took him along with us as a guide (SMO) [Cuban abbreviation for: Servicio Militar Obligatorio, compulsory military service.]

We camped near the house of a peasant where we waited for night to fall; meanwhile, we cooked. At dawn, in a rainstorm, we arrived at the house of a peasant who had very beautiful daughters. He was hostile toward us. We took an Englishman prisoner who said that he was an independent newspaperman.

April 20

Enroute to Muyupampa we met a peasant called [blank] who was very friendly, offering us coffee which we did not accept. Once at the highway, at Dantón's suggestion we let him talk to the newspaperman; and on his own authority he offered to let him go free on the condition he aid us with an interview with the guerrilla chief with photos and everything. The newsman accepted and he was given an interview with Inti, his camera, and a few documents. The operation for entering Muyupampa failed because a peasant gave warning and the town was mobilized. The town had been alerted to our people by 2 peasants and a member of the DIB. They were intimidated by Coco, who told them sternly to bring this warning to me here and that he would accept no excuses.

Carlos and Dantón asked permission to stay behind and try to get out. They were told to do whatever they considered prudent, they decided to stay behind.

They were given 3 weapons: two M-3s and one .22-calibre rifle.

April 21

We pulled back from the highway as fast as possible. By morning we had arrived at the house of [blank], who was not there. Some of the neighbors told us that he had gone to Camiri. (We were a little suspicious.) We made camp here. At about 12 noon, we were warned of the approach of a vehicle bearing a white flag. We took some precautions. It was the prefect of the town and the priest. They had come to ask us to leave because the Army was dug in and they did not want any blood spilled. We agreed on condition that they bring us some medicines and foodstuffs that we needed. At 3 or 4 p.m., more or less, they sent a plane against us which bombed the house in which we were staying.

Here we learned that two of our visitors, Debray and Carlos, had been taken prisoner.

April 22

At dawn we arrived at the house of a peasant called Raco. He is a man who knows the zone very well. He treated us well.

April 23

At dawn, we arrived at the road to the place called Tapera. The peasants wished us well and pointed out a locally born man who had arrived early and who, it would appear, is an informer, he was taken prisoner; he had a Mauser rifle. We stopped a light truck full of merchandise from which we bought various goods.

That night, we were attacked by the Army, which we fired back at as we were pulling out. We had to retreat hastily in the light truck. In the confusion, we think that we had lost $2,000.

April 24

In the early hours of the morning, we arrived at the ranch of the priest in El Mesón. That afternoon, we moved our camp a little farther down. Benigno and Aniceto left to look for Joaquín at the Iquiri River, going by way of an arroyo [east of?] the Iti school.

April 25

We moved the camp to avoid its being discovered by the Army and set up an O.P. on the mountain on the other side of the arroyo. This looked like a mistake because if there was fighting, it would be very difficult for those in the O.P. to cross.

April 26

While Pombo was on guard, an advancing column was discovered. We had not taken up planned positions ahead of time, so we were obliged to take up positions in places unsuitable for an ambush because they offered no chance for observation or camouflage and were practically out in the open. We tried to offset all these disadvantages with the courage that characterizes us. We suffered the unexpected loss of Rolando, who was cut down by a round. We helped carry him from the front, Antonio, Urbano, Inti, Chinchu and I. After this loss, I suppose I am in charge of the ambuscade. In Rolando, Ramón says, we have lost one of our most valuable members, both as a leader and a politician, and as a military man since he was a tried and proven fighter. For me, the reason above all, is that he was a man trained under our leadership.

We retreated along a trail recently traveled by the Army, that led to the Nacahuasu.

April 27

We continued our march to a somewhat more suitable and safe place and sent Benigno and Urbano ahead to explore. We rested. We ate *visna* hash.

April 28

It was decided to follow an old trail that led to the Río Grande, and from there to Vallegrande (river near La Florida). We camped in a place where there are (bitter) oranges.

April 29

After having walked a few hours, we realized that we had been advancing due west and that we were lost.

We camped, began the search for the trail and set up an ambuscade. (Coco and Camba returned with the news that they had found a trail which they believed led across the hills.)

April 30

We set out to cross the trackless hills since we learned what direction to go in. We camped on a small plain.

May 1

In the morning, we reached the plain. We heard the sound of a waterfall. We decided to go down because we had had no water since the previous day. At 11 a.m. we drank some coffee with milk. We camped at the headwaters of the little stream.

May 2

We turned back toward the south with the intention of finding an arroyo that would take us to the Iquiri, we marched across the plain.

May 3

We have only enough food for four days' light rations (soups and tinned meat). We stopped for the night on the slopes of an unnamed range.

May 4

In the afternoon, we came to an arroyo that runs toward the north. In the morning, we will send out two scouting parties to determine its route: 1) Coco and Aniceto downstream, and 2) Benigno and Pablito upstream. They will try to cut a path to a plain that will lead us toward the right bank.

May 5

At 6 p.m., we set out along the arroyo in a southerly direction, believing that the river ran into the Congri and even possibly to the Iquiri River.

On the radio, we heard about the arrest of Jorge [blank space] (El Loro) who was held by a peasant. In the afternoon we arrived at a deserted little camp which Benigno recognized as being one of those which had been built by them on their reconnaissance trip. So, we were on the Congri, presumably no more than one day's fast march from the Tres Cabezas camp and a half-day from the Oro.

The radio also told of Debray's mother's arrival in Bolivia; he is to be tried by a military court which is pressing the Congress for approval of the death penalty so that it can be applied against Debray.

May 6

We arrived at Marcos' little house, cooked *moche* and ate the last of our reserve of tinned meat. We hope to find some cans of milk, coffee and sugar with which to make breakfast when we get to the Oro.

May 7

On arriving at the Oro we found some coffee as we had hoped, a sign that Joaquín was not here.

We continued on toward the camp. Five men were sent on a scouting party to the farm. The Army had pitched camp there.

May 8

We set up an ambuscade and captured two men and, with very little food left, committed the error of shooting at them and wounding them although not seriously. At 2 p.m., I took command of the ambush and we captured two men without having to shoot them. During the night, a group of 28 Army men fell into the trap: six were made prisoners, three were killed, and one was wounded; we also captured 10 rifles. The rest of them fled. (1500 shots)

May 9

We arrived at the falls of the Oro River while enroute to Pirirenda Lagoon by way of a new route. We ate a piece of dried beef and the remains of the last cow we had killed.

May 10

Today I reach my 27th birthday, and I am hungry since for two days I have only been eating lard soup, which is all we have left.

May 11

While we were in the arroyo that leads to Pirirenda, after crossing a small elevation, we got word that a wild pig had been killed, with which we mitigated our hunger a bit. At 2 p.m., we continued our march and camped not very far from the plain, from which the lagoon could already be seen.

May 12

Now in Pirirenda, we camped near a hut, from which we took some *joco* and some calabash and which we ate like pigs. Two scouting parties were sent out along the road to find the house. We made a stew and began to roast corn.

In the newspaper taken from one of the prisoners (a lieutenant), there was a story about the lack of combat spirit among the troops, citing instances in which the troops broke down and cried when they learned of the presence of the guerrillas in their areas. It commented on how all the people in Pirirenda were evacuated and how, in their absence, their animals were eaten.

Our men moved to the house. I stayed in the camp with Willi, Arturo and Darío.

We had enough food for about ten days (corn and rice). We planned to rest here for about five days, and then to strike a blow at the highway or to take Gutiérrez.

May 13

We rested in this place and began making *frituras* [fritters] because we now have a corn mill and there is new corn.

May 14

Mother's Day, a day which has great significance for me because with all my heart, I would like to be with my adored Mother.

We had a meeting with Fernando at which we discussed the fact that he was very but *very,* pained by the thefts that we had been censuring in the past few days. This is something that completely demoralizes the troop.

With profound courage, he referred to the cases of Benigno and Urbano. (Benigno had eaten a box of Army supplies, according to El Médico.) Later, Tuma told me that this was true and that it was he who had given it to him; and Urbano was declared innocent by a number of the comrades of having been the one who took the dried meat at the Arroyo de los Monos.

Word came that the Army had arrived at the peasant's house.

May 15

We moved our camp very early in an effort to get closer to the shores of the lake, which was very beautiful. While some of our men were out looking for beans, the Army began to advance on us with air and ground forces. During this action, we crept up a hill and stayed there to watch. We came to a well-stocked house. We ate some fried chicken and rice. At dawn about 4 a.m., we left. Fernando became seriously ill and we had to inject him with drugs to control him. For this reason, we made a litter and carried him to a small mountain. At 7 p.m., we set out for a cart track that we had found during one of our scouting expeditions.

May 17

We camped on a sand flat where we had been two or three days ago. We found some things to eat and some water in Bisones (white flour, corn, lard, sugar, *mote,* etc.) Some time ago, Loro had reported the existence of this sand flat and of a road that goes to the Nacahuasu and which comes out about 9 km below our farm.

May 18

We found a place with water at the foot of a mountain. We

planned to rest for five days and set up an ambuscade on the road. We heard news of a battle on the Masicurí River.

May 19

We moved to the arroyo or lake [sic]. The owner is Benito Manfredi.

May 20

I was sent to take charge of the ambuscade. It is not in a suitable place, so Fernando is preparing to move it to some other place.

May 21

A quiet day in camp. Fernando appointed me cook's helper. Fernando is taking charge of all the cooking chores for these five days.

May 22

The man in charge of the sawmill (Bruno) arrived. He and his son had been stopped at our ambuscade. We are preparing to leave tomorrow night because we think they have been sent to spy on us. After they were brought in, he offered to collaborate with us and we decided to run the risk of his betraying us.

May 23

The man was sent out to get us a good supply of provisions. His son was left with us as a hostage. He was given until 11 at night to return. After the time was up, we waited three more hours and, as he had not returned, we set out for the road that leads to the Nacahuasu River.

May 24

We got to the river at 7 p.m. We walked in the water so as not to leave any tracks. We spent the night in the old camp from our previous trip.

May 25

In the morning we arrived at the Saladillo River, using this arroyo as our road to get to the Chacos del Abuelo of the [illegible], which is called [blank]. We spent the night at a farm at a place which the local people call La Cumbre.

May 26

We arrived at [blank]. Here we ate some sweet limes and, at night, pork and *yucca*. We set out for the hut of two peasants that the others told us was about an hour's walk from there. From them we will find out where the Army is located in Ipita.

May 27

We took the old man prisoner and a peon when they tried to follow us after finding our tracks. Bruno was the old man and he stated that he had tried to bring the supplies and had been arrested. They had taken the food and money from him.

The *habeas corpus* on Debray's behalf was refused on the grounds that he is under the jurisdiction of the Military Court.

May 28

In the morning, we crossed the Camiri-Santa Cruz road, capturing the ranch of Karatatama when we were discovered by a peasant woman. The peasants who had guided us were set free. We stocked up on supplies and, at 6 p.m., we set out on the road to Ipitarite, where we bought some food. We went to a large ranch house to buy chickens. They were so sorry that they had sold them that they gave us one of their own. Fernando was recognized by a female school teacher, later we ate a little bread.

BRAULIO'S DIARY

Braulio's diary begins with his arrival on October 25, 1966 and concludes August 9, 1967, only a few weeks before he was to die with Joaquín's separated command. Apparently the least literate of the diarists, Braulio was a stolid veteran of the Congo expedition. He seems to be keeping his diary almost in imitation of the other guerrillas, many of whom, including Tania, kept diaries which were destroyed during the campaign.

He has very little to add to the other diarists' accounts but he exemplifies at the less imaginative guerrilla in action. Braulio was a fairly high ranking Cuban officer and evidently a rough fighter. His was the first diary captured at Nancahuazú and the diary below (his second) was postdated in its first entries to make up for the diary he had lost earlier.

1966

October 25
Today I left home at 5:00 p.m.

October 29
Today I left my homeland.

November 25
I arrived in Bolivia after passing through the United States by mistake.

From La Paz, a two-day jeep ride before arriving at camp, which was a farm that had been bought. There had been corn planted and a house built. Also, two jeeps and a small truck had been bought and with these we confused the enemy. There were two Bolivians who worked there. Sometimes they worked as peons. The 1,200-hectare farm was in the name of a Bolivian who sometimes acted as boss; the little camp was in the brush, about 500 meters from the house. We stood watch beside a tree, and it was precisely under this tree, on my first watch, that I began this diary. . . .

All the neighbors and peons throughout the area thought that we were building a cocaine factory. Meanwhile, we brought in some arms and supplies.

I was Number 142, called "Braulio."

December 12
Some comrades arrived. Ramón called us together and we elected ourselves to posts. Days later we organized ourselves into three groups: Vanguard under Marcos, Center under Ramón, and Rearguard under Joaquín, So far, there were 22 of us.

December 24
Already in the new camp, we dined very well: a big suckling pig, with 29 [bottles] of beer, 10 of wine, 4 of rum, sweets, raisins, cheese and salad.

December 31
We had a similar meal and had a visitor. It was Mario Monje,

who had come to talk with Ramón. But he did not want an armed fight, and wanted to be the only chief of the guerrillas. Later, he excluded from the leadership of the party 2 comrades who were already at the camp who were in favor of fighting.

1967

January 17
The neighboring *patrón* arrived at the farm, trying to blackmail us, saying that he knew something, and wanted to join us, and was afraid of the Army.

January 19
A police lieutenant arrived, tipped off by the *patrón*. He took away a pistol and asked questions about the cocaine.

January 25
Guevara arrived to talk with Ramón about joining up with several more men.

January 31
Ramón spoke to us about how we would make our first march, which would be for reconnaissance and training. We figured on about 25-30 days for making contacts with the peasants.

February 1
With packs of about 50-60 pounds of supplies each, and a total of 25 men, we left.

February 5
At 3:00 p.m., the vanguard arrived at the Río Grande.

February 6
We conducted some explorations.

February 7
We made a raft for the vanguard, and part of the center, and took it to the river. We, the rearguard, had to make another raft, and at 10 o'clock we finished it.

February- 8

At 9:00 in the morning we crossed over.

February 9

The vanguard comes upon its first house. There, we ate fricasseed pork, and roast pork, and tamales. Here we found out that there were about 300 Army men building a road! they were mostly military engineers.

February 11

We left.

February 13

We made contact with another peasant and also ate a lot of tamales.

February 15

Another peasant. This one had a brother who was a *patrón* who had a daughter who was the girl friend of an Army officer. Here we ate tamales, fried pork, small ripe bananas, and sugar cane.

February 18

We left for the Río Rositas.

February 26

At 3 o'clock in the afternoon we lost our first man. It was comrade Serafin [Benjamín] who slipped on the bank of the river and did not know how to swim. When our comrades [got] to him, he had already drowned. We were already a little weak because of our low food supply. We had three cans in reserve and did not want to use them because we didn't know if we would come upon a house. We were eating, besides some birds, some [illegible] and [rabbits?] that we found.

February 27

At 6 o'clock in the afternoon we arrived at the Río Rositas, and, as a matter of fact, there was no house.

February 28

We made a raft and the vanguard begins to cross. The raft

drifts away and they are left stranded in the center and the rearguard on the other bank. That night the river rose and we could not get across. By March 2 we had returned to where we had begun, still without communications with the vanguard. I was having cramps. We ate the last of our food reserves, not knowing when we would find another peasant house, but the next day Miguel saw a gasoline motor in operation and a small corn field. Ramón ordered Ricardo and Inti to cross the river and look for food. Inti almost drowned, but on March 9 they returned with a raft loaded with bread, coffee, sugar, cigarettes, rice, corn, and a pig. Here we learned that Marcos had been across the river since March 5.

Restored a little, we continued toward the junction of the Río Nancahuazú with the Río Grande where we expected Marcos to be waiting for us with food. But, actually, he was already back at camp where things were not always going too well. Some new comrades had arrived with Guevara, and already, two had deserted. And Marcos had let himself be seen killing. The Army surprises our watch from behind, and Loro fires and kills one soldier, and wounds another. Meanwhile, we don't know anything about all this, and advance towards the Nancahuazú from the other side.

March 14

We arrive at the mouth of the Nancahuazú. There is nobody waiting on the other side. We made a raft and [it] crosses the river without difficulty after it swept us away, leaving us on the banks of the Nancahuazú.

March 17

At 9:00 o'clock in the morning, Miguel reached us with a bag of shredded meat of a colt which Ramón had ordered killed. It had been three days since we had eaten anything, and there the organism fortified itself again.

March 18

After more roast meat, we took off for camp.

March 19

We met comrades with provisions.

March 20

More provisions, and here we ate our fill.

March 22

We arrived at camp; we took over the defense since we were afraid that the Army was nearby. What is more, the Army had followed Marcos almost to the camp.

March 23

With Rolando and Benigno—at 7:00 o'clock in the morning, the Army falls into our ambush and we capture 27 guns, including three 60-mm mortars, two light machineguns, a 30-calibre machinegun and some Mauser rifles; seven dead, four wounded, and 10 prisoners. That same day, the 23rd, at 5:00 o'clock in the afternoon, a plane bombed the area for the first time. From that day on, they bombed daily.

March 24

We released the prisoners.

March 25

Ramón spoke to us for a long time and relieved Marcos and put Miguel in his place. Ramón said that they would try to publicize this first stage abroad so that the world would know about our guerrillas, and that some of the Bolivian papers would begin. He also said that four comrades would turn back, and he said that they were worthless.

April 1

We abandoned the base.

April 11

At 10:30 we attacked an Army patrol and captured 11 soldiers of the Army; two dead; five prisoners; 33 wounded. But they killed our first man in combat: El Rubio. We quickly organized another ambush and at 5:10 a patrol with 120 soldiers fell into our ambush. We captured 16 prisoners, 28 dead, and four wounded, and great quantities of guns and because . . .

April 12

The government of Barrientos declared the Bolivian Communist party illegal and orders that all of its leaders be prosecuted. Today we buried Rubio and retreated further up.

April 14

We returned again to base and had two days there before leaving for the upper Nancahuazú, as far as the first peasant village. The rearguard stayed here. Ramón, with the vanguard, left in the direction of a town called Bollipampa [sic., probably Muyupampa] with some other comrades who had to leave, among them a French writer and an Argentine. Tania was there; she had stayed with us because she had an injured leg. In those days, we could write [letters], but the Army had closed off all the exits and we weren't able to; a few days later, we heard over the radio that the Army had captured the French writer Debret [sic] when he tried to get out with five more guerrillas, including an Argentine. In a few days, the Army arrived where we were and we planned an ambush, but they saw through our ambush, and we were only able to fire at them, but we were able to keep them from advancing and remained in the area to wait for Ramón and find out the true story.

May 23

We had a deserter while we were waiting for Ramón. It was Pepe, one of the ones who took off.

June 2

Marcos and Victor disappeared while on an exploration mission.

July 8

The soldiers surprised Alejandro and Polo at an observation post. We abandoned the camp to others, but the Army followed us.

July 9

Guevara and Polo surprised them. We moved on towards the Río Yaquí. At 4 o'clock in the afternoon, Sarapio [sic] was leading, when the soldiers surprised him and killed him with several shots.

July 20

From that moment on we abandoned the area and began to

operate on our own. We moved along the road to Taperillas, and on the 20th an Army patrol surprised our camp, We scattered them after a few hours and retreated. In the fire fight, Eusebio and Chingolo deserted.

August 9

The Army surrounded us and during our retreat they killed Pedro and took a 30-calibre machinegun that he was carrying.

THE GUERRILLA FORCE DURING
THE BOLIVIAN CAMPAIGN

This list of 50 guerrillas represents Ché Guevara's maximum strength before the initial combat of March 23rd. Of this 50, two had drowned (Benjamín and Carlos) and three had deserted (Daniel, Orlando, and Salustio) before this first engagement. On March 23, 1967, Ché went into battle with the remaining 45. But of this 45, Tania was not a trained combatant and four others were considered by Ché to be his *resacas,* or the dregs of the unit and next to useless except as porters.

Accordingly, Ché's actual fighting force at its height in March 1967 totalled only 40. 17 Cubans, 20 Bolivians, and 3 Peruvians.

CUBANS (17)

Aliases	Real Names	Army Rank
Alejandro	Ricardo Gustavo Machín Hoed de Beche	Comandante
Antonio	Orlando Pantoja Tamayo	Captain
Arturo Chinaco	Nelson Aspuru	Rank unknown
Benigno	Daniel Alarcón Ramírez	Lieutenant
Braulio	Israel Reyes Zayas	Lieutenant
El Rubio Félix	Jesús Suárez Gayol	Captain
Joaquín Vilo	Juan Vitalio Acuna Nuñez	Comandante
Marcos Pinares	Antonio Sánchez Díaz	Comandante
Miguel	Manuel Hernández Ossorio	Captain
Moro Morogoro Mugamba Mugambo Tavito	Octavio de la Concepción de la Pedraja	Medical Lieutenant
Pacho Pachungo Pocho Pancho	Alberto Fernández Montes de Oca	Comandante
Pombo Carlos Negro	Harry Villegas Tamayo	Captain
Ramón Mongo Fernando Fernández	Ernesto Ché Guevara de la Serna	Comandante
Ricardo Papi Mbili Chincholín Chinchu Taco	Aspuru (?)	
Rolando San Luis	Eliseo Reyes Rodríguez	Captain
Tuma Tumani Rafael	Carlos Coello Coello	Lieutenant
Urbano	Leonardo Tamayo Nuñez	Captain

Government and Party Posts	Passport Names and Nationalities	Fate
Vice Minister of Industries; Military Chief, Matanzas City	Alejandro Estrada Puig Ecuadorian	Killed Aug 31, 67
Chief, Border Guard Forces, the Ministry of Interior; Chief, "Operation Camarioca"	Antonio León Velasco Ecuadorian	Killed Oct 9, 67
Chief of Bodyguards of Fidel Castro's son	Arturo Hernández Martínez Ecuadorian	Killed Oct 9, 67
Chief of Cane Cutters Camp, Central Españña, Perico, Matanzas Province	Benigno Soberon Pérez Ecuadorian	Escaped to Cuba from Bolivia via Chile. Arrived in Cuba March 6, 68
Bodyguard, Raúl Castro; Liaison Chief, Oriente Army	Braulio Tapia Reyes Panamanian	Killed Aug 31, 67
Vice Minister, Sugar Industry	Jesús Cuevas Ulloa Ecuadorian	Killed April 11, 67
Member, Central Committee, PCC *	Joaquín Rivera Nuñez Panamanian	Killed Aug 31, 67
Member, Central Committee, PCC *	Marcos Quintero Díaz Panamanian	Killed June 2, 67
	Miguel Espino Rivera Panamanian	Killed Sept 26, 67
Chief Surgeon, Calixto Garcia Hospital, Havana	Carlos Luna Martínez Ecuadorian	Killed Oct 14, 67
Director of Mines, Ministry of Industries; Member, Central Committee, PCC *	Raúl Borges Mederos Uruguayan Antonio Garrido García Uruguayan	Killed Oct 8, 67
	Carlos Suárez González Ecuadorian	Escaped to Cuba from Bolivia via Chile. Arrived in Cuba March 6, 68
President, National Bank of Cuba; Minister of Industries; Cuban delegate to UN; member, Secretariat of National Directorate of the PURS.	Ramón Benítez Fernández Uruguayan Adolfo Mena González Uruguayan	Killed Oct 9, 67
	Ricardo Morales Rodríguez Bolivian Marco Tulio Villamil Puentes Colombian Mario Rodríguez Pérez Bolivian ID Card	Killed July 30, 67
Member, Central Committee, PCC *	Rolando Rodríguez Suárez Panamanian	Killed April 25, 67
Bodyguard Ché Guevara, 1959 till death 1967	Rafael Acosta Moreno Ecuadorian	Killed June 26, 67
Secretary, Cuban delegation to the Conference of the Inter-American Economic and Social Council, Punta del Este, Uruguay, August 1961	Urbano García Nuñez Panamanian	Escaped to Cuba from Bolivia via Chile. Arrived in Cuba March 6, 68

* Partido Comunista Cubano

BOLIVIANS (29)

Aliases	Real Name	Fate
Aniceto	Aniceto Reynaga Gordillo	Killed Oct. 9, 67
Armando, Guevara, Moisés	Moisés Guevara Rodríguez	Killed Aug. 31, 67
Benjamín	Benjamín Coronado Córdoba	Drowned Feb. 67
Camba	Orlando Jiménez Bazán	Captured Sept. 29, 67
Carlos Hurtado	Lorgio Vaca Marchetty	Drowned March 67
Chingolo	Hugo Choque Silva	Deserted July 67
Coco	Roberto Peredo Leigue	Killed Sept. 26, 67
Daniel	Pastor Barrera Quintana	Deserted March 13, 67
Darío	David Adriazola Veizaga	Survivor
Eusebio	Eusebio Tapia Äruni	Deserted, July 67
Inti	Guido Peredo Leigue	Killed Sept. 10, 67
Julio, Julio Médico	Mario Gutiérrez Ardaya	Killed Sept. 26, 67
León, Antonio	Antonio Domínguez Flores	Deserted Sept. 29, 67
Loro, Bigotes, Jorge	Jorge Vázquez Machicado Viaña	Captured late May 67, probably executed
Luis, Chapaco	Jaime Arana Campero	Killed Oct. 12-14, 67
Médico Chino, Ernesto	Freddy Ernesto Maimura Hurtado	Killed Aug. 31, 67
Nato, Lucho Méndez	Julio Luis Méndez	Killed Nov. 14, 67
Orlando	Vincent Rocabado Terrazas	Deserted March 67
Pablo	Francisco Huanca Flores	Killed Oct. 12-14, 67
Paco, Paquito	José Castillo Chávez	Captured Aug. 31, 67
Pedro, Pan Divino, Pani	Antonio Jiménez Tardio	Killed Aug. 9, 67
Pepe	Julio Velasco Montana	Executed end May 67
Polo, Apolinar	Apolinar Aquino Quispe	Killed Aug. 31, 67
Ramón, Raúl	Raúl Quispaya	Killed July 9, 67
Salustio	Salustio Choque Choque	Captured March 67
Serapio	Unidentified	Killed July 9, 67
Víctor	Casildo Condori Vargas	Killed June 2, 67
Walter	Walter Arancibia Ayala	Killed Aug. 31, 67
Willy	Simón Cuba Sarabia	Killed Oct. 9, 67

PERUVIANS (3)

Eustaquio	Lucio Edilberto Galvan Hidalgo	Killed Oct. 12-14, 67
El Chino, Francisco, Emilio, Emiliano	Juan Pablo Chang Navarro	Killed Oct. 8, 67
Médico Negro, Negro	Restituto José Cabrera Flores	Killed Aug. 31, 67

EAST GERMAN (1)

Laura Gutiérrez Bauer de Martínez, Tania T.	Haydee Tamara Bunke Bider	Killed Aug. 31, 67

326

THE GUERRILLA FORCES
AFTER THEIR ACCIDENTAL DIVISION
ON APRIL 20, 1967

CHE'S GROUP		JOAQUIN'S GROUP
Aniceto	Serapio	Joaquín
Camba	Víctor	Tania
Chingolo	Willy	Ernesto
Coco	Eustaquio	Walter
Darío	El Chino	Moisés
Eusebio	Antonio	Negro
Inti	Arturo	Alejandro
Julio	Benigno	Paco
León	Marcos	Polo
Loro	Miguel	Braulio
Luis	Moro	
Nato	Pacho	
Pablo	Pombo	
Pedro	Ricardo	
Pepé	Rolando	
Raúl	Tuma	
	Urbano	

OTHER INDIVIDUALS MENTIONED IN THE DIARIES

Algarañaz—Ciro Algarañaz, owner of farm next to guerrillas' at Nancahuazú; former Mayor of Camiri.

Andrés—Guerrilla contact man who met Debray and Tania in La Paz and introduced them, after which Tania escorted the Frenchman to Nancahuazú. Identity unknown.

Arancibia—Félix Arancibia Berrera, member of urban organization.

Ariel—Code name for communications control officer in Havana.

Béjar—Héctor Béjar, member of urban organization.

Bleichner—Dr. Hugo Bleichner Taboada, member of urban general staff.

Carlos, Pelado, Pelao—Ciro Roberto Bustos, Ché's "coordinator" for Argentina, the artist who sketched the guerrillas, sentenced with Debray to 30 years' imprisonment. "Pelado" or "Pelao" means "bald one."

Comandante Fifo, Fidel, Leche—Cuban Premier Fidel Castro Ruz.

Dantón, Debre, Debray, Frenchman—Jules Régis Debray, Ché's principal liaison with Castro; prepared geopolitical study of guerrilla campsites for Ché. Sentenced to 30 years' imprisonment.

Estanislao—Mario Monje Molina, First Secretary of PCB until December 1967; Party's chief liaison with Castro and Havana, and its representative at January 1966 Tricontinental Conference in Cuba's capital.

Facundo, Tellería—Luis Tellería Murillo, member of PCB Central Committee, guerrillas' La Paz supply chief.

Flaco—member of urban organization; identity unknown.

Flores—Aldo Flores, PCB leader, at July-August 1967 OLAS Conference in Havana purported to be spokesman of Ché's guerrilla band.

Humberto, Rhea—Dr. Humberto Rhea Clavijo, Bolivian physician in charge of obtaining medicines, drugs, and surgical supplies for guerrillas; member of urban general staff; eluded police roundup of urban contacts and is in hiding.

Humberto—Humberto Vásquez Machicado Viaña, member of urban support group, brother of guerrilla Loro; eluded police roundup of urban contacts and fled to Cuba.

Iván—Left in charge of La Paz communications with Havana after guerrillas settled in Nancahuazú; identity unknown but apparently Cuban and trusted aide of Castro and Ché Guevara.

Kolle—Jorge Kolle Cueto, PCB second-in-command under Monje regime, thereafter Monje's successor.

La Loyo, Loyola—Loyola Guzmán Lara, national treasurer of urban organization; expelled from Juventud Comunista (Communist Youth) leadership for joining Ché; arrested and imprisoned in September 1967 roundup of Ché's urban contacts.

Laura, María, Mary, Tamara, Tania—Tamara Haydee Bunke Bider, a double agent spying on Ché for the KGB, Ché's first advance agent in Bolivia and his mistress, chief of his urban intelligence and security, liaison with Argentina (Bustos, et al.); also in guerrilla band, killed with Joaquín's group.

Lechín—Juan Lechín Oquendo, former Bolivian Vice President, former chief of mineworkers' union and Bolivian Labor Central (COB), head of Party of the Revolutionary Nationalist Left (PRIN); promised Castro he would aid guerrillas.

Lozano—Dr. Antonio Lozano Cazón, Bolivian dentist, member of urban organization.

Moreyra—Roberto Moreyra Montesinos, member of urban organization.

Norberta—Norberta Aguilar, member of urban general staff; arrested with Loyola Guzmán.

Paquita—Paca Vernal Leytón, member of urban general staff and wife of PCB leader Luis Leytón; arrested with Loyola Guzmán.

Pareja—Dr. Walter Pareja Fernández, Bolivian physician designated by Ché to head urban organization.

Ramírez—Humberto Ramírez Cárdenas, member of PCB Central Committee, participated in Havana discussions with Castro on helping guerrillas.

Renán—Renán Elías, member of urban general staff.

Rodolfo—Rodolfo Saldaña, operational Bolivian chief of Ché's urban organization, main liaison between it and guerrilla base; in hiding presently.

Rodríguez, Simón—Simon Reyes Rodriguez, member of PCB Central Committee, another participant in Havana discussions with Castro on helping guerrillas.

Sanchez (most used of about a dozen aliases)—Julio Dagnino Pacheco, Peruvian, Cuba-trained, Ché's go-between with Moisés Guevara, had charge of funds received from Havana for guerrillas after they settled in Nancahuazú; arrested in April 1968 with suitcase carrying $20,000 in guerrilla funds, and imprisoned.

Víctor—Casildo Condori Vargas, member of urban organization.